Financial Market Regulation

John A. Tatom
Editor

Financial Market Regulation

Legislation and Implications

Springer

Editor
John A. Tatom
Networks Financial Institute
Scott College of Business
Indiana State University
800 Sycamore St. #601
Indianapolis, IN 47809, USA
john.tatom@indstate.edu

ISBN 978-1-4419-6636-0
DOI 10.1007/978-1-4419-6637-7
Springer New York Dordrecht Heidelberg London

Printed on acid-free paper

Springer is part of Springer Science+Business Media (www.springer.com)

Preface

Financial regulatory reform has been critically important for several years. Even before the mortgage and financial crisis became apparent to most policymakers and analysts, Treasury Secretary Frank Paulson initiated, in spring 2007, a broad and sweeping review of financial regulation that was path breaking in its conceptual redesign. Moreover, the tenth anniversary of the passage of the Financial Modernization Act of 1999, also called the Gramm-Leach-Bliley Act (GLBA), at the time and perhaps still the most fundamental change in the nation's financial structure since the Great Depression, is a natural watershed for the evaluation of the structure and its regulation. The inevitable review of federal regulation was reinforced by the mortgage and financial crisis of 2007–2009. Several leading financial economists and analysts saw the problems of flawed financial regulation, especially the GLBA, as the fundamental cause of the crisis and demanded its repeal. There were many regulatory changes in 2008–2010 because of the crisis and Congress passed the Wall Street Reform and Consumer Protection Act of 2010. Also called the Dodd-Frank Act, it was signed into law on July 21, 2010.

The GLBA fundamentally changed the financial landscape in the United States and was the most sweeping financial legislation in 66 years. The GLBA allows the formation of financial holding companies that can offer an integrated set of commercial banking, securities, and insurance products. The tenth anniversary of such a sweeping change in the industry's structure is a natural benchmark for assessing the effects of the law and for questioning whether changes are necessary in the working of this historic legislation. But the importance of this review is reinforced by a variety of proposals that have been made in the last few years to reform the regulation of financial institutions; these reform proposals have attracted considerable attention among regulators and in the financial firms that they regulate. For example, many of these proposals follow the spirit of the GLBA by proposing that the regulatory system move toward a more integrated view of risks rather than continuing to follow the structure that was left untouched by the GLBA based on divisions across product lines or functional regulation for commercial banks, securities firms, and insurance companies. Most recently, the financial crisis and the failure of some large financial institutions have called into question the legitimacy of our current financial structure and its regulation, including to some degree the GLBA. There is no doubt that regulatory reform is front and center on today's policy agenda and that the lessons of the GLBA experience are critical to that discussion. This book examines financial regulation, especially the debate over the GLBA and its effects, and issues arising from the mortgage and financial crisis, "too big to fail" policy (TBTF), and the new Dodd-Frank financial reforms.

This book has four parts. Part I provides an overview of recent and prospective financial legislation and its effects. Part II presents more detailed empirical evidence of the global effects of the GLBA on banks and insurance companies. Part III provides six chapters on continuing issues in financial regulation. All of these chapters deal directly or indirectly with legislation and legislative failures to deal with TBTF, the implications of those failures, as well as serious proposals to deal with it more effectively than has been the case, at least through 2010. Part IV is a retrospective and prospective on financial legislation by Congressman James Leach, one of the original authors of the GLBA.

I explain in Chapter 1 that the GLBA was created to allow integrated financial service firms that could provide commercial banking, investment banking, and securities business and insurance under one roof, something that had been made illegal by the Glass-Steagall Act of 1933. The GLBA removed those barriers, boosting competition across all these product lines, driving down prices of financial services and boosting the quantity and quality of financial services. Moreover, the GLBA increased diversification of newly formed financial holding companies. In the recent financial crisis, provisions of GLBA reduced the damage of the failures of firms like Merrill Lynch, Bear Stearns, Lehman Brothers, Countrywide, and Wachovia by allowing large banks to acquire their remaining assets quickly and efficiently, something that would have been impossible under Glass-Steagall.

The GLBA did not lead to the overpowering of small- and medium-sized financial institutions by large financial conglomerates, as some had feared at the time. Consolidation has continued, but there are only about 600 financial holding companies in the United States today and most of them are small. There are several very large financial holding companies, but most of them were already large banks, investment banks or insurance companies.

In Chapter 2, Peter Wallison, Senior Fellow at the American Enterprise Institute and recently appointed member of the U.S. Congressional Commission on the Financial Crisis, reviews arguments that the GLBA caused or contributed to the financial crisis and rejects those arguments or suggestions. Ever since severe turmoil enveloped the financial markets in the fall of 2008, commentators have blamed deregulation of the financial system, and specifically the supposed "repeal" of the Glass-Steagall Act by the GLBA for the crisis. This led many to advocate a restoration of the separation of commercial and investment banking that was supposedly the essence of the Glass-Steagall Act. According to Wallison, these statements reflect a remarkable degree of ignorance about something that could be easily understood with a small amount of research. In this paper, he outlines the provisions of the Glass-Steagall Act, and shows that it did not and could not have had any significant effect in creating or exacerbating the financial crisis.

Wallison also reviews the implications of what he sees as the successful outcomes of the GLBA during its first 8 years and during the last 2 years of crisis. The effort to blame the Gramm-Leach-Bliley Act for the financial crisis–part of the general effort to blame deregulation or lack of regulation–is misplaced, in his view. GLBA permitted banks and securities firms to affiliate, but this was irrelevant to what happened in the financial crisis. Wallison argues that the banks that got into trouble in this crisis were the most heavily regulated financial institutions in the U.S., and hurt themselves in the traditional way for banks–by making bad loans. The securities firms or investment banks that got into trouble were not affiliated with banks, and they also created their financial problems in the traditional way–by underwriting bad securities. GLBA did not affect the potential for development of the new complex financial instruments, including mortgage backed securities, collateralized debt obligations, collateralized loan obligations, credit default swaps and auction rate securities, or financial institutions' ability to market or hold them. GLBA, accordingly, had nothing to do with the financial crisis, according to Wallison. He also argues that the capital markets and regulation should be reformed to widen the integration of markets and regulation; functional disparities in ownership and regulation that remained after the GLBA should be eliminated, in his view, to further enhance the efficiency, competitiveness and consumer welfare of the U.S. financial services industry.

In Chapter 3, Martin Mayer, Guest Scholar at the Brookings Institution and the author of numerous books on financial markets and policy, argues that the GLBA implicitly assumed that the TBTF policies of the 1980s had successfully been reined in or abolished by Congress in the early 1990s and that the GLBA, by implicitly encouraging the creation of larger and larger integrated financial service companies, required that abolition in order to be successful and develop a more stable and competitive financial system. Given the resurrection of TBTF in fall 2008, Mayer suggests that one option is to repeal the GLBA or perhaps replace it with a more stringent regulatory environment. Mayer explains that the growth of integrated financial institutions since the GLBA was passed makes repeal impossible, but that alternatives for financial institutions with narrower product focus and asset powers and some separation by function would be possible and desirable as approaches to limiting institution size, risk exposure and systemic risk.

According to Mayer, a dozen years ago, Randall Kroszner, soon to become one of George W. Bush's economic advisors and a Federal Reserve (Fed) Governor, could comment in a Levy Institute seminar, without fear of contradiction, that there was no evidence to back the "public interest rationale" for the separation of commercial and investment banking. Except for deposit insurance (and even here, there were mutterings about moral hazard), the limits imposed on banking by the Glass-Steagall Act of 1933 were roundly condemned through the entire cadre of academic and corporate economists, as the old law was unceremoniously junked 66 years later. A few of us did worry about the loss of information that could result as the veil of bank secrecy was extended over additional transactions, but we were not really respectable. Today, we few stand on the high ground of observed recent experience and watch the survivors of the still-acclaimed wave of financial innovation struggle defensively, if not repentantly, up the slopes of what Alan Greenspan called "shocked disbelief." Ten years after its repeal, Glass-Steagall has a constituency again.

Part III contains two chapters that contain empirical evidence on the global effects of the GLBA on the banking and insurance industries. In Chapter 4, the effects on global banking are discussed by Professors Kabir Hassan, Abdullah Mamun, and Ihsan Isik. Professor Hassan is Professor of Finance at the University of New Orleans and a Fellow at Networks Financial Institute. Professor Mamun is Associate Professor of Finance at the University of Saskatchewan, and Professor Isik is a Professor of Finance at Rowan University. Their paper investigates the impact of the GLBA on foreign banks. They find that the GLBA has had significant and negative spillover effects on the banking sectors of most developed countries, although the effects differ across countries. Most importantly, they show that the systemic risk of foreign banks relative to the world equity index increased following the passage of the GLBA and that the varying degrees to which this occurred accounts for the varying size of their adverse wealth effects. These effects are larger for large banks. According to Hassan, Mamun and Isik, these results imply that the GLBA reduced diversification opportunities for foreign banks by restricting their operations in the U.S., the most important banking market.

Chapter 5, also written by Professors Hassan and Mamun, investigates the impact of the GLBA on the insurance industries of developed countries. They find that the insurance industries of most of the developed countries were significantly and negatively affected by the GLBA, as U.S. insurance companies gained competitive advantage. Similar to the results with foreign banks, they find that the adverse effects of the GLBA on non-U.S. insurance companies vary across countries, although the effects on firms from the European Union do not vary by country. When they control for country-specific effects, they find that differing negative effects on profitability explain the adverse effect of the GLBA on non-U.S. insurance companies. This result is robust to various statistical techniques.

Part IV contains six chapters on continuing issues in financial regulation. All of these issues revolve around the cost of the financial sector safety net and the policy of TBTF, whether directly reducing or eliminating it and its public cost, or reducing its size by managing and controlling it, including the often neglected costs arising from regulatory actions themselves.

The most significant effort to deal with the TBTF problem was the Federal Deposit Insurance Corporation Improvement Act (FDICIA) of 1991, at the end of the savings and loan crisis. It set up a detailed process to ensure that no bank would ever again be in a position to have failed and yet be judged as TBTF. However, in the mortgage and foreclosure crisis, those barriers were hurdled with exceeding ease. Indeed, there were no media reports that institutions were approaching the threshold for a TBTF decision or of the official decision that institutions were TBTF. In the early stages of the mortgage and financial crisis, Professor George Kaufman recognized the flaws or loopholes in FDICIA and proposed a four pillar program to fix them and minimize the private and public cost of failure. Essentially his solution aims at minimizing the financial cost of failure and the financial safety net. Kaufman is the John F. Smith Professor of Finance and Economics and Director of the Center for Financial and Policy Studies in the School of Business Administration, Loyola University, Chicago, and he is a Senior Fellow at Networks Financial Institute. His analysis of how to minimize the cost of failure is contained in Chapter 6.

According to Kaufman, bank failures are often perceived to be more costly to the economy than the failure of other firms of comparable size and to generate widespread public fear. As a result, preventing bank failures is a major public policy concern in all countries. Kaufman argues that most public policy strategies adopted in nearly all countries to achieve this objective have eventually failed to do so, at a large cost, not only in reduced income and wealth to the failed bank's customers and in the bank's market area, but also to the taxpayers of the country as a whole, who have frequently been asked to finance most or all of the losses to bank depositors, other creditors, and, at times, even shareholders. The high cost of these policies has encouraged a search for more efficient ways of protecting the economy from bank failures, while permitting poorly managed or unlucky individual banks to exit but at no or little cost to either their customers or the economy. Kaufman's program is much simpler than the elaborately detailed processes developed in the Dodd-Frank Act of 2010. And these processes are unlikely to be used in most cases.

In Chapter 7, Professor Edward Kane, the James F. Cleary Chair of Finance at the Carroll School of Management at Boston College and a Senior Fellow at Networks Financial Institute, takes a different approach to TBTF. Instead of attempting to minimize the cost of failure, he focuses on monitoring and controlling the cost of the financial sector safety net so that when failures occur, the safety net cost is relatively low. He argues that the recent crisis is the product of shortcutting and eventual meltdown of due-diligence incentives in the securitization process. He maintains that the GLBA did not cause the crisis. Rather the two phenomena are linked by a common cause. The crisis and the GLBA both trace to difficulties of monitoring the effects of regulation-induced innovation on the cost of the financial safety net. These difficulties come from the ease with which clever managers can extract implicit subsidies to risk-taking from national safety nets by using advances in information, communications, and financial-contracting technologies to book traditional business in innovative and nontransparent ways, according to Kane.

Professor Kane says that the U.S. barriers between the banking, securities, and insurance industries that GLBA eliminated resemble the broken down remnants of ancient city walls visible in many European cities today. Before these walls were abandoned, blasts from the artillery of regulation-induced innovation had long since reduced them to rubble. Rebuilding cross-industry barriers would not lower the odds of future crises. What it would do is distract Congress and regulatory personnel from repairing the defects in supervisory incentives that brought about the shortcutting and outsourcing of due diligence. To fix these defects, Kane argues that the system needs a dose of better ethics. This requires that financial institutions and government supervisors be made formally accountable for pursuing the benefits of safety-net support in fair and efficient ways.

In Kane's view, effective programs of regulatory reform must address the incentive conflicts that intensify financial risk-taking and undermine government insolvency detection and crisis management. He notes that subsidies to risk taking that large institutions extract from the financial safety net encourage managers to make their firms riskier, harder to supervise, and politically and administratively more difficult to fail and unwind. In his view, repealing the GLBA or breaking up TBTF institutions would do little to arrest subsidy-induced activities. Rebuilding Glass-Steagall barriers between banking, securities, and insurance firms would instead make implicit taxpayer support of large institutions less transparent and serve foreign interests by encouraging conglomerate firms to operate affected businesses through foreign subsidiaries. To discourage financial institutions from abusing safety-net support, government supervisors must be made specifically accountable for delivering and pricing safety-net benefits fairly and efficiently. Kane argues that if Congress wants to make the system more stable, it should focus on: rewriting top officials' oaths of office; changing the ways top officials are paid and the ways they measure and report regulatory performance; and changing the kinds of securities that large institutions have to issue. The Dodd-Frank Act of 2010 did not take any of these recommended actions.

According to Professor Kane, TBTF, or the difficulty of failing a bank and unwinding it, or now a non-bank financial firm, has three dimensions, the size of institutions, their complexity and political clout. The GLBA deals with the complexity problem, but it does not address size or political clout. Tradeoffs in successfully dealing with one or even two of these problems intensify the other dimensions, making the problem of failing and unwinding virtually insoluble.

In Chapter 8, Professor Kane focuses on the fact that official definitions of systemic risk leave out the role of government officials in generating it. He claims that policymakers' support of creative forms of risk-taking and their proclivity for absorbing losses in crisis situations encourage opportunistic firms to foster and exploit incentive conflicts within the supervisory sector. To restore faith in the diligence, competence and integrity of officials responsible for managing the financial safety net, reforms need to rework operative incentives in the government and financial sectors. The goal should be to align the incentives of private risk managers, accountants, credit-rating firms, and government supervisors with those of ordinary taxpayers. Professor Kane describes a series of complementary ways of advancing toward this goal. The most important steps would be to measure regulatory performance in terms of its effect on safety-net risk exposures and to require insured institutions to support this effort. This entails estimating the explicit and implicit safety-net benefits they receive and issuing extended-liability securities designed to improve the accuracy of these estimates.

In Chapter 9, Christopher Whalen, cofounder and managing director of Institutional Risk Analytics and a Fellow at Networks Financial Institute, asserts that, in dealing with the 2007–2009 financial crisis, the Fed has placed its role as monetary agency and de facto steward of the market for U.S. Treasury debt ahead of its statutory responsibility for ensuring the soundness of the private banks. This behavior is a key illustration of the problem of political clout in addressing TBTF. The Fed sees itself as a national hero that can save the banks and financial system in order to save the economy and in the process be rewarded with expanded powers. The Fed was politically weak at the beginning of the crisis, as many analysts and politicians viewed the Fed as largely responsible for the crisis itself. But during the crisis, by surrendering its independence to the pressures of individual congressmen and the Treasury, the Fed was able to play its hero role and, in the end, to increase its powers. For example, the Fed becomes the central player in the Financial Stability Oversight Council (FSOC), having the key power to close or order the asset or liability structures changed, or to limit their overall size. This presumably would address the size problem of TBTF, but these powers conflict with the Fed's interest in being a hero and gaining more power, so it is not likely the Fed will act on these new powers unless strongly pressured to do so by a toothless, and likely ineffective committee, the FSOC, which has the same incentives not to act to limit the size of financial institutions. The Fed's enhanced political clout will render more difficult its incentives to fail and unwind.

While not central to Whalen's argument, the Fed, under pressure from the Congress early in the crisis, fundamentally altered its concept of monetary policy. It took on new lending powers to private financial firms and focusing on expanding direct placement of private credit rather than using traditional monetary policy, so-called quantitative easing, to increase the monetary base and money and credit supplies through relatively safe open market purchases of government securities. Indeed, the Fed began to act like a commercial bank, attempting to fund new private sector credit extensions by reducing other, safe holdings of U.S. government securities. Also the Fed, in a reversal of what might be called traditional banana republic central banking, asked the Treasury to sell such securities to them. In this case, however, the call was to further the Fed's commercial banking activity as it also asked the Treasury to hold the proceeds in special Treasury deposit accounts that are not used, thus sterilizing the potential to expand overall money and credit, and allowing the Fed, as commercial bank, to fund larger private lending by sales of these newly acquired Treasury securities.

As Whalen (2010) explains, the Fed's behavior was motivated by an attempt to placate Congress where the Fed's independence had come under serious question and threat. The Fed believed that it could play the national hero role by targeting private credit to financial firms, rather than simply targeting the federal funds rate, or a monetary aggregate such as the monetary base. In Whalen's view, the Fed changed its behavior rather than pursue another mandate to ensure the safety and soundness of the nation's large complex banking organizations and also to ensure the ability of the Treasury to borrow at low and stable interest rates. Apparently the Fed's actions were sufficient to placate Congress as regulatory reform has granted new powers to the Fed, including a lead role in financial stability monitoring and control and housing the new consumer financial protection bureau. Thus it appears that the Fed has regained its independence, but the path to that victory has shown congressional leaders that the Fed can be forced to act by congressional pressure and this lesson will not be forgotten by congressional leaders. In the end, the experience has seriously damaged the future independence of the Fed by demonstrating that Congress can influence policy through a threat of action.

Why did the Fed do this? In part it was due to a paradigm shift in understanding of how the Fed influences the economy and how it could stabilize the economy in the midst of a financial crisis and the developing recession. It also did so, however, because of a concern for systemic failure, normally understood as a desire to forestall failure in depository institutions, the traditional set of firms with whom central banks conduct business and on whose safety and soundness they attend, but now extended to "too interconnected" firms that could not be allowed to fail. Thus the Fed as hero was a key author of a new narrative that envisioned the country as exposed to a new and broader form of systemic risk that only it could fix. Whalen argues that the Fed was driven by its loss of credibility and reputation within the halls of Congress and its concern that as a result it would lose its independence and its ability to pursue long term goals of price stability, high employment and cyclical stability. The ironic result is that, while it appears that the Fed was successful because financial system reform has given the Fed new powers in monitoring and policing financial stability, with no loss of its supervisory powers over the nation's largest banks or its supervisory powers over the community banks, in fact the Fed has demonstrated convincingly that under pressure it has given up, and also will give up in future, its hard fought independence at the drop of a congressional hat. This will serve the Fed badly in all future crises when congressional pressures rise to dictate Fed actions.

The price of the Fed's victory is that the country is now shackled with a notion of the Fed's role as protector of private sector financial institutions, at least of those that are too interconnected to fail. The size of the Fed's balance sheet, which had hitherto been feared as a harbinger of inflation, is now encouraged to expand because it provides the new insurance of the largest financial (and probably eventually non-financial) institutions. This introduces a new level of moral hazard, potentially socializes normal and crisis-driven losses of private firms, heightens the threat of productivity and growth, kills new financial regulations and poses new risks to the achievement of the fed's traditional goals, especially for price stability. As with any congressional response to crisis, it is likely that recent steps will be revisited and polished to remove rough edges. Whether Congress can or would want to reign in the Fed in its new regulatory posture and reverse the Fed's new monetary policy is less likely, however.

In Chapter 10, Professors Ronnie J. Phillips and Alessandro Roselli explore an older approach to limiting the size of the financial safety net by reducing the risk that a bank can fail, which is called the narrow bank proposal. Professor Phillips is a Professor of Economics at Colorado State University and a Networks Financial Institute Senior Fellow; Professor Roselli is currently at the Cass Business School in London. Phillips and Roselli argue that the normal crisis response of Congress would be passage of legislation that increases oversight and regulation by the federal financial regulatory agencies, rather like Dodd-Frank. But they indicate that a superior approach would be to limit the risk of a liquidity and insolvency in a financial crisis by adopting a "narrow bank" structure. This is another way to manage the cost of the financial safety net but avoiding failure, even in the event of a bank run. A narrow bank is one that holds only U.S. government securities and cash as assets behind deposits and other liabilities that are payable on demand. The heart of the proposal, they argue, is to make checkable deposits as safe a means of payment as currency, but without the need for the elaborate supervisory and regulatory structure required when federal deposit insurance and the discount window are part of the financial safety net. It works because it separates the role of banks in providing a safe and stable means of payment from the system of credit creation by financial institutions. Those liabilities would not be insured, nor would they keep a bank from becoming TBTF because regulators would focus only on protecting the payment system, minimizing runs and protecting banks from failure. In the current environment where regulators are concerned with interconnectedness of credit instead of liquidity and solvency, such a scheme might be deemed to be inadequate.

Congress, regulators and pundits have viewed financial institution compensation as a contributing factor to the recent crisis. The argument is that bankers and others took on undue risk that led to the downfall of some institutions. Such behavior is unfathomable for long-term employees or their managers because the incentives for "excessive" compensation that might promote "excessive" risk taking are not in the long-term interest of either party. More importantly, the usual argument in the crisis was that the instruments that became illiquid and fell in value were viewed by the marketplace, banks and employees as relatively low risk. Thus taking such risks could not have contributed to excessive, not to mention normal, compensation. In Chapter 11, Professor David VanHoose addresses the case for regulating bank compensation and its pitfalls. VanHoose is the Herman W. Lay Professor of Private Enterprise and Professor of Economics at the Hankamer School of Business at Baylor University and a Senior Fellow at Networks Financial Institute.

According to VanHoose, the government has been explicitly and implicitly regulating the compensation of top managers at a number of U.S. banks since passage of the Economic Stabilization Act of 2008. Bank regulators also have added evaluations of bank management compensation packages to the list of factors taken into account in supervisory safety-and-soundness examinations. He also notes that pending legislation would require the Federal Reserve to establish explicit standards for evaluating the risk implications of bankers' pay. The FDIC has proposed incorporating the structure of bank management compensation into the determination of banks' deposit insurance premiums, according to VanHoose. He reviews the academic literature on the empirical relationship between bank management compensation and risk, discusses theoretical considerations that may underlie the mixed evidence regarding this relationship, and assesses potential pitfalls associated with actual and proposed regulations of the structure of management compensation in the banking industry. His main conclusion is that there is neither persuasive empirical evidence nor an unambiguous theoretical argument in favor of either direct or indirect regulation of bankers' pay.

In Part IV, former Congressman and GLBA author James A. Leach reprises the missing link between the crisis and the GLBA, the performance of the GLBA and the shortcomings in existing regulation, before Dodd-Frank, and the problems with this new regulation. He calls attention to the role of excessive leverage at investment banks, promoted by erroneous regulatory changes at the U.S. Securities and Exchange Commission, in creating the crisis and the difficulties of the so-called "invisible government," the armies of regulators that use their political clout to expand their powers, yet in doing so boost the cost of the financial safety net, and create disincentives to effective regulatory behavior. Leach reinforces the arguments about political clout emphasized by Kane and Whalen, focusing laser attention on what he calls the invisible government, the growing number and increasingly powerful group of financial regulators. Congressman Leach is currently the Chairman of the National Endowment for the Humanities. He served as a representative in Congress for 30 years, where he chaired the Banking and Financial Services Committee when he sponsored the GLBA.

Congressman Leach reviews the legislative framework of financial regulation, assesses public and private sector accountability for the crisis, and appraises the legislative aftermath. According to Leach, his "thesis is that the economy and the financial security of the country were unnecessarily jeopardized by the unchecked greed of a few; that, at critical moments, politics and ideology dominated regulatory decision making; that the regulators, the invisible government, allowed excess leveraging out of excess confidence in risk-based mathematical modeling; that a conflicted Congress emboldened risk taking at Fannie Mae and Freddie Mac; and that problems in commercial bank regulation related less to what Congress did than what it did not do. As both a participant and observer in the legislative process, [Leach] has designed this review in part as a chronicle of Congressional interactions between the parties and with the Executive branch and in part as a take on regulation itself."

Networks Financial Institute is pleased that we have been able to make this work available. Regulatory reform issues are central to our research agenda and there is perhaps no more important topic that we could address today. We began work on this material in the early days of the mortgage crisis, largely because of an interest in what research has to say about the effectiveness and success or weaknesses of the GLBA. As the crisis emerged, it became clear that the problems of financial regulation extend well beyond, or more accurately, are largely unrelated to the GLBA, but those issues are readily placed in context by a consideration of financial structure.

A book such as this depends on the support and cooperation of many people. I am very grateful to all of the authors for their excellent work. It is truly and completely their work. I would also like to thank the editorial staff at Springer for their willingness to take on this project and their production staff. I am also very grateful to our team here at Networks Financial Institute, especially our research coordinator Martha Henn McCormick and research assistant Nicholas Ochieng, for making this work possible.

Indianapolis, Indiana John A. Tatom

Contents

Contributors

M. Kabir Hassan Department of Economics and Finance, The University of New Orleans, 438 Kirschman Hall, 2000 Lakeshore Drive, New Orleans, LA 70148, USA, mhassan@uno.edu

Ihsan Isik College of Business, Rowan University, 201 Mullica Hill Road, Glassboro, NJ 08028, USA, isik@rowan.edu

Edward J. Kane Boston College, Chestnut Hill, MA 02467, USA, edward.kane@bc.edu

George G. Kaufman Department of Finance, Loyola University, 1 East Pearson Street, Chicago, IL 60611, USA, gkaufma@luc.edu

James A. Leach National Endowment for the Humanities, Washington, DC, USA, jleach@neh.gov

Abdullah Mamun Edwards School of Business, University of Saskatchewan, 25 Campus Drive, Saskatoon, SK, Canada S7N 5A7, mamun@edwards.usask.ca

Martin Mayer The Brookings Institution, 1775 Massachusetts Avenue NW, Washington, DC 20036, USA, mmayer2a1@aim.com

Ronnie J. Phillips Networks Financial Institute, Indianapolis, IN 46208, USA; American Institute for Economic Research, PO Box 1000, Great Barrington, MA 01230, USA, rphillip@me.com

Alessandro Roselli Faculty of Finance, Cass Business School, London, EC2Y 8HB Great Britain, aleroselli@alice.it

John A. Tatom Scott College of Business, Networks Financial Institute, Indiana State University, 800 Sycamore St. #601, Indianapolis, IN 47809, USA, john.tatom@indstate.edu

David VanHoose Baylor University, One Bear Place #98003, Waco, TX 76798, USA, david_vanhoose@baylor.edu

Peter J. Wallison American Enterprise Institute for Public Policy Research, 1150 Seventeenth Street, N.W., Washington, DC 20036, USA, pwallison@aei.org

Christopher Whalen Institutional Risk Analytics, 371 Van Ness Way, Suite 110 Torrance, CA 90501, USA, chris@rcwhalen.com

Part I
Overview: Recent and Prospective Financial Legislation

Chapter 1
Financial Legislation: The Promise and Record of the Financial Modernization Act of 1999

John A. Tatom

On November 12, 1999, President Clinton signed the most significant piece of financial services regulation to be enacted since the Great Depression, at least up to that time. When the Financial Service Modernization Act of 1999, better known as the Gramm-Leach-Bliley Act (GLBA), was signed, the financial services industry faced strong pressures for deregulation of the rigid structure imposed during the Great Depression. During the 2007–2008 financial crises and ensuing debate regarding financial services regulation, the GLBA became a target as members of the financial sector, academia, and government considered possible triggers that may have precipitated the crisis.

The dramatic events that shook the U.S. financial services sector in 2008, including the deployment of the Troubled Asset Relief Program (TARP) and the failures of some of the nation's largest financial firms, made financial services regulation a heated topic on the national policy agenda. In June 2009, the Obama Administration set forth a new proposal for financial services regulation [see U.S. Treasury (2009)] and the Congress completed action on the reforms in July 2010 in the Wall Street Reform and Consumer Protection Act of 2010, or Dodd-Frank, signed into law on July 21, 2010. While the effects of the new legislation are still uncertain, some lessons about the role of legislation and its implications can be gleaned from reviewing the experience with the GLBA and the recent crisis. Most of the provisions of Dodd-Frank require studies or new regulatory specifics from regulatory authorities, an estimated total of at least 243, according to the law firm of Davis Polk and Wardell, and even more according to others. Thus, until those new regulations are fleshed out, it is difficult to assess the effects of the Act except to assert that it is the largest intrusion of federal regulatory authority since the Glass-Steagall Acts of

---

J.A. Tatom (✉)
Scott College of Business, Networks Financial Institute, Indiana State University, 800 Sycamore St. #601, Indianapolis, IN 47809, USA
e-mail: john.tatom@indstate.edu

This chapter also appeared as Networks Financial Institute *Policy Brief* 2010-PB-05.

J.A. Tatom (ed.), *Financial Market Regulation*, DOI 10.1007/978-1-4419-6637-7_1,

1933 and 1935.[1] This chapter reviews the contribution of the GLBA, its critics, and its effects on the 2007–2008 financial crisis and the new Dodd-Frank legislation.

Why Regulate Banks and Other Financial Institutions

After the foreclosure and financial crisis of 2007–2009, it may seem strange to ask why political leaders might want to regulate banks or other financial institutions. But this question does not have an answer that is as obvious as it may seem. There are three main reasons that have been put forward as justifications for financial regulation. The first is asymmetric information, that is, that corporations have unequal access to private information that belongs to stockholders, and this information is necessary for sound private decision making by stockholders and other investors. Regulations aim to avoid market failures that would occur if valuable information, which is essentially free or relatively inexpensive, but otherwise private, is not provided to markets; such a failure would reduce capital formation and the size of the corporate sector. This is the main justification for the regulatory authority of the Securities and Exchange Commission, which was founded in 1934. This explanation leads to informational reporting requirements for corporations and disclosure of key financial information that might not exist, or might not be uniform, otherwise. Note that this does not lead to a special case for regulation of banks or financial institutions, only all corporations.[2] Some financial economists and analysts, however, believe that these issues are more significant for banks and other financial institutions. VanHoose (2010) reviews theories of bank regulation and concludes that there is no compelling case for "market failure" to warrant a case for bank regulation. Market failures arising from large external spillovers, significant market power or so-called informational asymmetries, are not found in the empirical literature on banking.

The second rationale is regulatory capture, where efforts by industry incumbents to use legislation and political authority to secure competitive advantages lead to industry regulation. In this theory, banking firms demand and use state regulation

[1] Developing and promulgating new regulations dictated by Dodd-Frank is not the only obstacle. Most of the issues presented by the financial crisis are unaddressed or not fully addressed by Dodd-Frank so at least another major round in regulatory reform can be expected in the next few years in the United States. These include a large number of issues raised about fixing too-big-to-fail and how to repair critical holes in the regulation of complex financial institutions, retirement saving and credit default swaps, and other new and complex instruments, where thoughtful proposals have been developed by the Squam Lake group. See French et al. (2010).

[2] On the basis of a data set of 150 countries, Barth et al. (2006) conclude that regulation based upon disclosure and market-based monitoring provide superior outcomes based on a broad range of desirable regulatory outcomes. Regulations employing entry restrictions, government ownership or restrictions on banking activities, such as those arising from regulatory capture, adversely affect banking system performance.

as a means to protect themselves from competitive entry. VanHoose (2010) concludes that this alternative theory better explains patterns of bank regulation than the asymmetric information theory.

Another rationale for financial regulation is that fractional reserve banking, the fact that banks hold cash assets that are a fraction of their liabilities, many of which are payable on demand, gives rise to an inherent risk of runs on banks that can lead to failure of otherwise solvent banking institutions. Because of this, legislation providing for government insurance of bank deposits was adopted in 1933 to create the Federal Deposit Insurance Corporation (FDIC). Not surprisingly, this action led to a further justification for bank regulation to ensure solvency of banks in order to minimize taxpayer exposure to losses of the FDIC should industry paid premiums be insufficient, as, for example, in a financial crisis. Such a rationale has led to regulations aimed at limiting competition, such as limits on interest rates paid by banks, entry regulation to protect profit, and a variety of requirements on asset composition and other operational decisions in order to protect bank profitability and avoid losses and insolvency. This rationale has been extended, without serious examination or evidence, to all financial institutions, not just banks, by the Federal Reserve (Fed) and the U.S. Treasury, with tacit endorsement by the Congress, to encompass the notion that financial institutions can be "too interconnected," so that shocks in some part of the industry can lead to failures elsewhere. This may appear to be similar to the "bank runs" problem, but it is not. There is no end to the potential for losses due to interconnectedness, whether in banking, the rest of the financial industry, or even nonfinancial business, because all consumers and producers are connected to varying degrees to other consumers and producers.

VanHoose (2010) points out that another rationale for financial regulation, consumer protection, is inadequate. He quotes Benston (2000), who wrote that "most nations already have broad social regulations to address such issues."[3] This rationale was an important component of the GLBA and more recently of Dodd-Frank. VanHoose cites studies that show that the cost of bank regulation is substantial relative to overall bank expenses; these estimates are striking, given the popular notion that deregulation since the 1970s has reduced regulatory costs to negligible levels.

Looking Back at the GLBA—Great Expectations and Some Skepticism

The Glass-Steagall Act of 1933, which created the FDIC and other significant banking reforms, contained provisions that prohibited a bank holding company from owning other financial companies. The GLBA repealed these legal separations, allowing bank holding companies to own insurance, financial planning/investment firms, and other financial service businesses. The "financial holding company" structure allowed banks, securities firms, and insurance companies to offer each

[3]See VanHoose (2010), p. 198.

other's products. For example, a bank could create a financial services holding company to offer insurance or security services; and an insurance company could provide retail or investment banking services. Essentially, the GLBA broke down the barriers to competition across the financial services portfolio.

The authors of the GLBA expected that the Act would enhance competition between firms and allow financial services to be provided more efficiently through a streamlined enterprise. The emergence of electronic and Internet-based banking services largely negated many of the barriers that had served to make banking a geographic-based delivery system in the past, even without the GLBA. By providing consumers with a "one stop shop" where they could take care of all of their financial business, the GLBA was intended to optimize consumer convenience. Under the GLBA, banks, insurance companies, security companies, and investment banks could offer their customers products and services beyond their traditional product portfolios. Besides enhanced competition and efficiency, many thought that the GLBA would open the doors for more product innovation. The reasoning was that if bank holding companies were able to offer a broader menu of products, they would be inclined to develop new products that would meet customers' evolving needs while generating additional revenue for the bank.

The primary innovations that arose from the GLBA were changes in how products were distributed as opposed to the development of new products. Under the Act, retail banks, investment banks, insurance companies, and securities firms were able to leverage economies of scope and scale to distribute traditional products from other sectors to better serve the portfolio of financial needs of their customers. This increased competition in distribution not only resulted in lower profit margins but also provided new profit centers in each sector of the industry. For example, while community banks increased marketing of insurance products and security services, they tended to secure these services from external sources as opposed to developing the services in-house. This arrangement resulted in security and insurance companies enjoying a sales boost as other institutions promoted their products. Money center and super-regional banks benefited from the ease of expanded sales of both variable and fixed annuities and development of their own security products.

The GLBA allowed banks to develop private equity businesses that could hold investments for up to 10 years, allowing banks to provide equity financing to small- and medium-sized firms. Additionally, the Act made it easier for banks of all sizes to underwrite municipal securities and develop securities sales and origination services, as well as insurance products. Likewise, insurance companies used the GLBA to cultivate new revenue streams. MetLife became one of the largest financial holding companies. Allstate Insurance's interstate bank emerged as a truly national competitor in retail banking services by using its agent network to cross-sell banking services.

The ability to provide bank financing to investment banks' corporate clients was an attractive service for large corporations which increased competition for investment banking services. However, not all investment banks actually became part of financial holding companies with banking affiliates. This changed after the financial crisis arose. Following the failure of Bear Stearns and Lehman Brothers, two investment banks without significant attachments to bank affiliates, Goldman Sachs and Morgan Stanley became bank holding companies. Today there is no major investment bank that exists outside of a financial holding company structure. As the credit crisis continued, commercial bank charters offered the attractive benefit of immediate access to liquid funds through the Federal Reserve. The GLBA made possible the bank mergers that quickly and efficiently resolved two of the largest institutional failures in the financial crisis, Bear Stearns and Merrill Lynch.

A key financial innovation brought about by the financial integration permitted by the GLBA was reduced systematic risk.[4] Stock prices rose for banks, insurance companies, and security firms on the passage of the GLBA. Bank stocks, especially money center and super regional bank stocks, gained the most, followed by insurance companies and then security firms. Meanwhile, overseas insurers' stock prices dropped significantly. Evidence shows that part of the gain in rates of return on stocks was due to lower systematic risk premiums associated with these firms.

As with most new legislation, the GLBA was not accepted warmly by all portions of the industry. One of the primary concerns in the drafting and eventual passage of the GLBA was the protection of customer privacy. Critics questioned whether the vast amount of information held by one institution would compromise the privacy of account holders. Extensive restrictions on intra- and inter-company sharing of customer information were included in the Act to address these concerns.

Another criticism was that the GLBA was enacted to formalize a *fait accompli*—the merger of Citibank and Travelers Group to create Citigroup, announced in 1998. However, this was not true. The merger of Travelers Group and Citicorp was approved by the Fed on the basis that "nonpermitted businesses would be divested within a pre-defined time frame." The passage of the GLBA eased the burden of an agreement that had already been negotiated and eliminated the concerns about the cost or difficulties of complying with the divesture requirements.

A third concern was that the GLBA would enable large mega-institutions to dominate commercial banking, investment banking, brokerage, and insurance business. By creating "superstore" banks, some feared that smaller institutions including community banks would not be able to compete.

Did the GLBA Achieve Its Intentions?

Interestingly, many of the outcomes of the GLBA did not play out as both authors and critics thought they might. The GLBA did not result in a rush of financial services firms delving into new lines of business, except among the largest institutions. Beyond notable mergers (e.g., Citigroup and Travelers, JP Morgan, and

[4]See Hassan, Mamun and Isik, Chapter 4, and Hassan and Mamun, Chapter 5, as well as their references to other studies.

Chase), the industries' response was primarily in the sale of nontraditional products, rather than the "manufacturing" of new products. As of June 29, 2009, there were only 592 financial holding companies authorized by the Federal Reserve, and most of them were small and had limited availability of nontraditional products.

The GLBA seems to have been more effective at fostering product delivery than creating new types of products. Around the same time that the GLBA was being introduced, new technology was providing the financial services industry with sophisticated tools such as marketing customer information files (MCIF) and data warehousing programs. These tools made it easy for marketers to categorize customers by life stage and create bundles of products tailored to life stages or product usage. For example, a customer with an auto loan would be a prime candidate to cross-sell an insurance policy; a senior club member might be interested in a money market or other high-yield deposit account.

To some extent, primarily through acquisition, holding companies were formed to allow broader menus of products to be manufactured in house. However, over time, many institutions have opted to source specific financial products from specialists, focusing on the distribution of products in response to consumer needs.

Skeptics' concerns about privacy have also not borne out. The newly formed Citigroup led the way in crafting privacy restrictions that are included in the GLBA. The three principal parts to the privacy requirements of the GLBA include the Financial Privacy Rule, Safeguards Rule, and pretexting provisions. The language and restrictions within each section of the Act's privacy components seem to have served their purpose in protecting customer information from wide dissemination across subsidiaries.

The GLBA and the Financial Crisis

As the financial crisis emerged, debate arose regarding any role that the Act may have played in creating products that were not by definition innovative, but rather, controversial, or other changes that may have contributed to the crisis. Some questioned whether the innovation that the GLBA fostered had included financial products linked to the subprime crisis—specifically mortgage loans and the array of new investment products created during the housing bubble. It must be noted that rapid growth in home buying and thus the growth in mortgage assets was a result of public policy pressures to increase homeownership in the United States. The resulting growth of mortgage companies, especially some tied to real estate companies and to thrift institutions, led to substantial changes in the processing of mortgage applications and to new channels of financing at increasingly competitive prices. This trend was reinforced by banks' movement away from the "originate and hold" model to an "originate and distribute" model. Under the new model, banks made and serviced mortgage loans, but sold the loans to investment banks and government sponsored entities (GSEs) Fannie Mae and Freddie Mac, who, in turn, packaged the loans into pools against which they issued securitized mortgages. These purchasers, especially some investment banks, went one or more steps further, pooling these securities to create collateralized debt obligations and even more esoteric versions of these instruments. The initial mortgage securitization instruments and process were not new, however; they had existed for 15–20 years. What was new and especially problematical was including risky subprime mortgages and especially adjustable rate subprime mortgages, in these packages. Adjustable rate subprime loans grew rapidly in 2004–2007 just as market interest rates were rising, so that earlier loans of this type were resetting to, in many cases, unaffordable levels.

These new products were the creation of investment banks that could have developed them with or without the GLBA. And they were part of a pattern of new instruments developed there that failed when a more normal appetite for credit risk returned to markets in 2007 and subsequently. The illiquidity of instruments such as auction rate securities and structured finance products, was stunning, following the rapid growth of such new products during the previous few years as investors abandoned caution in search of yield on their investments in what was essentially a very low rate of return environment. Riskier and higher yielding new assets became the rage.

Even though none of these new instruments could be linked to the GLBA, some critics were quick to blame the law for the financial crisis. Nobel Laureate Paul Krugman lays blame on Senator Gramm, the lead author of the GLBA, and on the GLBA noting: "Aha: the Politico notices that Phil Gramm, McCain's presidential economic guru, can also be viewed as the father of the financial crisis."[5] Nobel Prize-winning economist Joseph Stiglitz called for the repeal of the GLBA in the January 2009 issue of *Vanity Fair*. While political opposition to the GLBA exists, no political leader stepped forward to champion, repeal or revision of the GLBA. President Barak Obama, while a presidential candidate in 2008, expressed the view that the GLBA was responsible for the mortgage crisis, but neither he nor congressional leaders followed up with the repeal of the GLBA.[6] Henry Kaufman argues that the GLBA caused the crisis and advocates a return to a narrow bank regime in line with the Glass-Steagall regulatory structure.[7] Paul Volcker has also expressed regret over the passage of the GLBA and the failure of Dodd-Frank to repeal it.[8]

One could argue that the partial adoption of the Volcker Rule, which would have prohibited banks from conducting private equity, hedge fund or proprietary trading businesses, in Dodd-Frank reflected a repeal of the most dangerous elements of the GLBA. This would be wrong, however, for at least two reasons. First, Volcker did not regard his original proposal as repealing the GLBA,[9] and second, Dodd-Frank

---

[5] See Krugman (2009).

[6] See Paletta and Scannell (2009)

[7] See Kaufman (2010).

[8] See Uchitelle (2010). Volcker has argued elsewhere that financial deregulation introduced no new innovations beyond the automatic teller machine, but in this article he cites derivatives, securitizations and credit default swaps as products that did not exist before deregulation.

[9] See Uchitelle (2010).

did not implement the Volcker Rule. Instead, it put limits on the extent of two of these businesses, with private equity and hedge fund assets limited to no more than 3% of total assets, required these activities to be conducted in separate subsidiaries, and eliminated proprietary trading activities of banks. The latter is hard to define and is likely to prove difficult to eliminate since similar activities are routinely conducted in other traditional parts of the asset management of banks. Its effectiveness will be determined, as so much of Dodd-Frank, by regulators' new processes to enforce it.

Opposition to the GLBA appears to be more advanced in Britain, where the Tory leadership is advocating adoption of a Glass-Steagall type separation of banking from financial services. This is unique in that the British financial system has not had such a separation structure in the past. George Osborne, new Chancellor of the Exchequer, advocated this approach when he was shadow Chancellor, as did the former Tory Chancellor, Nigel Lawson, who noted "Capitalism needs a revived Glass-Steagall Act."[10] Nonetheless, when the Tories came to power in June 2010, adoption of a policy like Glass Steagall was not part of the program.

The mortgage crisis arose because of the growth of subprime mortgage products developed by mortgage bankers and investment banks, most of them unregulated, and whose products were certainly not under the auspices of the GLBA provisions that govern bank holding companies or of other commercial banking laws. Significant pressure from Congress, supported by mandates and federal subsidies to foster homeownership helped accelerate the growth and development of subprime products.

As a result of the growth in home ownership and specifically the growth of subprime mortgage assets, incentives were created for investment banks to develop financial products to leverage and manage their mortgage portfolios. These products were often created by nontraditional companies and thus, marketed outside of traditional regulatory structures. These new products included subprime-based mortgage-backed securities, collateralized debt obligations, collateralized loan obligations, auction rate securities, and credit default swaps. While some of these products were sound, many were complex and unknown, creating a misunderstood risk profile.

Indeed, during the crisis, the large failures of institutions occurred not among banks, but among nonbank financial conglomerates such as Bear Stearns, Lehman Brothers, Merrill Lynch, and American International Group (AIG). In short, the financial crisis was the result of poor regulation of new intermediaries acting outside the traditional regulatory structure that existed before and after the GLBA. The GLBA did not deregulate the financial services industry beyond allowing for integration of institutions across product lines. As Wallison points out in the next chapter, without the GLBA, the failures of investment banks and large thrift institutions would not have been so easily resolved and the spillover to all financial institutions and the economy would have been severe.

---

[10] See Lawson (2009).

The notion that the financial crisis was a banking crisis has been fostered by the political posturing of both the Bush and Obama administrations, led by the adoption and implementation of TARP. The TARP program began by forcing banks and a few nonbank financial institutions to accept government funds without evidence that they were confronting any meaningful liquidity or solvency problems. Most of the banks paid back these funds as soon as they were allowed. While TARP had authority to spend up to $700 billion, originally to acquire toxic assets of banks, less than $300 billion was ever disbursed to banks, most of that was repaid within the next 18 months and in 2010 losses to TARP were projected to arise from funds provided to automobile producers and AIG, with little loss arising from funds advanced to commercial banks.

Another perspective on whether there was a GLBA or financial-crisis-induced failure of banks is that the failure experience of depository institutions (banks and thrifts) has not risen to the level of the last real crisis, the savings and loan (S&L) crisis of the late 1980s and early 1990s. In a new broad historical review of financial crises, Reinhart and Rogoff (2009) refer to the S&L crisis as a "bank-centered financial crisis" and they include it in their comparison of the subprime crisis to such crises. It must be noted that they use the term "milder," and not their terms "severe" or "systemic," in referring to the S&L crisis and they conclude that the subprime crisis was worse than other banking crises in advanced countries or in the five crises that they call the "Big Five," "severe," and "systemic," crises. Certainly, this suggests that the subprime crisis was the worst since at least Great Depression, but one natural indicator that Reinhart and Rogoff do not review, the number of bank failures, suggests otherwise. In 2008–2009, there were 165 failures (there were only three in 2007, the first year of the crisis), and it is likely that there will be 150–200 failures in 2010. It is possible that, in 2010, the number of failures will reach or surpass the previous high of 179 in 1992, which came toward the end of the S&L crisis. But a total of 300–350 failures for 2008–2010 pale in comparison with the three to four times larger number of failures in the worst 3 years of the S&L crisis (1989–1991), or the six times larger number of failures during the worst 5 years of the earlier crisis, 1808 in 1987–1992. For the full 13-year period of elevated bank failures from 1981 to 1993, there were 2,335 failures, about seven times as many as are likely in and following the subprime/financial crisis. At least for this indicator of banking crisis, the recent mortgage and financial crisis is hugely dwarfed by the so-called mild S&L bank-centered financial crisis.

A supporting view is offered by Bullard (2010), who argues that commercial banks, especially the smaller community banks, did not cause the crisis, and therefore, do not need to be reregulated. He points out that 20 financial firms made up 80% of the assets of the Standard and Poor's 500 at the end of 2007. Only one-third of the assets of these financial firms were controlled by bank holding companies, regulated by the Fed, while two-thirds were nonbank financial firms, which are not in the bank regulatory system and not under the authority of the Fed. In his view, there were runs on the shadow banking system and these and the nonbank financial firms caused the crisis. He does not recognize that the Fed did have regulatory control over the holding companies, though he is correct that they did not have authority over nonbank financial firms.

Dodd-Frank provides more authority for the Fed and FDIC to close bank holding companies and other financial firms, but it is not likely that this will be the end of "too big to fail" (TBTF) despite claims that it will. The experience in the recent crisis extended the notion of TBTF to nonbanks and even to nonfinancial firms, such as auto companies. Improved discretionary ability to close banks and bank holding companies was unnecessary and expanded discretionary control to close other financial and nonfinancial companies is not likely to be used in the event of another crisis. The only new power is the ability to use a discretionary threat to private sector firms that is likely to be abused in ways that are wholly unrelated to a real financial crisis. Fortunately, this congressional overreach is unlikely to survive future judicial challenge.

The Profitability Perspective

How did the GLBA impact U.S. banks' overall profitability? Despite gains in stock prices, there is no conclusive evidence that profitability or productivity rose for the banking industry as a whole. From an asset growth perspective, however, total assets of all banks grew at an 8.1% annual rate from 1999 to 2008, much faster than the gross domestic product (GDP) (4.9%). Assets at the nation's four largest holding companies (Citigroup, JP Morgan Chase, Bank of America and Wells Fargo) grew more than twice as fast, however, expanding at a rate of 16.6%, more than three times as fast as the economy's GDP. The rest of the banking industry grew a little more slowly than the overall economy, with assets expanding at a 4% rate.

Certainly, the GLBA appears to have helped create jobs in the financial services sector. Prior to the GLBA (1987–1999), employment in the financial services sector grew more slowly than overall employment, reflecting stagnation within the industry. However, from 1999 to 2007, financial services employment outpaced overall employment, reflecting the improving performance of the financial sector.

An increased level of competition within the banking sector is also indicated by the decline in net interest margins. From 1984 to 1999, the average net interest margin of all commercial banks was 4.17%. This number declined sharply (54 basis points) after the GLBA, averaging 3.63% from 1999 through the second quarter of 2009. The transformation of banking is reflected in a sharp shift in the importance of traditional financial intermediation (borrowing and lending) toward more fee income from services such as insurance and security sales, origination fees, and service fees for overdrafts, loans of credit, and other services. From 1969 to 1986, the share of interest income in total commercial bank income was about 90%. As the GLBA removed walls separating banks, insurance, and securities firms, the share of interest income fell to 72% in 1999 and to 64% in 2003. Since then, the share rose to 73% in 2008 as traditional banking has reasserted its importance.

Senator Gramm laid out a market test of the future success of the GLBA:

> The test that I believe we should use—the test I will use, the test I hope people looking at this bill years in the future will use—is, 'Did it produce a greater diversity of products and services for American consumers? Were those products better? And did they sell at a lower price?' I think if the answer to those three questions is yes, then this bill will have succeeded.[11]

According to the evidence above, the GLBA was a success, especially for the largest banks. On the other hand, Gramm's ultimate test of its success is its survival, though his explanation has come under a cloud of doubt, at least temporarily, because of the mortgage and financial crisis. Gramm argued,

> Ultimately, the final judge of the bill is history. Ultimately, as you look at the bill, you have to ask yourself, 'Will people in the future be trying to repeal it, as we are here today trying to repeal—and hopefully repealing—Glass-Steagall?' I think the answer will be no. I think it will be no because we are doing something very different from Glass-Steagall. Glass-Steagall, in the midst of the Great Depression, thought government was the answer. In this period of economic growth and prosperity, we believe freedom is the answer.[12]

The GLBA survived the assault of leading intellectual and political critics in the United States and the United Kingdom, at least in their post-crisis reform efforts.

What About "Wallet Share"?

An early concern upon passage of the GLBA was that financial behemoths would take over the financial services industry. By 2009, only about 600 mostly small local and regional financial holding companies exist to facilitate cross-sector product availability. There is some question whether even this small number really provides full service product availability. The expansion of new products and services allowed by the GLBA has not resulted in increased products per household within institutions. Banks did not lure large numbers of customers away from insurance firms, nor did insurance companies lure significant numbers of customers away from traditional banks. As a result, the GLBA has not resulted in a meaningful diversification of product shares within individual firms.

The GLBA may have helped foster customer retention. While customers appear to have a preference for doing business with specialists across the product spectrum, customers who have concentrated their buying across banking, insurance or securities within a single holding company are likely to be more loyal, and less likely to flee when they encounter a more attractive offer for a single product.

---

[11] See Simpson (2009).

[12] See Simpson (2009).

Examining the Legacy

Like most regulation, the GLBA has been both condoned and vilified, particularly, in the context of the economic meltdown. However, the GLBA appears to have been a significant factor in supporting the vigor and health of U.S. banks by enabling them to deliver products and services that enhance competition and deliver the services consumers demand. Notably, the solvency of the nation's banks has improved dramatically in the past decade. Banks reached a historical peak in their ratio of capital to assets, or lowest leverage ratio, in mid-2008—about the same time the financial meltdown was capturing national headlines. Over the past 10 years, the GLBA has played a role in the growth of the U.S. banking industry, making it more internationally competitive and more resilient to economic and financial shocks. Despite its critics, the GLBA has increased innovation as well as enhanced the convenience of financial services for both consumers and businesses. The GLBA broke down restrictive barriers brought about during the Great Depression. Despite the criticisms of the GLBA during the financial crisis and early stages of the legislative debate for financial regulatory reform, no effort to repeal the GLBA surfaced.

In the development of the GLBA, primary concerns focused on consumer protection and privacy issues. Today, systemic risk, subprime credit, and mortgage credit crisis issues introduce new concerns. Dodd-Frank created a new Consumer Financial Protection Bureau, housed within the Federal Reserve, but independent of them. The new bureau will have power to write regulation, examine, and enforce it for banks, thrifts, and credit unions with assets over $10 billion, mortgage-related businesses, payday lenders, and certain nonbank financial firms, though auto dealers are explicitly exempt. Dodd-Frank did not retire or consolidate any of the existing financial regulatory bodies, however, except for merging the federal chartering and regulation of thrifts with that of banks within the Office of the Comptroller of the Currency (OCC) in the U.S. Department of Treasury. This transfers consumer protection rules for thrifts to oversight by the OCC, as well as the new bureau. Thus, Dodd-Frank continues the pursuit of stronger consumer protection regulation and in this regard it touches on one area that some analysts believed contributed to the mortgage and financial crisis of 2007–2009, the concern to protect consumers from predatory lending. There is no evidence that predatory lending contributed to the mortgage crisis, however, as predation with unsustainable mortgage lending ran from borrowers to lenders and to mortgage-backed asset investors.

As new regulatory structures are considered, these "new" questions will need to be addressed. The subprime crisis was largely due to credit extensions among mortgage bankers and thrift institutions. Additionally, the creation of complex new products such as mortgage-backed securities, collateralized mortgage obligations, collateralized debt obligations, auction rate securities, and credit default swaps were developed and marketed outside traditional regulatory structures. These gaps will certainly be considered in any new system of regulation and oversight.

On the other hand, some analysts have noted that, without the GLBA, the ability of the financial system to insulate investors from larger losses and instability would have been more restricted [see Chapter 2 below, for example]. Some banks that had extensive investment banking operations have experienced relatively large losses (Citigroup, Bank of America); but, it was the largely nonbank affiliated institutions, such as Bear Stearns and Lehman Brothers, whose failure is most closely linked to the financial crisis.

Looking forward, new regulation may or may not affect the GLBA. As noted above, Dodd-Frank did not alter the financial structure or other aspects of the GLBA very much. Dodd-Frank left the product offerings of financial institutions largely intact. The exceptions are that banks will no longer be able to undertake proprietary trading and their offerings of hedge fund services and private equity services will each be limited to 3% of total assets. Paul Volcker, former chairman of the Fed and adviser to President Obama, had recommended that all three of these activities be prohibited in the new legislation. Instead, only proprietary trading was prohibited and the other activities were limited. Of these three activities, only private equity had been expanded for U.S. banks in the GLBA.

In 2008, Secretary of Treasury Henry Paulson's *Blueprint* [see U.S. Treasury (2008)] called for a move to regulation by risk type rather than function, referred to as a move from functional regulation to objectives-based regulation. Essentially, the regulatory structure had remained unchanged by the GLBA, regulating various financial firms along product lines, despite the possibility of merging products lines under the GLBA. These regulatory "silos," regulating according to types of products rather than types of risk were a target of the Paulson *Blueprint*. This proposal did not survive into the Obama proposal of 2009 [see U.S. Treasury (2009)], though there was otherwise broad agreement in the two regulatory reform proposals and indeed, Dodd-Frank incorporated many of the proposals in both documents. For example, Dodd-Frank consolidated the Office of Thrift Supervision in the Office of the Comptroller of Currency and ended the thrift charter, as both sets of proposals had agreed earlier. It also set up a Federal Office of National Insurance to serve as a national center for insurance information and federal policy, as well as a coordinator for federal insurance policy in international policy coordination. Perhaps most importantly, it established a separate and independent consumer protection regulator, the Consumer Financial Protection Bureau, as both earlier proposals had recommended and, most notably, the most significant aspect of the Paulson plan's objectives-based regulation that carried through to the new legislation.

Another component of the objectives-based regulatory structure proposed in the *Blueprint* called for a regulator of financial stability. Dodd-Frank includes a Financial Stability Oversight Council composed of all the various existing regulators and chaired by the Secretary of Treasury. It does not abolish the Fed's role in monitoring and controlling financial stability, however, as envisioned by the *Blueprint*. Creation of the Consumer Financial Protection Bureau and the Financial Stability Oversight Council may be only the first steps in moving toward the new structure envisioned in the *Blueprint*. However, the *Blueprint*'s notion of having a single regulator for prudential regulation suffered major setbacks in its omission from the Obama proposals, its omission from Dodd-Frank, and from the abolition of the Financial Services Authority, the world's leading example of an objectives-based regulator, in favor of moving prudential regulation back under the Bank of England, the central bank and principal institution for financial stability.

Despite the criticism that the GLBA contributed to the financial crisis, the only two large investment banks that were not previously part of financial holding companies (Morgan Stanley and Goldman Sachs) became financial holding companies in order to improve their strength during the crisis. Smaller investment banks that do not also function as banks may remain so over the next decade if they survive as independent investment banks. Several large financial holding companies have emerged over the past 10 years including JP Morgan Chase, Bank of America, Citigroup, and Wells Fargo. There are about seven large foreign universal banks that rely primarily on deposit taking but also have securities. It is likely that efforts to expand product offerings, which have occurred over more than three decades, will continue, even among the large financial holding companies. Moreover, some midsize and small banks will continue to offer a broad portfolio of financial products and services. Whether financial holding companies will remain so in the future will depend, in part, on how new regulations under Dodd-Frank play out. Since all financial institutions are now subject to the Fed's new financial oversight and the new law gives significance to the Fed's notion of financial firms, broadly conceived, being "too interdependent to fail," there will be little advantage to being a bank, a bank holding, or a financial holding company and only more regular and pervasive costs associated with the tighter oversight of bank and bank holding companies. While the Fed could intervene, it is likely that as time makes the financial crisis and passage of Dodd-Frank more distant, some large financial firms that specialize in nonbank activity may give up their status as a financial holding company with a commercial bank affiliate.

References

Barth JR, Caprio G Jr, Levine R (2006) Rethinking bank regulation: till angels govern. Cambridge University Press, New York, NY

Benston G (2000) Consumer protection as justification for regulating financial-services firms and products. J Financ Serv Res 17:277–301

Bullard J (2010) Containing risk in the new global financial landscape. In:19th Annual Hyman P. Minsky conference on the state of the U.S. and world economies, New York, 10 Apr. http://research.stlouisfed.org/econ/bullard/BullardLevyMinskyFinalApril15.pdf

French KR et al (2010) The squam lake report. Princeton University Press, Princeton, NJ

Kaufman H (2010) The road to financial reformation: warnings, consequences, reforms. Wiley, Hoboken, NJ

Krugman P (2009) The Gramm connection. Personal blog, 29 Mar

Lawson N (2009) The future of capitalism. Financial Times, 12 May

Paletta D, Scannell K (2009) The question for those fixing the financial mess. Wall Street J, March 10

Reinhart CM, Rogoff KS (2009) This time is different. Princeton University Press, Princeton, NJ

Simpson AG (2009) Would Gramm Leach Bliley pass senator Gramm's own test? Insur J, 4 Apr. www.insurancejournal.com/news/national/2009/04/20/99770.htm

Uchitelle L (2010) Volcker pushes for reform, regretting past silence. New York Times, 9 July

U.S. Department of the Treasury (2009) Financial regulatory reform: a new foundation: rebuilding financial supervision and regulation, 17 June. http://www.financialstability.gov/docs/regs/FinalReport_web.pdf

U.S. Department of the Treasury (2008) Blueprint for a modernized financial regulatory structure, 31 Mar. http://www.ustreas.gov/press/releases/reports/Blueprint.pdf

VanHoose, D (2010) The industrial organization of banking. Springer, Berlin

Chapter 2
Did the "Repeal" of Glass-Steagall Have Any Role in the Financial Crisis? Not Guilty. Not Even Close

Peter J. Wallison

Introduction

The law that separates investment banking from commercial banking, popularly known as the Glass-Steagall Act, initially consisted of only four short statutory provisions. Section 16 generally prohibited banks from underwriting or dealing in securities,[1] and Section 21 prohibited securities firms from taking deposits.[2] The remaining two sections, 20[3] and 32,[4] prohibited banks from being affiliated with firms that are principally or primarily engaged in underwriting or dealing in securities. The Gramm-Leach-Bliley Act of 1999 (GLBA) repealed Sections 20 and 32, so that banks could thereafter be affiliated with securities firms; but Section 16 was left intact, so that whatever banks were forbidden or permitted to do by Glass-Steagall—before the enactment of the GLBA—remained in effect. The fact that Glass-Steagall, as it relates to banks, remains in full force and still governs the securities activities of banks is apparently not generally known. Those who blame the financial crisis—and specifically the weak financial condition of banks—on the "deregulation" of Glass-Steagall or the GLBA, seem to have only a fuzzy idea of what deregulation they are talking about. When challenged for specifics, they generally cite the "repeal" of Glass-Steagall. This chapter is intended to demonstrate that the significant elements

---

P.J. Wallison (✉)
American Enterprise Institute for Public Policy Research, 1150 Seventeenth Street, N.W., Washington, DC 20036, USA
e-mail: pwallison@aei.org

This chapter also appeared as Networks Financial Institute *Policy Brief* 2009-PB-09.

[1] Section 16, as incorporated in 12 U.S.C 24 (Seventh), both prohibits banks from underwriting and dealing in securities and permits them to act as brokers, as follows: "The business of dealing in securities and stock by the association shall be limited to purchasing and selling such securities and stock without recourse, solely upon the order, and for the account of, customers, and in no case for its own account, and the association shall not underwrite any issue of securities or stock."

[2] 12 U.S.C. 378.

[3] 12 U.S.C. 377.

[4] 12 U.S.C 78.

J.A. Tatom (ed.), *Financial Market Regulation*, DOI 10.1007/978-1-4419-6637-7_2,

of Glass-Steagall—those that apply to banks—were never repealed, and thus that neither the financial problems of banks, nor the financial crisis itself, can be blamed on the GLBA's supposed "repeal" of Glass-Steagall.

The term "bank" is often misused, and it is important to clarify how the term will be used in this chapter. A bank is a very specific type of entity, chartered by the federal government or a state, to take deposits that are withdrawable on demand—the hallmark of a bank—and make loans. In the discussion that follows, I will use the term "bank" to refer to depository institutions chartered by national or state banking authorities and insured by the Federal Deposit Insurance Corporation (FDIC). Recently, it has become common—especially in the media—to refer to other kinds of financial institutions as "banks" or part of something called the "shadow banking system," even though these nonbank financial institutions—securities firms (also called investment banks), insurance companies, finance companies, hedge funds and others—do not take deposits, and their deposits are not insured by the FDIC. To be sure, these nonbank financial institutions make loans, but lending alone is not banking, and the consistent misuse of the term "bank" to describe nondepository institutions has sown a great deal of confusion about what real banks can and cannot do.

Since we are interested in the effect of Glass-Steagall's repeal on the financial condition of banks, and the possible role of repeal in the banking crisis, it is important to distinguish between banks and other nonbank financial institutions—particularly, bank holding companies (BHCs) and investment banks. As we will see, banks can engage in securities trading for only a very limited category of securities—primarily government securities or those backed by the government—but a BHC or an investment bank is not subject to these restrictions. A BHC is an ordinary business corporation that controls a bank; it is not specially chartered like a bank and not permitted to take deposits. Nor does a BHC have other attributes of a bank, which include automatic access to the Federal Reserve's (Fed) discount window, participation in the nation's payment system, and deposits insured by the FDIC. In addition, BHCs are regulated by the Fed, while most banks—and virtually all large ones—are regulated by the Office of the Comptroller of the Currency, a unit of the Treasury department that charters and supervises national banks. State chartered banks are regulated by their home state regulators and the FDIC at the federal level.

An investment bank is a securities firm—a firm specializing in the business of trading securities of all kinds. Investment banks are not backed by the government in any way and—unlike banks—are intended to be risk-takers. The Glass-Steagall Act was designed to separate commercial banks from investment banks; it did that simply by prohibiting affiliations between the two and by prohibiting commercial banks from engaging in the business of investment banks—that is, underwriting and dealing in securities. After 65 years, and many academic studies showing that this separation was unnecessary and misplaced,[5] the GLBA repealed the affiliation

[5]See, e.g., the work cited by Barth, Brumbaugh and Wilcox, "The repeal of Glass-Steagall and the advent of broad banking. J Econ Persp, May 2000.

prohibitions of Sections 20 and 32, but—as noted above—left the restrictions on bank securities activities intact.

A good example of the misuse of the term bank appears in a recent article by reporter Louis Uchitelle in the *New York Times*. The article notes that Paul Volcker "wants the nation's banks to be prohibited from . . . trading risky securities, the very practice that got the biggest ones into trouble in 2008."[6] After scanning this sentence, readers might be forgiven for believing that banks trade risky securities. But that would be incorrect. Because of the continuing applicability of Glass-Steagall, banks are still prohibited from trading securities—other than various government-issued or government-backed securities that are generally risk-free. Under these circumstances, it's not clear what institutions Uchitelle is referring to as banks; he could have meant the BHCs that control banks, or he could be referring to subsidiaries of these BHCs that trade securities, or even to subsidiaries of banks that are permitted to trade securities after the GLBA. But he could not have been referring to banks themselves. Imprecise use of language like this is one of the reasons that many people have the mistaken view that Glass-Steagall was repealed by the GLBA, and that banks can now trade risky securities. But as I will show, banks—the government insured entities that are permitted to take deposits—are still forbidden by Glass-Steagall to trade any but the safest kinds of securities.

Glass-Steagall in the Context of Banking Law

U.S. banking laws are designed to separate a bank from the risks that might be created by the activities of its affiliates—particularly, its holding company or any subsidiary or affiliate of the bank that is permitted to engage in securities trading. This separation is effected by severely restricting the transactions between banks and their affiliates. There are two principal reasons for these restrictions: (i) to ensure that the so-called bank "safety net"—deposit insurance and access to the discount window—is not extended beyond banks to their holding companies or their nonbank affiliates, and (ii) to protect the bank's financial position from exposure to the risks that are taken by its affiliates and securities subsidiaries. Insofar as possible, the idea is to allow a holding company—and even a bank securities affiliate—to fail without endangering the health of any related bank.

In order to reduce the range of bank risk taking, banking laws and regulations also limit the activities in which banks themselves can engage. That is the context in which the Glass-Steagall Act should be viewed. As noted above, Glass-Steagall continues to prohibit banks from "underwriting or dealing" in securities. "Underwriting" refers to the business of assuming the risk that an issue of securities will be fully sold to investors, while "dealing" refers to the business of holding an inventory of securities for trading purposes. Nevertheless, banks are in the business of making investments, and Glass-Steagall did not attempt to interfere with that

---

[6]Uchitelle, Op. cit., note 1.

activity. Thus, although Glass-Steagall prohibited underwriting and dealing, it did not interfere with the ability of banks to "purchase and sell" securities they acquired for investment. The difference between "purchasing and selling" and "underwriting and dealing" is crucially important. A bank may purchase a security—say, a bond—and then decide to sell it when the bank needs cash or believes that the bond is no longer a good investment. This activity is different from buying an inventory of bonds for the *purpose* of selling them, which would be considered dealing.

Nor did Glass Steagall ever prohibit banks from buying and selling whole loans, even though a loan could be seen as a security. When securitization was developed, banks were permitted—even under Glass-Steagall—to securitize their loan assets and sell their loans in securitized form. Similarly, banks were always permitted to purchase and sell securities based on assets, such as mortgages, that they could otherwise hold as whole loans. Glass-Steagall did not affect this authority, but the act was interpreted to make clear that they could not deal in or underwrite these or other securities. Under this interpretation, banks could not underwrite or deal in mortgage backed securities (MBS), but they were free to buy these securities as investment securities and sell them when they believed that would be appropriate. Again, these restrictions remained in force after GLBA; the only difference was that GLBA now permitted banks to be affiliated with firms that engaged in underwriting or dealing in securities, including MBS, and this affiliation could be through a subsidiary of the bank's holding company (both the bank and the securities firm would then be under common control) or through a subsidiary of the bank itself. In both cases—whether the securities firm is a holding company affiliate or a subsidiary—there are severe restrictions on transactions between the bank and the securities firm. These are outlined below.

Finally, Glass-Steagall permitted banks to underwrite and deal in government securities, or securities backed by a government, and this was unaffected by GLBA. For example, banks could, before and after Glass-Steagall and GLBA, underwrite and deal in U.S. government securities, the securities of Fannie Mae and Freddie Mac, and the general obligation bonds of states and municipalities. This exemption applies mostly to securities that are backed by the U.S. government or by a state or municipality, although it also applies in cases—such as Fannie Mae and Freddie Mac—where the issuer of the security is performing a government mission but not strictly backed or guaranteed by the federal government or a state or municipal government.

From this analysis, it should be clear that the GLBA's repeal solely of the affiliation provisions of the Glass-Steagall Act did not permit banks to do anything that they were previously prohibited from doing. Accordingly, it is incorrect to suggest that Glass-Steagall's repeal had any affect whatever on the ability of banks to engage directly in the risky business of underwriting and dealing in securities. Nevertheless, it is reasonable to ask whether the repeal of the affiliation provisions of Glass-Steagall could have caused banks to suffer the losses that were a prominent feature of the financial crisis, and whether the possibility of affiliation with banks could have caused the losses to the large securities firms—also known as investment banks—that drove one of them into bankruptcy (Lehman Brothers), two of them into becoming subsidiaries of banks (Merrill Lynch and Bear Stearns), and two more into recasting themselves as BHCs under the supervision of the Fed (Goldman Sachs and Morgan Stanley). The remaining portions of this chapter will review the specific restrictions that Glass-Steagall imposes on banks, the restrictions on transactions between banks and their securities affiliates and subsidiaries, and the possibility that affiliations with a bank—permissible after GLBA—might have caused the losses suffered by the large investment banks.

Regulation of the Securities Activities of National Banks

Almost all the big banks—Citibank, Wachovia, Bank of America, JP Morgan Chase, and Wells Fargo—are (or were in the case of Wachovia) national banks, chartered, regulated, and supervised by the Comptroller of the Currency, an official of the Treasury Department. National banks are creatures of the federal government and derive all their powers from federal law. State-chartered banks are subject to the different legal regimes of the chartering states, but if they are insured by the FDIC—and virtually all state-charted banks are federally insured—they are subject to substantially the same Glass-Steagall rules as those applicable to national banks. Since national banks are chartered under federal law, their powers as banks are outlined in 12 U.S.C. 24 (Seventh), the basic statute that enumerates the specific activities in which national banks are permitted to engage. If an activity is not listed in or implied by this statutory section, national banks cannot engage in it.

The Office of the Comptroller of the Currency (OCC) has issued extensive regulations outlining what national banks are authorized to do under 12 U.S.C 24 (Seventh), which is the statutory provision that incorporates Section 16 of the Glass-Steagall Act. Section 16, as outlined above, permits banks to act as agents or brokers for securities, but prohibits them from underwriting or dealing. Since GLBA made no change in the provisions of Glass-Steagall concerning bank securities activities, these regulations were not modified as a result of the GLBA. Under the OCC regulations, banks could underwrite or deal in only two categories of securities, called Type I and Type II.

Type I securities are as follows:

(1) Obligations of the United States;
(2) Obligations issued, insured, or guaranteed by a department or an agency of the U.S. government, if the obligation, insurance, or guarantee commits the full faith and credit of the United States for the repayment of the obligation;
(3) Obligations issued by a department or agency of the United States, or an agency or political subdivision of a State of the United States, that represent an interest in a loan or a pool of loans made to third parties, if the full faith and credit of the United States has been validly pledged for the full and timely payment of interest on, and principal of, the loans in the event of nonpayment by the third party obligor(s);

(4) General obligations of a State of the United States or any political subdivision thereof; and municipal bonds if the national bank is well capitalized as defined in 12 CFR 6.4(b)(1);
(5) Obligations authorized under 12 U.S.C. 24 (Seventh) as permissible for a national bank to deal in, underwrite, purchase, and sell for the bank's own account, including qualified Canadian government obligations; and
(6) Other securities the OCC determines to be eligible as Type I securities under 12 U.S.C. 24 (Seventh).

Type II securities are as follows:

(1) Obligations issued by a State, or a political subdivision or agency of a State, for housing, university, or dormitory purposes that would not satisfy the definition of Type I securities pursuant to paragraph (j) of §1.2;
(2) Obligations of international and multilateral development banks and organizations listed in 12 U.S.C. 24 (Seventh);
(3) Other obligations listed in 12 U.S.C. 24 (Seventh) as permissible for a bank to deal in, underwrite, purchase, and sell for the bank's own account, subject to a limitation per obligor of 10% of the bank's capital and surplus; and
(4) Other securities the OCC determines to be eligible as Type II securities under 12 U.S.C. 24 (Seventh).[7]

The regulations relating to Type III, IV, and V securities are detailed and technical, but generally these categories include corporate bonds, municipal bonds that are not general obligation securities, small business-related securities that are investment grade, and securities related to commercial or residential mortgages.[8] The OCC's regulations place limits on the size of bank holdings of securities in these categories, but banks are permitted to purchase and sell these securities in the same way that they can purchase and sell whole loans. However, banks are not permitted to underwrite and deal in Type III, IV, or V securities.

Accordingly, under the OCC's regulations, before and after GLBA, banks could not underwrite or deal in MBS or other nongovernmental securities. They could, of course, invest in MBS, but they could do this before and after the adoption of both Glass-Steagall and the GLBA, just as they were permitted to invest in the whole loans that the MBS represented. In other words, to the extent that banks suffered losses on MBS, collateralized debt obligations, or other instruments that were securitized versions of whole loans, their losses came from imprudent investments and not from trading—that is, underwriting or dealing—in these instruments. It would be correct to say, therefore, that banks suffered losses on these securities by acting as

[7]CFR Title 12: Banks and Banking, Part 1—Investment Securities, Sec 1.2 (a) and (b), available at http://www.occ.gov/fr/cfrparts/12CFR01.htm# § 1.02 Definitions.
[8]Ibid.

banks—as lenders—and not as the securities traders that some commentators seem to imagine.

Bank Affiliations with Securities Firms

Although banks themselves could not underwrite or deal in MBS or other non-governmental securities under Glass-Steagall, the GLBA permitted banks to be affiliated with securities firms. Did this newly permitted affiliation cause banks to take risks and suffer losses they would not have sustained if the GLBA had not repealed the affiliation prohibitions in the Glass-Steagall Act? The answer again is "no." Banking law and regulations prevent the activities of a bank securities affiliate or subsidiary from adversely affecting the financial condition of a related bank.

As noted above, banking laws and regulations are designed to separate banks as fully as possible from the risks that are taken by their holding companies, or by any affiliate that is a subsidiary of the holding company. Although it is possible after GLBA for a bank to hold a securities firm as a subsidiary, the OCC regulations require that this subsidiary be treated like a subsidiary of the holding company, rather than like a subsidiary of the bank. The principal statutory provisions that wall off the bank from its holding company and from its own securities subsidiary are sections 23A and 23B of the Federal Reserve Act,[9] which are applicable to all banks, whether federal or state chartered.

Section 23A limits the financial and other transactions between a bank and its holding company or any holding company subsidiary. For extensions of credit, the limit on a bank's exposure to its holding company or any holding company subsidiary is 10% of the bank's capital and surplus for any one holding company affiliate and 20% for all affiliates in the aggregate. All such lending or extensions of credit must be collateralized with U.S. government securities up to the value of the loan, and must be overcollateralized if other types of marketable securities are used as collateral.[10] All transactions between a bank and its affiliates must be on the same terms as the bank would offer to an unrelated party.[11] Other restrictions also apply, including prohibitions on the bank's purchase of a low quality asset from an affiliate,[12] or the bank's issuance of a guarantee, acceptance, or letter of credit on behalf of an affiliate.[13] All these restrictions are applied by the Comptroller of the Currency to a national bank's relationship with a securities subsidiary.[14]

---

[9] 12 U.S.C. 371c and 371c-1

[10] 12 U.S.C. 371c (c) (1)

[11] 12 U.S.C.-1(a) (1)

[12] 12 U.S.C. 371c (a) (3)

[13] 12 U.S.C. 371c (b) (7)

[14] CFR Title 12, Sec 5.39 (h) (5), available at http://ecfr.gpoaccess.gov/cgi/t/text/text-idx?c=ecfr;sid=1362d767c96a0fe1dccee11e2b313524;rgn=div5;view=text;node=12%3A1.0.1.1.5;idno=12;cc=ecfr#12:1.0.1.1.5.3.4.8.

Of course, if the securities firm is a subsidiary of the bank rather than a holding company affiliate, the bank will have an investment in the subsidiary which could be lost if the subsidiary fails. However, the OCC's regulations require that the bank "must deduct the aggregate amount of its outstanding equity investment, including retained earnings, in its [securities subsidiary] from its total assets and tangible equity and deduct such investment from its risk-based capital . . . and . . . may not consolidate the assets and liabilities of [the securities subsidiary] with those of the bank."[15]

These restrictions substantially reduce any likelihood that the business of a securities affiliate or subsidiary will have an adverse effect on the bank. The bank's lending to a securities affiliate or subsidiary is severely limited, must be collateralized, and must be made on the same terms that the bank would offer to an unrelated third party. In addition, the bank's investment in a securities subsidiary is not recorded as an asset on its balance sheet. In other words, they are effectively written off at the time they are made. Thereafter, if the securities subsidiary should fail, there will be no impact on the bank's balance sheet. Under these circumstances, it is highly unlikely that any activity carried on in a securities affiliate or securities subsidiary of a bank could have an adverse effect on the financial condition of the bank.

It is very doubtful that the restrictions of Sections 23A and 23B would be ignored either by a bank as an institution or by any director, officer, or employee of a bank or its holding company. The law permits civil and criminal penalties for knowing violations of the 23A and 23B, or any other regulation, and the civil fines involved can be enormous. For example, banking regulators can impose a *personal* civil money penalty of up to $1 million per day on any bank director or officer, for every day that a violation continues, if the director or officer engaged in a knowing violation of an order or regulation, or a breach of fiduciary duty, that causes a substantial loss to a bank.[16]

Accordingly, it is reasonably clear that GLBA's repeal of the affiliation provisions of the Glass-Steagall Act did not have and could not have had any adverse effect on the financial condition of any parent or affiliated bank, and thus did not contribute and could not have contributed in any way to the financial crisis.

What Caused the Financial Instability and Possible Insolvency of the Largest Banks?

Since banks themselves could not engage in any securities activities after the enactment of the GLBA that they could not do before the act's adoption, one must look elsewhere for the causes of the financial weakness that many U.S. banks suffered.

[15] CFR Title 12, Sec 5.39(h)(1)(i) and (ii). Available at http://ecfr.gpoaccess.gov/cgi/t/text/text-idx?c=ecfr;sid=1362d767c96a0fe1dccee11e2b313524;rgn=div5;view=text;node=12%3A1.0.1.1.5;idno=12;cc=ecfr#12:1.0.1.1.5.3.4.8.

[16] 12 U.S.C. 1818(i).

As noted above, there is strong evidence that, despite heavy regulation, many of the banks that got into trouble did so by failing to act prudently in their investment or lending activities—in other words, in their capacity as banks—and not because they engaged in securities trading or were affiliated with securities firms that were underwriting and dealing in securities. If this is true, bank losses should show up in the types of assets that banks traditionally hold—mortgages, commercial and industrial loans, and investments—and not in their trading accounts. That, in fact, is what we see.

In the spring of 2009, at the request of the Treasury Department, the Fed and the Comptroller of the Currency supervised a special process of stress testing by the 19 largest U.S. financial institutions (most of which were banks). Table 2.1 is taken from a report by the Fed on the stress tests, and shows the projected aggregate losses for all 19 institutions in an adverse economic and financial scenario.[17] For purposes of this discussion, it is important to note that the projected losses that these 19 institutions were likely to suffer came from the usual assets that are found in banks—residential and commercial mortgages, commercial loans, credit card receivables, and the like. The relatively high level of trading and counterparty losses in the table—still a relatively small portion of the total—is probably attributable to including the holdings of the independent investment banks (Goldman Sachs and Morgan Stanley) among the 19 institutions, and the consolidation of the assets of the investment banks acquired in 2008 by JP Morgan Chase (Bear Stearns) and Bank of America (Merrill Lynch). Thus, the projected aggregate trading and counterparty losses for those four banks were over $80 billion, out of a total of $99 billion for all 19 institutions as a group.[18] Similar losses for all the other banks in the survey were negligible.

Table 2.1 Estimated losses for 2009 and 2010 for the more adverse scenario

Loan category	Estimated loss (in billions of dollars)	Percentage of losses within category
First lien mortgages	102.3	8.8
Second/junior lien mortgages	83.2	13.8
Commercial and industrial loans	60.1	6.1
Commercial real estate loans	53.0	8.5
Credit card loans	82.4	22.5
Securities (AFS and HTM)	35.2	N/A
Trading and counterparty	99.3	N/A
Other[a]	83.7	N/A
Total estimated losses (before purchase accounting adjustments)		$599.2 billion

[a]Includes other consumer and nonconsumer loans and miscellaneous commitments and obligations.

[17]Board of Governors of the Federal Reserve System, "The Supervisory Capital Assessment Program: Overview of Results," May 7, 2009, available at www.federalreserve.gov/newsevents/press/bcreg/bcreg20090507a1.pdf (accessed May 29, 2009).

[18]Ibid., Appendix.

Accordingly, it would be accurate to conclude that the enactment of GLBA—to the extent that it allowed banks to affiliate with securities firms—did not result in major losses at the banks as the result of their own securities activities or the securities activities of their subsidiaries or affiliates. On the contrary, it seems clear that the banks got into trouble, and precipitated the financial crisis and the recession, by doing exactly the things we expect them to do—make loans and hold normal and traditional financial assets. The absence of any major source of projected losses coming from securities trading activities shows that the repeal of the affiliation provisions of the Glass-Steagall Act did not induce the banks to take on unusual amounts of trading assets. Nor was trading a significant source of their projected financial losses.

Did the Securities Firms (Investment Banks) Get into Trouble Because of Their Affiliations with Banks?

There is still one other possibility—that GLBA's repeal of the affiliation provisions in Glass-Steagall enabled securities firms to establish relationships with banks and that these relationships caused the near-insolvency of Merrill Lynch, Goldman Sachs, and Morgan Stanley, and the bankruptcy of Lehman Brothers. However, this seems highly unlikely. Each of these investment banking firms had a subsidiary bank—something that would not have been possible before the repeal of the affiliation provisions of Glass-Steagall—but these bank affiliates were far too small to cause any serious losses to their massive parents.

The following table shows the relative size of the parent and the subsidiary bank for each of the four major securities firms (Table 2.2).

Table 2.2 Subsidiaries of investment banks are relatively small

Investment bank	Investment bank assets (2008)	Subsidiary bank's assets
Goldman Sachs	$800 billion	25 billion[19]
Morgan Stanley	660 billion	38.5 billion[20]
Merrill Lynch	670 billion	35 billion[21]
Lehman Brothers	600 billion	4.5 billion[22]

[19]Federal Reserve Board, "Order Approving Formation of Bank Holding Companies," The Goldman Sachs Group, Inc., September 21, 2009, p.1.

[20]Federal Reserve Board, "Order Approving Formation of Bank Holding Companies," Morgan Stanley, Inc., September 21, 2009, p.1.

[21]iBanknet, Merrill Lynch Bank & Trust Co, FSB, October 22, 2009; available at http://www.ibanknet.com/scripts/callreports/getbank.aspx?ibnid=usa_2577494.

[22]Investigative Reporting Workshop, Woodlands Commercial Bank, available at http://www.ibanknet.com/scripts/callreports/getbank.aspx?ibnid=usa_3376461.

In light of the huge disparities between the size of each major investment bank and the size of its depository institution subsidiary, it is highly unlikely that the insured bank subsidiary could cause any serious financial problem for the parent investment bank, or significantly enhance the financial problems that the parent company had created for itself through its own operations.

Conclusion

Accordingly, it seems clear that the banks that encountered financial problems got into trouble the old fashioned way—by making imprudent loans. There is no evidence of significant amounts of risky securities trading activities. Similarly, the investment banks got into trouble as traders and risk takers—their traditional business—and not because of their affiliations with the small banks they held as subsidiaries. Thus, it is possible to conclude without much question that GLBA's repeal of the affiliation provisions of the Glass-Steagall Act had no significant effect whatever on the financial crisis.

Chapter 3
Glass-Steagall in Our Future: How Straight, How Narrow

Martin Mayer

A dozen years ago, Randall Kroszner, soon to be one of George W. Bush's economic advisors and a Governor of the Federal Reserve (Fed), could comment in a Levy Institute seminar, without fear of contradiction, that there was no evidence to back the "public interest rationale" for the separation of commercial and investment banking. Except for deposit insurance (and even here, there were mutterings about moral hazard), the limits imposed on banking by the Glass-Steagall Act of 1933 were roundly condemned through the entire cadre of academic and corporate economists, as the old law was unceremoniously junked 66 years later. A few of us did worry about the loss of information that could result as the veil of bank secrecy was extended over additional transactions, but we were not really respectable. Today, we few, still not a happy few, stand on the high ground of observed recent experience and watch the survivors of the still acclaimed wave of financial innovation struggle defensively, if not repentantly, up the slopes of what Alan Greenspan called "shocked disbelief."

Ten years after its repeal, Glass-Steagall has a constituency again. Lord Turner, in his report to the Financial Services Authority (FSA), summed up the moral argument: "We have to prevent large commercial banks from taking the benefit of retail deposit insurance, lender of last resort access, and too big to fail status, and using these advantages in risky proprietary trading activities of little social value."[1] Mervyn King, Governor of the Bank of England, has called for firm separation of the "public utility" banks from the merchant banks. Paul Volcker has publicly complained that nobody in the White House or the Treasury Department has listened to his counsel that, if you wish to avoid more fiascos like those we have witnessed in the last year, you'd better take control of what insured depositories can do with the money. Giving the finger to Sandy Weill, with whom he had built the

M. Mayer (✉)
The Brookings Institution, 1775 Massachusetts Avenue NW, Washington, DC 20036, USA
e-mail: mmayer2a1@aim.com

This chapter also appeared as Networks Financial Institute *Policy Brief* 2009-PB-07.

[1] Griffiths (2009).

J.A. Tatom (ed.), *Financial Market Regulation*, DOI 10.1007/978-1-4419-6637-7_3,

monstrous and dysfunctional Citicorp, John Reed then contributed a laconic statement of support for Volcker's position on the letters page of the *New York Times*.[2] The September/October 2009 issue of *Harvard Magazine* offers an article by David A. Moss, professor at that university's business school, with the flat statement: "The simple truth is that New Deal financial regulation worked. In fact, it worked remarkably well."[3] I am going to dissent from that comment, too, because the net effect of the New Deal reforms in a time of rapid technological change was to diminish the franchise value of the banking license, from which much evil flowed. Then, perhaps, we can look ahead.

We start with the fact that the separation of commercial banking from investment banking, a shorthand term for the securities business, was not a new idea in 1933. It was the British custom and had been American law and custom until the turn of the twentieth century, when deposit-taking banks began forming "securities affiliates." Such affiliates were first recognized in law by the McFadden Act of 1927. By 1929, they had taken over half the corporate underwriting business in the United States. The phenomenon was not entirely welcome. In 1930, an article in the first issue of *Fortune* worried that a commercial bank involved with the sale of securities might "get into promotional difficulties of which it should be judge rather than advocate."[4] Herbert Hoover in 1932 called for an end to "conditions which permit the credit machinery of the country to be made available without check for wholesale speculation in securities."[5] On the day after he succeeded Albert Wiggins as president of the Chase National Bank in 1933, Winthrop Aldrich announced his bank would cut its ties with its securities affiliate, proclaiming it "impossible to consider the events which took place during the past 10 years without being forced to the conclusion that intimate connection between commercial banking and investment banking almost inevitably leads to abuses."[6] More recently—earlier this year, in fact—Henry Kaufman agreed, arguing that "these problems are likely to be particularly acute in the context of a bank holding company with an incentive to cross-sell its products among its diverse customer base."[7]

Abuse of securities powers by banks had not, in fact, played much of a role in the financial disasters of 1929–1933. Most of the banks' worst violations were manipulating the stock market price of their own shares, and the activity that was most resented—the drainage of cash away from productive uses to the "call money" market that fed stock speculation—was done by the big corporations without the mediation of the banks in what we have recently and insistently been taught to call a shadow banking system. There has grown up a revisionist history that really there wasn't anything all that bad about the stock market of the late 1920s, led as it

[2]Reed (2009).

[3]Moss (2009, 24).

[4]*Fortune Magazine* (1930, 138).

[5]Hoover (1932).

[6]Perkins (June 1971, 525).

[7]Kaufman (2009, 121).

was by a combination of the partnership investment banks and the rapidly growing securities affiliates of the commercial banks.

In fact, there was a lot of misbehavior with other people's money in the 1920s. Looking back from his old age, George Moore, who would go on to create Citicorp from the chassis of First National City Bank, wrote that "People who did not live through it can scarcely imagine the Wall Street of the 1920s. It seemed that money was something you played with: everybody had it." (Moore did not himself buy stocks: "If you work in the undertaker's parlor," he wrote, "you're a little more careful how you cross the street.")[8] Some of the stories are quite like our current interests. Albert Wiggins in 1933, for example, was president and CEO of Chase, a member on 56 corporate boards of directors, and part of the executive committee of the Federal Reserve Bank of New York. His own board voted him a retirement salary of $100,000 a year, and during his last 4 years with the bank he received total salary and bonuses of $1,500,000. That's in 1933 dollars. "Wiggins," historian Donald Ritchie wrote in 1987 in a paper for the Senate Banking Committee, "protested that his associates from the bank had determined these generous emoluments. 'And I helped to fix theirs,' he added. . . ."[9]

There are three reasonable arguments that blame our recent financial disaster on the repeal of Glass-Steagall. The most obvious is that it invited bankers to venture out into water that was way over their heads. Martin Wolf, in the *Financial Times*, makes the obvious point, commenting that "Financial liberalisation and financial crisis go together like a horse and carriage."[10] George Moore, sent to represent National City Bank at the final conference between the House and Senate in 1933, said that the argument against deposit insurance was that the competence of bankers was not an insurable risk. Academics and mathematicians found it easy in recent years to peddle what were in reality very risky strategies because bankers had no notion of the dangers inherent in selling volatility.

Andrew Sheng in his new book *From Asian to Global Financial Crisis* makes the technical argument, presenting the modern financial system as a network subject to viral attack. "In network terms," Sheng writes, "Glass-Steagall set up firewalls between networks to prevent contagion between them. Repeal of the act in 1999 set the stage for complete network integration and therefore massive contagion."[11]

The third argument is psychological, and it stresses the basic incompatibility of commercial banking and investment banking. The commercial banker looks at a loan and asks how the borrower is going to repay it, and, if he's any good, he expects a detailed answer; the investment banker looks at a financing and asks how he is going to sell the paper, and he will proceed happily with any plausible answer. In Sheng's more elegant formulation, "You cannot mix the culture

[8]Moore (1987, 70–71).

[9]*Modernization of the Glass-Steagall Act,* Hearing Before the Committee on Banking, U.S. Senate. Washington, DC: GPO, July 30, 1987, 45.

[10]Wolf (2009, 8).

[11]Sheng (2009, 326).

of investment banking (where risk taking is key) and commercial banking (where prudence is vital) under one roof." Within the bank, the proponent of originate-and-distribute enjoys a big advantage from day one in his competition on with the old-fashioned banker who wants to lend-and-hold: his profit comes at the start, off the top.

Twenty years ago, I wrote an article about Darla Moore of Chemical Bank, who with the lawyer Harvey Miller re-invented Debtor-in-Possession financing. She was about to marry the billionaire Richard Rainwater and saw no reason not to give her views about how the bank was run. Her description of how large loan applications were considered was, "You send it to Jimmy Lee. If he says he can blow it out the door, you make the loan; if he says he can't sell it, you don't make the loan." Mr. Lee now performs these same functions for JP Morgan Chase, which is the name we now give to Chemical Bank. One should note that when Lee started his activities, Glass-Steagall was still the law; the only difference Gramm-Leach-Bliley made was that the new law expanded his list of potential customers. Joe Grundfest, when he was an U.S. Securities and Exchange Commission (SEC) Commissioner, liked to say that a term loan is nothing but an illiquid junk bond. This is not true, because the two instruments are on different ends of the great continuum that leads from relationship to transaction—but one can (and one did) behave as though it were true.

Government-supported securitization as a way to multiply the funds banks can lend goes back to the Federal Housing Administration in 1934, offering to insure 20-year self-amortizing mortgages so Walter Bimson of Valley National Bank in Phoenix could sell them to insurance companies in the northeast and replenish his lendable funds. But those were real sales to third parties. Not until Bill Seidman's Federal Deposit Insurance Corporation (FDIC) invented the collateralized debt obligation (CDO), looking to resolve the savings and loan (S&L) mess by selling with partial government guarantees the entire asset portfolios of failed depositories, did it become acceptable procedure to form structured investment vehicles (SIVs) that, with support from the sponsoring bank, could pretend to transfer the ownership of defective assets. Part of the rationale for Glass-Steagall had been to prevent such concealment.

Perhaps the closest link between the repeal of Glass-Steagall and the recent disaster is that they share a tap-root: the belief within the industry, in academia and especially among the government supervisors, banking (defined as lending money and getting it back) is no longer a profitable business. The job of pricing loans can be done more cheaply, if perhaps not so well, in securities markets. But the banks are too important for the government to let them be chopped up by Schumpeterian creative destruction. Banks are special, as E. Gerald Corrigan, now of Goldman Sachs, insisted when he was president of the Federal Reserve Bank of Minneapolis; their deposit liabilities are the transaction balances of the economy. When a securities house goes bankrupt, its shareholders and creditors absorb the loss. There is no court-supervised bankruptcy procedure for banks despite the obvious need for some system to permit limiting the protection of careless lenders to a failing bank. The losses of a decapitalized banking system, as Andrew Sheng pointed out a dozen years ago in his study for the World Bank,[12] are an implicit fiscal deficit, whether or not the institutions involved are formally declared too big to fail. It is worth remembering that the phrase "too big to fail" goes back to testimony in 1984 before the House Banking Committee by Todd Conover (an accountant, not a banker), defending his decision as Comptroller of the Currency that Continental-Illinois, then the tenth largest bank in the United States, could not be permitted to collapse, even if that meant that the FDIC had to borrow money from the Federal Reserve to pay off the purchasers of the holding company's commercial paper, some of which had been issued in the Caribbean as a tax dodge. Bernanke and Paulson and Geithner did not invent the expenditure of money *ultra vires* for pious purposes.

The effort of this chapter is to get people to think a little more in new directions, so I am going to be discursive. There is certainly a case to be made that who regulates is more important than the laws themselves. Bill Martin, who really believed his job was to take away the punch bowl just when the party was getting interesting, would not have had Alan Greenspan's problem in deciding whether or not there was a bubble in housing. (Bill Martin, after his retirement from the Fed, warned his successor Arthur Burns that the quality of the nation's savings had been dropping. Burns said that the numbers looked okay, and Martin said, "People aren't saving any more so they can send their kids to college. They don't think they can do that now. They're saving to buy a piece of land in Virginia. That's a very different kind of savings."[13]) I am prepared to argue that, if Chris Cox had been chairman of the SEC and Ben Bernanke chairman of the Fed in 1992, we would have rescued Drexel Burnham—and if Richard Breeden had been chairman of the SEC in spring 2008, Bear Stearns would have been dissolved. The Fed has always refused to accept that it regulates the banking system. The approved word has always been "supervised." What was not understood in Maiden Lane and still isn't is that when you supervise you become complicit.

The Glass-Steagall Act was intended to keep banks out of activities that might threaten the stability of the payments system or the financial markets. Farmers and merchants all over the country resented the call money market in New York that drained cash from their local banks, because speculative use of the money in the national money market was more profitable than conventional lending. A debt deflation nobody understood very well had placed immense burdens on enterprise, and there had been just enough skullduggery in the management of the large banks to give Congress a rationale for control. This was still the age of prohibition, before the Great War taught government that the easy way to get something from an economy or a society was to pay a little extra for it.

So deposit-taking banks were forbidden to pay interest on demand deposits and were limited in the rates they could offer for time deposits, which could not be called savings accounts. They were prohibited from owning nonbank businesses,

---

[12] Sheng (1996).

[13] Mayer (1980, 334).

from offering their services interstate and from providing insurance or underwriting securities issuance, except for municipal paper. Private ownership of monetary gold was forbidden, and Federal Reserve banknotes were to become the national currency, except for dollar bills, which remained Treasury paper surrogates for silver ("payable in silver to the bearer on demand") for another generation. Checks written on member banks of the Federal Reserve System had to be accepted for face value by other member banks of the System. The Federal Reserve was empowered to limit the use of margin in securities trading, and did.

Most important of all, to prevent runs on the banks, consumer deposits up to a maximum of $2500 per account were insured by a new Federal Deposit Insurance Corporation that had a call on the Treasury if necessary. (The $2500 figure was the same as the maximum size of a postal savings account.[14]) Member banks had to keep a fraction of their money on deposit at the Federal Reserve Bank where they were a member, and this fractional reserve system was the engine of monetary policy, providing a multiplier for the actions of the open market committee. If the Fed added a thousand dollars to bank reserves by purchasing paper in the market or making a loan at the discount window, the result with a 10% reserve would be an increase of $10,000 in the assets and liabilities of the banks. If the Fed sold a thousand dollars of paper into the market, pocketing the proceeds, banks would be compelled to cut their collective balance sheets by $10,000. The banks had to square their accounts at the Fed every Wednesday afternoon.

Ralph Leach of JP Morgan used that bank's correspondent relationships around the country to create a market in "Fed Funds" that served the purposes once served by the call money market. Walter Wriston and John Exter then found a way to fund the money center banks through the issuance of negotiable CDs—and in 1969 the Fed, terrified by the collapse of the market for Chrysler paper following the bankruptcy of Penn Central, agreed to eliminate interest rate ceilings on bank liabilities expressed as negotiable CDs of more than $100,000. Fear that a nascent Eurodollar market could create dollars offshore if foreign central banks got in the habit of making Eurodollar loans abroad led Fed chairman Arthur Burns to negotiate a deal with his European fellows that they would ship their excess dollar receipts to New York to be invested by the Fed in U.S. government securities "held for foreign official account." Recurrent bouts of inflation gave a weird cast to the Fed's limits on the interest banks could pay on time deposits, as the Federal Reserve Board sat in solemn conclave to determine how large a television set a bank could give in return for a 5-year certificate of deposit at below-market interest rates. A New England savings bank offered a Negotiable Order of Withdrawal, a "Now Account" that was in effect an interest-bearing checking account, and the facade of interest rate controls gradually fell off the system. Indeed, the Fed refused to interfere when Charles Keating's Lincoln Savings and Loan paid more than four percentage points of commission to what was then called Prudential-Bache to broker in deposits that

[14] I am indebted to Carter Golembe for pointing this out.

would pay their customers two and three percentage points more than other S&Ls were paying.

Then, quite suddenly—and this is still the age of Glass-Steagall—the Fed abdicated its control of the money supply, permitting Banc One to pass on through the banks' clearing systems the checks issued by Merrill Lynch for its Cash Management Account. There soon followed the home equity loan, sponsored by the banks, enabling American households to monetize the equity in their homes. I wrote the first article about the Cash Management Account, for Fortune, in 1981, and I asked Paul Volcker why he had permitted it, and he said, "It was one of those things where you look at it and think, 'That's interesting, I wonder where it will go,' and the next time you look at it it's so big you don't dare do anything about it."

On the asset side of the ledger, the steps away from Glass-Steagall were more tentative. Senator Carter Glass regretted the separation of deposit banking and investment banking almost from the beginning, and history chipped away at the other controls. The law permitted banks to underwrite municipal bonds; in the 1960s, Comptroller James Saxon extended this power to revenue bonds. In 1956 and again in 1970, Congress enacted laws that expanded the asset powers of "bank holding companies," to be supervised by the Fed, which took a somewhat restricted view of what these holding companies should be permitted to do. For example, though the traditional banker gives the traditional borrower quite a lot of advice, the Fed prohibited bank holding companies from owning or operating management consulting firms. One of the "Article 20" powers the Fed granted the holding company was the right to form special purpose vehicles (SPVs) that would purchase the banks' loans and take them off the bank's balance sheet, the sort of thing that got the securities affiliates in such trouble in 1933. This happened on Volcker's watch and over his dead body—the vote was one of very few where the chairman dissented. Years later, in 2007, the majority that overruled him turned out to be right (for ill, not for good) in one significant aspect—the bank couldn't escape ultimate responsibility for the SPVs and SIVs its holding company underwrote. But by the time that became clear, it was the taxpayer who was on the hook (Bamber and Spencer 2008; El-Erian 2008; Wessel 2009; Zandi 2009). Like the blind Indian savants confronted with an elephant, each of these sees a different reason why the banks diverted their own blood to transfuse the purchasers of the paper they had originated and distributed.

If we could make the world afresh, we would re-regulate banking by control over the instruments that insured depositories were permitted to trade and to hold as investments. Thirty years have passed since Scott Pardee, then the chief foreign exchange trader at the Federal Reserve Bank of New York, first proposed the creation of a financial Food and Drug Administration empowered to prevent the marketing or use of instruments with the potential to destabilize our financial systems. Scott lived in a world where periodically, as he put it, everybody ran to the same side of the boat. The damage was to some extent controlled because foreign exchange contracts, like wheat or oil futures contracts, involved deliverables. Elizabeth Warren at Harvard made a similar suggestion about a year ago, urging a vetting process especially for the trading instruments that can be created ad lib. Jan

Kregel has pointed out that our markets are now organized to price the risk of future events rather than to value future income flows, which makes them much less useful in the allocation of resources.[15]

Change in the current disastrous markets isn't going to happen this time around. The industry has squared the Congress, and the Treasury, having played along with the game for lo these many years, is not well situated to throw any weight behind Secretary Geithner's correct instinct that we can never have financial stability until the derivatives trade is forced out of the over-the-counter nexus and into mandatory standardization and exchange trading. I note in passing that I first said this in a book published in 1997. The most strongly argued objections to Geithner's original proposal are in fact the strongest arguments for it. Lufthansa complained that exchange-traded oil futures require players to post margin, and thus eat liquidity, but from the point of view of the taxpayers who have to supply the liquidity when the players in the OTC markets get it wrong, the exchanges stand sentinel—as the regulators so frighteningly don't—over the public's money.

One of the instruments that should simply be banned is the CDO that jumbles together various loans, notes, receivables, mortgages, etc. The CDO is a fixed-income mutual fund with adverse selection in its construction. What may be gained in diversification is lost in incomprehensibility. The real-life origin of this instrument was Bill Seidman's desire to sell off the portfolios of the busted S&Ls as "whole banks" rather than have his Resolution Trust Corp. break out the assets in conventional categories so they could be valued and sold to an informed market where the participants had the time, talent and resources to do due diligence. The questions the buy side might reasonably wish to have answered could be buried under the rubric of the rating. We have very bad experience in the art world in the selling of paintings where the expert is paid by the dealer. For two generations, the art historians who authenticated or failed to authenticate an alleged old master were paid a fixed percentage of the sales price, with the result that our museums are burdened with many paintings not really by the advertised artist. Not to put too fine a point on the matter, the CDO was developed as a way to conceal value, or the lack of it. This means that you couldn't sell it without guarantees or find some way to swap assets in and out of the package, leading us through the swamp of the total return swap to the tar sands of the Credit Derivative Swap and the tar baby of the enormous taxpayer gift to Goldman Sachs in the rescue of AIG.

We could, in fact, keep banks from playing the CDO game. The big shillelagh in the closet is the power to award or deny—or adjust the premium on—deposit insurance. Even in today's lets-be-kind-to-the-banks regulatory atmosphere, insured depositories obviously should be banned from investing in or trading a CDO-squared, or options with all-or-nothing triggers, or the lower tranches of collateralized mortgage obligations. The purpose, as Lord Turner wrote in his FSA report, is to "make the banking system an economic shock absorber, not itself a source of shocks."

---

[15] Kregel (2009, 16–17).

If the regulators are too timid to use their control of deposit insurance as a weapon, the derivatives problem can be dealt with by a revision of the bankruptcy law that ends the preference now given to such instruments by the securities legislation of 1999 and the bankruptcy legislation of 2005. There is no good reason in law or economics—no explanation other than pure political clout—why bilateral over-the-counter derivatives contracts, which are simply bets on the direction of prices, should be settled before the rest of a bankrupt estate and the claims on it. Exchange-traded contracts, of course, would continue to clear and settle as they do today.

Too big to fail is of course the worst problem. We have been forced to accept the idea that giant failed banks are not only entitled to blank checks from the government but may use those checks to expand. Banking is now a seriously overconcentrated industry. And there is no societal or economic benefit from the elephantiasis of banking. There are no economies of scale in banking once the bank's deposits are greater than, say, \$5 billion, and the economies of scope claimed by the industry are in reality the profits that can be made by exploiting conflicts of interest. The work that should be done now by the economists and regulators would look to the separability of the parts of the holding company. For many years, the Fed insisted as part of its approval process in granting new powers to bank holding companies that the activities for which permission was requested would be "a source of strength" to the bank. The Congress could, I think, breathe life into such a requirement, keeping the capital of the "utility" side of the bank save from depredation by the "casino" bank. By denying the other subs access to the holding company's capital unless the safety of the bank is beyond question, traders across the market and geographic spectrum could be compelled to pay close attention to the quality of their counterparties What we really want is an internalized private-sector Glass-Steagall.

What lies ahead of us right now is more serious than these arcana of banking powers and supervision. Quite inadvertently, the Federal Reserve has created a new and original banking system, destroying the fractional reserve control procedures with which we all grew up and substituting what is at the margin, though nobody at the Fed seems to recognize it, a 100% reserve plan, a throwback to Henry Simons and Irving Fisher and Lauchlin Currie. "Quantitative easing" leaves the community of banks with what are now again called "excess reserves," after a generation when there were no excess reserves, if only because everything left over after a bank had met its reserve requirement was called "Fed Funds" and had market value. And as part of this process the Fed showed a profit from the seigniorage, which was paid to the Treasury and reduced the federal deficit.

Other than jawboning and pious declarations about preventing inflation, monetary policy is pretty close to out the window in the new dispensation. Previously, with a 10% reserve requirement and a loaned up system where the books had to be squared every other Wednesday, the Fed could pull, say, \$100 million out and know that the banks as a group would have to cut back on their loans by \$900 million. Conversely, a stimulating Fed could be confident that the injection of \$100 million of what Milton Friedman called "high-powered money" would produce a billion dollars of new banking assets (loans and reserves).

Now it's one for one at best—and that only on the heroic assumption that a banking system unwilling to lend money from its existing pile of excess reserves will allocate new excess reserves to loans when the Fed seeks to stimulate, and when the purpose is stringency will cut back on lending rather than reduce its stash of excess reserves. We are assured by those Fed governors who give speeches that the Fed will be able to control what happens to the excess reserves because Congress now permits the Fed to pay interest on them, and for the same interest rates banks would rather keep their money at the Fed than lend it out. The New York Fed talks about taking money out through third-party repo; even if that works, it doesn't restore the multiplier.

Lord Turner has suggested that regulation of banks and securities houses should look to economic substance, not legal forms. If the economic function of the instrument is insurance, banks should be kept off the playing field. If the trading activity involves the pledging of liability structures that include insured deposits, the bank should be barred access to the trading room. (And meanwhile we need a little more understanding by regulators, academics, commentators, and politicians that the banks as a group do not lose money by making wild bets on long shots; they lose by huge bets on what their algorithms and computers tell them are sure things. There are no sure things.) In all trading activities conducted over-the-counter, banks should be held to high know-your-customer standards, with inviolable rules for the posting of collateral and the maintenance of records that permit each participant in the market to know continuously the full degree of its exposure to every counterpart across the full range of markets.

I have been trying to find a cheerful thought to leave with you. About the best I can do is note that one of the worst worries of my generation can now be abandoned. When information technology was still new, law professor Harry Kalven noted his fear that through the agency of the computer, mankind would lose its benign capacity to forget. We know now that despite the violence of the shock, both the big banks and the cadre of bank regulators and supervisors—and academics—are shaking off the awful memories of 2008 and are setting up the same pins in the same alleys for the same players to try again. We will have to do this, at least, once more before we even try to get it right.

References

Bamber B, Spencer A (2008) Bear trap: the fall of bear stearns and the panic of 2008. Brick Tower Press, New York, NY

El-Erian M (2008) When markets collide. McGraw-Hill, New York, NY

Fortune Magazine (1930) Banking, group and branch, Fortune Feb 1930, 63–180

Griffiths K (2009) FSA's last weapon in the new financial world will be discretion. Telegraph, 19 Mar. http://www.telegraph.co.uk/finance/newsbysector/banksandfinance/5012735/FSAs-last-weapon-in-the-new-financial-world-will-be-discrection.html

Hoover H (1932) Address accepting the Republican Presidential Nomination, 11 August. http://americanhistory.about.com/library/docs/blhooverspeech1932.htm

Kaufman H (2009) The road to financial reformation. Wiley, New York, NY

Kregel J (2009) Managing the impact of volatility in international capital markets in an uncertain world. Summary (Levy Institute of Bard College), Fall
Mayer M (1980) The fate of the dollar. Times Books, New York, NY
Modernization of the Glass-Steagall Act (1987) Hearing before the committee on banking. U.S. Senate, GPO, Washington, DC
Moore GS (1987) The banker's life. W. W. Norton & Co, New York, NY
Moss DA (2009) An ounce of prevention. Harvard Magazine, 24 Sept/Oct
Perkins EJ (1971) The divorce of commercial and investment banking: a history. Bank Law J (June) 88(6):438–528
Reed JS (2009) Volcker's advice. New York Times, 21 Oct. http://www.nytimes.com/2009/10/23/opinion/l23volcker.html?_r=1&scp=1&sq=reed%20volcker&st=cse
Sheng A (ed) (1996) Bank restructuring: lessons from the 1980s. The World Bank, Washington, DC
Sheng A (2009) From Asian to global crisis. Cambridge University Press, New York, NY
Turner LA (2009) The turner review: a regulatory response to the global banking crisis. Financial Services Authority, London, Mar
Wessel D (2009) In fed we trust. Crown Business, New York, NY
Wolf M (2009) This time will never be different. Financial Times, September 28
Zandi M (2009) Financial shock. FT Press, Upper Saddle River, NJ

Part II
Some Empirical Evidence on the Effects of the Gramm-Leach-Bliley Act

Chapter 4
Cross-Border Impact of Financial Services Modernization Act (FSMA): Evidence from Large Foreign Banks

M. Kabir Hassan, Abdullah Mamun, and Ihsan Isik

Introduction

The Financial Services Modernization Act (GLBA) of 1999 was sought to modernize the U.S. financial services industry, which was regulated by depression era regulation such as the Glass-Steagall Act (1933) and the Bank Holding Company Act (1956), and to introduce more competition in the U.S. financial services industry. It is argued that the GLBA is going to shape the future of the U.S. financial services industry. Empirical studies have documented that this regulation has created opportunities for domestic financial institutions. However, is the GLBA going to affect foreign banks? Does the regulation offer opportunity for foreign banks or is it going to create a barrier to entry, expansion, and operation of foreign banks in the United States? The resolution of these questions has implication for policy makers and for the banking industry. In this study we seek to provide answers to these questions.

Whether the GLBA has created opportunity for foreign banks is not clear from the current studies. Carow and Heron (2002) and Akhigbe et al. (2005) examine the spillover effect of the GLBA on foreign banks. Carow and Heron include ten foreign banks that are traded in the United States in their study, which analyzes the impact of the GLBA on domestic institutions. They find a significant negative spillover for the foreign banks and argue that the capitalization requirement imposed by the GLBA is the most likely reason for these wealth effects. Akhigbe et al. (2005) analyze a sample of 44 foreign banks from seven different countries to test whether the GLBA is a local or a global event. They find limited evidence of wealth effect and argue that the wealth effects of foreign banks surrounding the events leading to the GLBA are attributable to country-specific events.

In this study we analyze a larger sample of foreign banks (215 foreign banks) representing the banking industry of ten developed countries (Canada, France,

M.K. Hassan (✉)
Department of Economics and Finance, The University of New Orleans, 438 Kirschman Hall, 2000 Lakeshore Drive, New Orleans, LA 70148, USA
e-mail: mhassan@uno.edu

J.A. Tatom (ed.), *Financial Market Regulation*, DOI 10.1007/978-1-4419-6637-7_4,

Denmark, Germany, Greece, Italy, Japan, Spain, Switzerland, and the United Kingdom (U.K.)). We find that most of the foreign banking industries have a significant and negative welfare effect from the events leading to the passage of the GLBA. This result collaborates with the findings of Carow and Heron (2002). Banking industries of six (Canada, Denmark, Germany, Greece, Japan, and Spain) out of the ten countries that we investigate have a significantly negative impact, while the banking industries of France, Italy, and the U.K. are largely unaffected by this regulation. The most important contribution of this study is that we show that the wealth effect of foreign banks can be explained by an increase in systematic risk exposure with respect to world index. This implies that GLBA has reduced the capability of foreign banks to diversify their portfolio by restricting their entry and/or expansion to the U.S. market. We argue that a higher capitalization requirement on foreign banks may be a likely explanation for this result. In addition, by abolishing the barrier to entry to the banking sector for other sectors of the financial services industry that have home field advantage, and restriction on scope of activities of foreign banks may also explain this result. Finally, we also find that larger banks are affected more from the GLBA. This result is intuitive; the larger banks which need more diversification opportunity are the most affected by the GLBA.

Literature

Empirical evidence on the impact of the GLBA on domestic financial institutions is mixed. Hendershott et al. (2002) investigate the market response of the GLBA on financial services industries. They do not find any market response for commercial banks, while they find a significantly positive wealth effect for both the insurance and brokerage firms. They argue that loopholes in the laws have long allowed banks to have a "fairly substantial presence in other sectors" as a reason to why there is no wealth effect for commercial banks. For all three industries, they find that the firm size can explain the cross-sectional variation of the wealth effect. In addition, for commercial banks they also find that profitability can explain the cross-sectional variation in return. Similarly, Carow and Heron (2002) find that brokerage firms and insurance companies benefit from the GLBA, but banks do not. In addition, they find that foreign banks have negative wealth effect.

Akhigbe and Whyte (2001), on the other hand, find that all three financial services industries benefit from the passage of the GLBA and that larger and well-capitalized banks benefit more from this law. They also find that brokerage firms benefit regardless of size, but the gains are inversely related to their capital position. Insurance companies benefit regardless of size and capitalization. Mamun et al. (2005) find a positive wealth effect for banks. They show that money center and super regional banks benefited the most. In addition, banks with section 20 investment subsidiaries benefited more from the regulatory changes. They identify that opportunity to diversify is a major source of the wealth effect from the GLBA. Finally, Barth et al. (2000) argue that the GLBA is just ratifying the status quo rather than being revolutionary. They also argue that this law favors larger banks and financial institutions.

With the growing integration of financial markets and institutions, the existing literature predicts that the GLBA may produce international spillover effects. For example, Bruner and Simms (1987) find a spillover effect from Mexico's loan crisis on U.S. banks. Similarly, Musumeci and Sinkey (1990) find that Brazil's announcement of a debt moratorium in 1987 had a spillover effect on the U.S. money center banks. Madura et al. (1991) find that Citicorp's announcement of a significant increase in loan-loss reserves in 1987 had a significant negative impact on British banks.

The available empirical research suggests that at least some types of cross-border consolidation can improve the risk-expected return tradeoff for banks. McAllister and McManus (1993), Hughes et al. (1996, 1999), Hughes and Mester (1998), and Demsetz and Strahan (1997) find that larger, more geographically diversified institutions tend to have better risk-expected return tradeoffs. In addition, Cummins and Weiss (2000) find that international diversification can improve both the risk-expected return tradeoff and profit efficiency for the insurance industry.

Grosse and Goldberg (1991) investigate the foreign banking activity in the United States by country of origin. Their results show that foreign direct investment (FDI) and foreign portfolio investment into the United States, bilateral trade, and the size of each countries' banking sector (demand deposits and time deposits) are positively correlated with that countries' bank presence in the United States. Hultman and McGee (1989) find that foreign presence of the U.S. bank subsidiaries are directly related to FDI and exchange rate, and inversely related to price to earnings P/E ratios. They find that the growth of foreign bank branches and agencies in the United States is directly related to FDI, and exchange rate. Goldberg and Saunders (1981) show that important determinants in foreign banks' growth in the United States are the size of interest differentials between the United States and foreign deposits and loans, the falling P/E ratio for the US bank stocks, increased size of FDI, the persistent depreciation of the U.S. dollar and the expectation that the International Banking Act (IBA) of 1978 would have a restrictive effect on foreign banking activity in the United States. Seth et al. (1998) show that one of the major determinants of financial institutions' growth abroad has been the parallel growth of FDI and foreign trade by globally oriented multinational corporations from the institutions' home country.

GLBA and Foreign Banks

Under the GLBA, foreign banks can engage in commercial banking, merchant banking, and insurance in ways consistent with their business strategies. If the foreign bank chooses to be a financial holding company (FHC), there is no limit to the revenue generated by its insurance activity, merchant banking activity or investment banking activity. To qualify as an FHC, it must notify the Federal Reserve (FRB) about the activities in which it will engage and obtain certain required approvals for those activities. In order to become an FHC, its depository institution must be well capitalized and well managed; and no insured institutions within the FHC can have less than a satisfactory rating under the Community Reinvestment Act (CRA).

Foreign banks under the GLBA have to decide whether they want to keep their current structure and continue to engage in current activities or to engage in other activities permitted under the new regulation. If foreign banks engage in traditional commercial banking in the United States, via a branch or agency, they may still do so without changing their structure. But if the U.S. branch or agency engages in certain securities, merchant banking or investment banking activities in the United States, it has to stop (unless they are grandfathered[1]). Under the new regulation, the activity, and not the entity, determines the primary supervisory authority.

Most foreign banks that engaged in significant insurance activities before the GLBA did so through a domestic bank or through an insurance subsidiary of a domestic bank. Now foreign banks must either operate via an existing licensed insurance subsidiary, or establish a new subsidiary and obtain a license from the state insurance department where they want to sell the insurance, in order to take full advantage of the opportunities provided by the new regulation.

Most of the foreign banks carry out their investment or merchant banking activities in the United States through Section 20 investment subsidiaries. These banks can continue to engage in these activities so long as they are grandfathered, but they cannot engage in any new activities. Some of the foreign banks in the United States engage in investment banking through domestic bank and trust companies. These operations must cease under the new law. The GLBA requires foreign banks to engage in these activities through a registered broker dealer.

In order to engage in any activity in the United States, a foreign bank must be well capitalized and well managed by the standards set by the FRB. The FRB will review worldwide operations of a foreign bank to determine whether they can engage in commercial banking, or any other activities in the United States.

Hypotheses

Hypothesis 1: GLBA will have significant spillover effects on foreign banks.

There are several reasons to expect that foreign banks will have significant wealth effects due to the passage of the GLBA. First, the literature on foreign spillover effects predicts that if the banking sector of a country has exposure to any foreign market, then an event in that foreign market can have spillover effects on the financial sector of that country. Any bank that wants to have foreign coverage has to have its operation in the United States[2] Table 4.1 shows that all of the developed

[1]Grandfathered means the bank may continue to engage in the activity because it did so before the restrictions became law. New activities are not covered by the grandfather provision.

[2]Blanden (2000) claims that the "U.S. remains a magnet for foreign banks, with a presence in New York essential for any group with pretensions to international coverage."

Table 4.1 Foreign banks' operation in United States: Number of banks, revenue from US operation, and FHC status of foreign banks

Country	No. of banks in USA in (9/98)	No. of banks in USA in (9/99)	Total asset booked in USA (9/98) $million	Total asset booked in USA (9/99) $million	No. of banks claimed FHC status by November 30, 2001	Percentage of foreign banks claiming FHC structure (%)
Canada	6	6	122, 524	125, 095	6	100
Denmark	2	2	–	–	1	50
France	14	10	171, 358	163, 618	2	14
Greece	1	1	–	–	0	0
Germany	14	15	147, 458	209, 228	2	14
Italy	17	15	31, 013	26, 355	0	0
Japan	50	39	279, 591	213, 625	0	0
Spain	5	5	17, 651	20, 319	1	20
Switzerland	8	8	83, 336	56, 120	2	25
UK	11	10	83, 540	88, 551	1	9
All foreign banks	320	284	1, 162, 669	1, 126, 516	21	7

Source: Board of Governors of the Federal Reserve System.

countries (included in this study) have exposure to the U.S. banking market. So we expect a spillover effect on the foreign banks from the GLBA. Second, Goldberg and Saunders (1981) and Hultman and McGee (1989) document that the IBA of 1978 influenced the growth of foreign banks in the United States. Similarly, we argue that the GLBA may also impact the growth of foreign banks in the United States.

Finally, Berger et al. (2000) report a growing trend in foreign banks acquiring the U.S. banks. In the mid 1990s the total value of such consolidations was $10 billion (in 1998 dollars) and, by 1998, that amount had increased to $12 billion. One of the major reasons for such mergers is that cross-border consolidation generally improves the risk-expected return tradeoff. Table 4.2 shows the correlation of bank earnings between the U.S. and foreign banks from 1988 to 1997. The correlation is quite low and mostly negative, except with the U.K. This data suggests very strong diversification possibilities and opportunities to improve the institutions' risk-expected return tradeoff through cross-border consolidation (Berger et al. 2000). Given the diversification opportunities, added with the size of the market (of the U.S. banking industry), any major regulatory change in the U.S. banking industry should have spillover effects on foreign banks.

Hypothesis 2: Foreign banks will have negative wealth effect from the passage of the GLBA because of reduced the diversification opportunities.

The GLBA creates opportunities for foreign banks to engage in activities that were not permitted under previous regulation. Under the GLBA, foreign banks have no revenue limits from any of their investment, merchant banking, insurance or depository activities, when they choose to become an FHC. But these advantages are also available to local banks, insurance, and securities firms. So for all the new opportunities, a foreign bank still has to compete with local firms who have "home field advantage"[3] over the foreign banks. Thus we expect that foreign banks may have negative wealth effects from the passage of GLBA.

Under the new regulation, the insurance activities conducted by foreign banks through domestic banks and insurance subsidiaries of domestic banks have to cease. In addition, a portion of the investment and merchant banking activities conducted via domestic banks and trust companies has to be discontinued. Foreign banks will be allowed to retain only the part of their investment and merchant banking activities (the most important operation in the United States) carried out through Section 20 investment subsidiary, and will be restricted to those activities that are grandfathered. The same grandfathering provision applies to their traditional commercial banking activity. But for all the activities that are allowed, they will still have to comply with the FRB's capitalization and management standards for their U.S. operations, as well as their worldwide operations. In fact, the permissible activity of foreign banks will become more restricted under the GLBA unless foreign banks claim a FHC structure. To claim FHC structure, foreign banks must meet the FRBs capitalization and management standards. The capital adequacy and management

[3]See Berger et al. (2000) for a detailed discussion of the Home Field Advantage hypothesis.

Table 4.2 Correlation of bank earnings between the United States and selected G-10 and E.U. countries between 1988 and 1997

	Canada	Denmark	France	Germany	Greece	Italy	Japan	Spain	Switzerland	UK	USA
Canada	1.000										
Denmark	0.648	1.000									
France	−0.344	−0.229	1.000								
Germany	0.129	0.500	−0.513	1.000							
Greece	−0.705	−0.279	0.084	0.394	1.000						
Italy	−0.391	−0.455	0.803	−0.264	0.170	1.000					
Japan	−0.320	−0.563	0.259	0.098	0.202	0.733	1.000				
Spain	−0.085	−0.195	0.782	−0.522	0.089	0.498	0.088	1.000			
Switzerland	−0.275	−0.246	0.155	0.107	0.309	0.310	0.301	−0.138	1.000		
UK	0.592	0.689	−0.734	0.446	−0.169	−0.854	−0.708	−0.431	−0.426	1.000	
USA	0.413	0.399	−0.880	0.258	−0.329	−0.938	−0.603	−0.702	−0.336	0.811	1.000

Source: "Bank Profitability": OECD Publications 1999 and 2000.

standards set by the GLBA can also be a potential reason for negative wealth effects. Carow and Heron (2002) argue that many countries impose lower capital requirements than the United States, thus these eligibility requirements may impose new costs for foreign banks that want to do business in the United States as a FHC, or in any other structure.

Hypothesis 3: The banking industries of any two countries will not have the same impact from the GLBA.

Studies that investigate foreign bank presence, activity, and growth in the United States find that there are country-specific characteristics such as exchange rate, size of the source country's banking sector, P/E ratio, and trade with the source country which can explain such activities. Table 4.3 presents the distribution of sample banks across the countries, some bank-specific information, information regarding bilateral trade with the United States, form of operation of these banks in the United States, and concentration of the banking sector in the respective countries. We argue that since such characteristics, and also exposure to the U.S. banking market, are not same for any two countries, the impact on any two countries' banking industry will not be the same from the GLBA.

Data and Methodology

Data

This study mainly concentrates on banks from European Union (E.U.) for several reasons. First, the United States and the E.U. are frequently compared in the literature because they have roughly equal shares of world population and gross domestic product (GDP). Second, the E.U. accounts a larger share of the world's banking assets compared to that of the United States.[4] We include Japan because, until 1999, Japanese banks had the highest total banking assets in the United States and Japan has the most restricted financial services industry in the developed world. Canada is included in the sample because all large Canadian banks (Schedule 1 banks) have large operations in the United States and Canada has control over a sizeable amount of assets in U.S. operations.

We test the above hypotheses using daily common stock returns over a period from January 1998 to December 2000. Daily stock returns and balance sheet information for large banks from Canada, Denmark, France, Germany, Greece, Italy, Japan, Spain, Switzerland, and the U.K. are obtained from the DataStream database and BankScope database. Daily stock returns for 45 large U.S. banks (over $10 billion total assets in 1998) are obtained from the Center for Research in Security Prices (CRSP) database. We identify 13 major events from the *Wall Street Journal* and Lexis-Nexis wire service. In Table 4.4, we summarize these important events.

[4]See Barth et al. (2000).

Table 4.3 Descriptive statistics

Country	No. of firms	Three bank concentration Ratio[f] (%)	Total asset in 1999[a, b]	ROE in 1999[b]	Total no. of agencies in 1999[d]	Total no. of branches in 1999[d]	Total no. of representatives in 1999[d]	Total no. of subsidiaries in 1999[d]	No. of FHCs in 11/30/2001[e]	Export from USA 99[a,e]	Import to USA 99[a,e]
Canada	8	65.20	$106,498.89	14.60	3	2	0	1	6	$166,600.00	$198,711.10
Denmark	36	63.70	$197,443.91	9.12	0	1	0	0	1	$1,725.60	$2,818.70
France	18	63.60	$69,747.42	12.38	0	3	0	0	2	$18,877.40	$25,708.60
Greece	8	98.30	$16,701.70	25.57	0	0	0	0	0	$995.50	$563.10
Germany	11	89.50	$234,317.24	9.66	0	3	0	1	1	$26,800.20	$55,228.40
Italy	17	35.90	$62,000.18	12.13	0	6	2	0	0	$19,436.60	$8,475.00
Japan	73	28.30	$38,019,876.81	−10.87	1	14	6	0	0	$57,465.70	$130,863.90
Spain	15	50.10	$40,494.54	16.21	0	0	0	0	0	$6,133.40	$5,059.20
Switzerland	21	79.80	$57,467.31	8.29	0	2	0	1	2	$8,371.30	$9,538.60
UK	8	29.10	$243,770.56	21.32	0	4	0	0	1	$38,407.10	$39,237.20
USA	45	13.30	$66,903.15	1.22[c]					570		

[a]In millions of U.S. dollars
[b]*Source*: DataSream
[c]*Source*: Compustat
[d]*Source*: *The Banker* March 1999
[e]*Source*: Board of Governors of the Federal Reserve System
[f]*Source*: Barth et al. (2000)

Table 4.4 Timeline of the Gramm-Leach-Bliley Act

Date	Event
11/4/98	1. (i) Senator Alfonse D'Amato lost his re-election bid (11/03/98-night). (ii) Senator Gramm to take over as a chair of senate banking committee. (11/04/98)
1/8/99	2. Financial services reform bill is reintroduced in congress
2/17/99	3. Draft bill was unveiled in the senate.
4/12/99	4. Senator Gramm meets with senate minority leader to work on the bill
4/28/99	5. Senate banking committee formally files the financial services modernization act in the senate
5/4/99	6. Clinton raises the privacy issue to be included in the bill
05/06/99 -Midnight	7. Senate passes S. 900. Senate version of the bill is passed
7/1/99	8. House version of the bill is passed
10/15/99	9. Federal reserve and treasury announce agreement on the regulation
10/22/99	10. Gramm makes deal with White House on CRA
11/02/99	11. Joint house conference report signed by the majority of the conferees, clearing the way for the votes in both the House and the senate
11/4/99	12. Senate passes the bill (90-8) and House passes the bill (362-57)
11/12/99	13. President Clinton signs the bill into law

Note: The first column 'Date' is the event date. If the event occurred after the trading closed for a day, then the next trading day is the event date. Event Window is defined as Event Date, −1 day and +1 day. The second column, 'Event,' describes the main event.

Portfolio Analysis

First, we adapted the model used by Blinder (1985), then following Wagster (1996) we introduce long-term and short-term interest rate to control for the interest rate risk. We also include return on exchange rate with the U.S. dollar because return on foreign investment will depend on return on the assets within its own market and changes in exchange rate. We then modify the model following Cornett and Tehranian (1990) and introduce the lagged value of the market index for possible nonsynchronous trading effects. We use dummy variables to identify the major events that led to the passage of the GLBA. The dummy variable is equal to 1 over each event window and zero otherwise. The coefficient estimate associated with the dummy variable measures the impact of the event on the portfolio. The model we estimate is:

$$
\begin{aligned}
R_{it} = \alpha_i + \alpha_i{}'D + \sum_{j=1}^{2} \beta m_{ij} Rm_{i,t+j-2} + \sum_{j=1}^{2} \beta m_{ij}{}' DRm_{i,t+j-2} + \sum_{j=1}^{2} \beta w_{ij} Rw_{t+j-2} \\
+ \sum_{j=1}^{2} \beta w_{ij}{}' DRw_{t+j-2} + \delta l_i Rrl_{i,t} + \delta s_i Rrs_{i,t} + \kappa_i Rf_{i,t} + \gamma_i DG + e_{it} \qquad (4.1)
\end{aligned}
$$

where, R_{it} is the return on portfolio i ($i = 11$, and each country has one equally weighted portfolio) at day t, $Rm_{i,t}$ is the return on market index of country i at day t, Rw_t is the return on Morgan Stanley Capital International (MSCI) world equity index at day t, DG is a dummy variable that is equal to 1 over every event window[5] and zero otherwise, γ_i is the coefficient of a dummy variable that captures the impact of the GLBA on the banking industry of ith country. $Rf_{i,t}$ represents the return on exchange rate between U.S. dollar and the currency of ith country at day t; $Rrs_{i,t}$ represents the return on short term interest rate for country i at day t; $Rrl_{i,t}$ represents the return on long term interest rate for country i at day t. D is a dummy variable that is equal to 1 after the enactment of the regulation and zero otherwise, thus $\beta m'_{i1} - \beta m'_{i2}$ captures the change in exposure to systematic risk between pre-act and post-act time for country i with respect to its own country equity index and $\beta w'_{i1} - \beta w'_{i2}$ captures the change in exposure to systematic risk between pre-act and post-act time for country i with respect to its MSCI world equity index.

We estimate the model presented in Eq. 1 using seemingly unrelated regression methodology. Schwert (1981) argues that individual asset returns of the firms in the same industry measured over a common time period are contemporaneously correlated because the firms will react similarly to any unanticipated event. So in events such as regulatory changes, the residuals will not be *iid*. If there is a contemporaneous correlation among the disturbances across equations but not correlated over time, seemingly unrelated regression (SUR) model estimates will be more efficient than Ordinary Least Squares (OLS). We use a likelihood ratio (LR) test suggested by Berndt and Savin (1977) to test the null hypothesis that the off-diagonal elements of the variance-covariance matrix are zero.[6] We perform this test to check for contemporaneous correlation among the disturbances across equations. The result of the specification test for our portfolio model shows that the null hypothesis that off-diagonal elements of the variance-covariance matrix is zero is rejected at the 1% level. Statistically that means that coefficient estimates from SUR are more efficient as opposed to the OLS estimates.

The main advantage of using the SUR is that it allows us to test the cross-country restriction (Hypothesis 3). In order to test for Hypothesis 3, we test the following null hypothesis:

$$H_0 : \gamma_1 = \gamma_2 = \gamma_3 = \ldots\ldots = \gamma_{11} \tag{4.2}$$

---

[5]Event windows are defined in Table 4.4.

[6]This test in principal determines whether the off-diagonal elements of the *variance covariance matrix* (Σ) of error terms are zero or not. Excluding the diagonal elements, there are $1/2m*(m-1)$ unknown parameters in Σ that can be arranged in a vector, θ. Here m is the number of equations. The null hypothesis is:

$H_0{:}\theta = 0$

This test is based on the following statistic:

$$\lambda_{LR} = T\left[\sum_{i-1}^{m} \log \hat{\sigma}_i^2 - \log\left|\hat{\sum}\right|\right]$$

Here $\hat{\sigma}_i^2$ is $e_i'e_i/T$ from the individual least squares regression and $\hat{\sum}$is the maximum likelihood estimator of Σ. This statistic has a limiting χ^2 distribution with $1/2m*(m-1)$ degrees of freedom under the null hypothesis.

Cross-Sectional Analysis

In order to test for our second hypothesis, we generate average abnormal return, i.e. γ_i ($i = 1$–215) for each firm using the model presented by Eq. 1. We then estimate the following model using OLS, where γ_i is the dependent variable. The cross-sectional model is:

$$\gamma_{i,j} = f(CAN, DEN, FRA, GER, GRE, ITA, JAP, SPA, SWI, UK, \beta m'_{i,j}, \beta w'_i, SIZE_i, ROE_i) \tag{4.3}$$

where, *CAN, FRA, ..., UK* are country dummy variables, which are equal to one if a firm is from that country, and zero otherwise. These dummy variables will control for country specific variations. $\beta m'_{i,j}$ and $\beta w'_i$ are changes in exposure to systematic risk with respect to a home country market index and the MSCI world equity index. $SIZE_i$ is defined as the log of total asset value (in U.S. dollars) in 1998 for firm *i* and ROE_i is the return on equity of firm *i* in 1998.

Empirical Results

Estimates of the parameters of the portfolio model are presented in Table 4.5. We find that, for most of the countries, the own country equity index is significant and positive (except Spain) while we find that MSCI world equity index is positive and significant for the United States only. We find that 7 out of 10 countries we analyze have significant average abnormal returns from the 13 events that we analyze. Banking industries of six countries have negative spillover effect from the passage of the GLBA; these are Canadian banking industry (it has an average abnormal return of −0.15%, which is also significant at 1%), Denmark's banking industry (it has an average abnormal return of −0.02%, significant at 1%), Germany's banking industry (it has an average abnormal return of −0.02%, which is significant at 5%), Greece's banking industry (it has an average abnormal return of −0.12%, which is also significant at 1%), Japan's banking industry (it has an abnormal return of −0.03%, which is significant at 1%), and Spain's banking industry (it has a significant abnormal return of −0.07%, significant at 1%). The banking industry of Switzerland has a positive spillover effect, but it is marginally significant. The banking industries of France, Italy, and the U.K. seem to be unaffected from the passage of the GLBA. These results support our first hypothesis that there are significant spillover effects of the GLBA on banking industries of developed countries and the second hypothesis that these spillover effects are negative.

Our third hypothesis, that the information produced over these 13 events has the same impact on the banking industry of any two countries, is rejected at the 1% level. This hypothesis is tested using a Wald test (presented by Eq. 2) with a test statistic of 76.78. The underlying distribution under the null hypothesis is $\chi^2(10)$.

In order to identify the cross-sectional variation in average return from the events that led to the GLBA, we perform a cross-sectional analysis. We estimate Eq. 3 using OLS. The result of the estimation is presented in Table 4.6; the *t*-statistics

Table 4.5 Estimation results of model parameters of the portfolio model (Eq. (4.1)). The following table presents the estimation results of portfolio model

Country	Intercept	Change in the intercept	Own country equity index (1 day lag)	Own country equity index	Change in the own country equity index (1 day lag)	Change in the own country equity index	MSCI world equity index (1 day lag)	MSCI world equity index	Change in the MSCI world equity index (1 day lag)	Change in the MSCI world equity index	Exchange rate with USA	Long-term interest rate	Short-term interest rate	Average return on 13 events	R^2
Canada	−0.013	0.053[a]	0.000	0.000[b]	0.000	0.000	0.109	0.058	−0.003	−0.112	0.054	0.017	−0.026	−0.0015[a]	0.39
	−1.48	4.36	0.12	2.33	0.47	−1.39	1.03	0.45	−1.47	−0.56	0.44	0.38	−0.49	−4.01	
Denmark	0.008[a]	0.008[a]	0.000[c]	0.000[a]	0.000	0.000	0.004	0.001	0.000	−0.003	0.000[c]	−0.005	0.002	−0.0002[a]	0.75
	5.72	3.99	1.73	2.76	0.00	−0.97	0.24	0.09	−0.42	−0.12	−1.92	−0.92	0.32	−3.38	
France	0.006[a]	0.003[b]	0.000[c]	0.000[c]	0.000	0.000	−0.005	0.003	0.000	−0.016	−0.001	−0.001	−0.002	0.0000	0.87
	13.39	2.47	1.71	1.83	−0.23	−0.18	−0.51	0.30	−1.36	−0.89	−0.13	−0.43	−0.67	−0.35	
Germany	0.003	0.056[a]	0.000	0.000[a]	0.000	0.000[b]	−0.022	−0.011	0.000	−0.009	−0.033	−0.010	0.028[c]	−0.0002[b]	0.81
	1.45	14.79	−0.28	4.73	0.03	−2.24	−1.02	−0.42	−0.15	−0.23	−1.56	−0.72	1.80	−2.52	
Greece	−0.114[a]	0.004	0.000	0.000[a]	0.000	0.000	−0.023	0.118	0.000	−0.012	0.068	0.036	0.027	−0.0012[b]	0.96
	−31.94	0.35	−0.53	9.11	0.85	−1.25	−0.15	0.78	−0.02	−0.05	0.51	0.47	0.55	−2.27	
Italy	−0.022[a]	0.077[a]	0.000	0.000[a]	0.000	0.000[a]	0.000	0.015	−0.001	−0.064	0.018	0.009	−0.008	0.0001	0.89
	−7.94	14.37	1.12	6.80	0.14	−2.63	0.01	0.32	−0.95	−0.88	0.47	0.55	−0.41	0.49	
Japan	0.012[a]	−0.003[a]	0.000[b]	0.000[a]	0.000	0.000	0.005[c]	0.000	0.000	0.003	0.003	0.000	0.000	−0.00003[a]	0.59
	75.93	−8.16	−2.34	3.13	0.87	−0.51	1.77	0.16	−1.13	0.59	1.64	−0.08	−0.66	−2.85	

Table 4.5 (continued)

Country	Intercept	Change in the intercept	Own country equity index (1 day lag)	Own country equity index	Change in the own country equity index (1 day lag)	Change in the own country equity index	MSCI world equity index (1 day lag)	MSCI world equity index	Change in the MSCI world equity index (1 day lag)	Change in the MSCI world equity index	Exchange rate with USA	Long-term interest rate	Short-term interest rate	Average return on 13 events	R^2
Spain	0.076[a]	0.020[b]	0.000	0.000	0.000	0.000	−0.028	−0.069	0.000	0.067	−0.022	−0.008	−0.019	−0.0007[a]	0.44
	17.27	2.14	1.50	−0.24	−1.33	0.60	−0.62	−1.23	0.48	0.78	−0.50	−0.25	−0.95	−4.61	
Switzerland	−0.020[a]	−0.019[a]	0.000[b]	0.000[a]	0.000	0.000	−0.034[a]	−0.011	0.000	−0.006	−0.012	0.005	−0.001	0.0001[c]	0.94
	−18.27	−8.98	2.34	6.29	−0.13	1.38	−3.61	−0.95	0.90	−0.35	−1.41	1.08	−1.01	1.86	
UK	−1.661[a]	1.250[a]	0.000	0.000[a]	0.000	0.000[b]	−0.228	0.202	−0.010	−1.337	0.001	0.127	0.042	−0.0010	0.67
	−32.02	7.29	0.76	5.92	−0.02	−2.03	−0.33	0.27	−0.87	−1.10	0.00	0.53	0.13	−0.40	

$R_{it} = \alpha_i + \alpha_i{'}D + \sum_{j=1}^{2} \beta m_{ij} Rm_{i,t+j-2} + \sum_{j=1}^{2} \beta m_{ij}{'} DRm_{i,t+j-2} + \sum_{j=1}^{2} \beta w_{ij} Rw_{t+j-2} + \sum_{j=1}^{2} \beta w_{ij}{'} DRw_{t+j-2} + \delta l_i Rrl_{i,t} + \delta s_i Rrs_{i,t} + \kappa_i Rf_{i,t} + \gamma_i DG + e_{it}$ where, R_{it} is the return on portfolio i at day t, $Rm_{i,t}$ is the return on own market index of country i at day t, Rw_t is the return on MSCI world equity index at day t, DG is a dummy variable that is equal to 1 over every event window and zero otherwise, $Rf_{i,t}$ represents the return on exchange rate between U.S. dollar and the currency of ith country at day t; $Rrs_{i,t}$ represents the return on short term interest rate for country i at day t; $Rrl_{i,t}$ represents the return on long term interest rate for country i at day t. D is a dummy variable that is equal to 1 after the enactment of the regulation and zero otherwise

[a,b,c]Denote significance at 1, 5, and 10% levels respectively

Table 4.6 Cross-sectional analysis of wealth effect on each firm in the banking industries of selected developed countries

Parameter	Estimate	*T*-statistics
CAN	0.0290	1.03
DEN	0.0208[a]	1.97
FRA	0.0275[b]	2.67
GER	−0.0011	−0.06
GRE	−0.0585[a]	−2.43
ITA	0.0217[c]	1.69
JAP	0.0518[b]	2.46
SPA	−0.0034	−0.17
SWI	0.0251[a]	2.56
UK	0.0541[b]	3
$bm'_{i,j}$	−0.0099	−0.79
$bw'_{i,j}$	0.0001[b]	3.27
SIZE	−0.0034[c]	−1.76
ROE	0.0000	0.27
R^2	0.54	
***F*-Statistics**	15.36	

We estimate the following model:
$\gamma_{i,j} = f(CAN, DEN, FRA, GER, GRE, ITA, JAP, SPA, SWI, UK, \beta m'_{i,j}, \beta w'_i, SIZE_i, ROE_i)$
We estimate the model using OLS using 215 firms in the sample. Here $\gamma_{i,j}$ is the abnormal return of firm *i* of country *j*., *CAN, DEN,. . ., UK* are dummy variables for a particular country; these variables are equal to one for that country and zero otherwise. $\beta m'_{i,j}$ is the change in exposure to systematic risk with respect to home country market index, while $\beta w'_{i,j}$ is the change in exposure to systematic risk with respect to home country market index. *Size* is log of book value of total asset and *ROE* is return on equity.
[a,b,c]Denote significance at 1, 5, and 10% levels respectively.

are computed using the formula suggested by MacKinnon and White (1985). We use country dummy variables to control for the country specific effects. The variables that are significant may be due to the country specific variables (like trade with the United States, exchange rate, size of the source countries financial sector as suggested by the literature on the determinants of foreign bank presence, activity, and growth in the United States) or due to country specific events in those periods.

The main hypothesis we want to test is whether the GLBA created or reduced the diversification opportunity for foreign banks. We find that $\beta w'i,j$ is positive and significant. This means diversification opportunities for these banks, with respect to world index, has been reduced. This validates our major hypothesis (Hypothesis 2) that the GLBA reduced diversification opportunities for foreign banks. We use *Size* and profitability measures in the cross-sectional regression because Hendershott et al. (2002) and Mamun et al. (2005) find that both of these variables can explain the cross-sectional variation in wealth effects for domestic commercial banks from the passage of the GLBA. We find evidence that larger banks have more negative wealth effects. Since larger banks generally would be interested in foreign diversification and have more U.S. exposure, a reduction of such opportunities should affect them more.

Conclusion

We examine the impact of the GLBA, a major regulatory change in U.S. financial services industry, on a sample of 215 non-U.S. banks from 10 countries. In the era of globalization of financial markets, it is argued that deregulation like the GLBA, or single market program of E.U. should have an impact beyond the boundaries of the jurisdiction.[7] In this chapter, we present further evidence of globalization of financial institutions. We find that banking industries of 7 out of 10 developed countries have significant wealth effects from the passage of the GLBA. We also find that the impact of the GLBA is not the same for any two banking industries of foreign countries.

The cross-sectional investigation suggests that a part of negative reaction is due to country specific attributes in that period. But most importantly, we show that the negative wealth effect is due to the reduction in the diversification opportunities for foreign banks that is due to the passage of the GLBA. This reduction in diversification opportunity from the GLBA can be due to increased competition from domestic participants, restrictions imposed on the scope of activities permissible to foreign banks, restructuring the way certain business were carried out, or due to the FRB's capitalization and management standards for its worldwide operation. Anecdotal evidence also supports the argument that the GLBA adversely affected the presence of foreign banks in the United States. For example, Blanden (2000) reports that the number of foreign banks in the United States has been declining. In addition, Table 4.1 shows that only 7% of the foreign banks present in the United States have adopted the FHC structure, a structure through which most of the new opportunities are available to foreign banks. Finally, we argue that the GLBA will restrict the expansion and entry of foreign banks in the United States.

References

Akhigbe A, Whyte AM (2001) The market's assessment of the financial services modernization act of 1999. Financ Rev 36:119–138

Akhigbe A, Fry M, White AM (2005) Financial modernization in U.S. banking markets: a local or global event? J Bus Finance Account 32(7–8):1561–1585

Barth JR, Brumbaugh RD Jr, Wilcox JA (2000) The repeal of glass-steagall and the advent of broad banking. J Econ Perspect 14:191–204

Barth JR, Nolle DE, Rice TN (2000) Commercial banking structure, regulation and international comparison. In: Papadimitriou DB (ed) Modernizing financial systems. St. Martin's Press Inc, New York, NY, pp 119–250

Berger AN, DeYoung R, Genay H, Udell GF (2000) Globalization of financial institutions: evidence from cross-border banking performance. Brooking-Wharton Papers in Financial Services 3

Berndt ER, Savin NE (1977) Conflict among criteria for testing hypotheses in the multivariate linear regression model. Econometrica 45:1263–1277

[7]Berger et al. (2000).

Binder JJ (1985) Measuring the effects of regulation with stock price data. Rand J Econ 16: 167–183

Blanden M (2000) Shrinking in the big apple. The Banker, p 150

Bruner RF, Simms JM (1987) The international debt crisis and bank security returns in 1982. J Money Credit Bank 19:46–55

Carow KA, Heron R (2002) Capital market reactions to the passage of the financial services modernization act of 1999. Q Rev Econ Finance 42:465–485

Cornett MM, Tehranian H (1990) An examination of the impact of the Garn-St. Germain depository institutions act of 1982 on commercial banks and savings and loans. J Finance 45:95–111

Cummins JD, Weiss MA (2000) The global market for reinsurance: consolidation, capacity and efficiency. Brooking-Wharton Papers in Financial Services 3

Demsetz RS, Strahan PE (1997) Diversification, size, and risk at U.S. bank holding companies. J Money Credit Bank 29:300–313

Finch S, Macdonald G, Walker J (2000) Getting in on the act. The Banker (January) 88–89

Demsetz R, Strahan P (1997) Diversification, size, and risk at bank holding companies. J Money Credit Bank 29:300–313

Goldberg LG, Saunders A (1981) The determinants of foreign banking activity in the United States. J Bank Finance 5:17–32

Grosse R, Goldberg LG (1991) Foreign bank activity in the United States: an analysis by the country of origin. J Bank Finance 15:1093–1112

Hendershott R, Lee DE, Tompkins JG (2002) Winners and losers as financial service providers converge: evidence from the financial modernization act of 1999. Financ Rev 37:53–72

Hultman C, McGee L (1989) Factors affecting the foreign banking presence in the U.S. J Bank Finance 13:383–396

Hughes JP, Mester LJ (1998) Bank capitalization and cost: evidence of scale economics in risk management and signaling. Rev Econ Stat 80:314–325

Hughes JP, Lang W, Mester LJ, Moon C-G (1996) Efficient banking under interstate banking. J Money Credit Bank 28:1043–1071

Hughes JP, Lang W, Mester LJ, Moon C-G (1999) The dollars and sense of bank consolidation. J Bank Finance 23:291–324

MacKinnon JG, White H (1985) Some heteroskedasticity consistent covariance matrix estimators with improved finite sample properties. J Econ 29:305–325

Mamun A, Hassan MK, Maroney N (2005) The wealth and risk effects of the Gramm-Leach-Bliley act (GLBA) on the U.S. banking industry. J Bus Finance Account 32:351–388

McAllister P, McManus D (1993) Resolving the scale efficiency puzzle in banking. J Bank Finance 17:389–405

Madura J, Whyte AM, McDaniel WR (1991) Reaction to the British bank share prices to Citicorp's announced $3 billion increase in loan loss reserves. J Bank Finance 15:151–163

Musumeci JJ, Sinkey JF (1990) The international debt crisis, investor contagion, and bank security returns in 1987: the Brazilian experience. J Money Credit Bank 22:209–220

Schwert GW (1981) Using financial data to measure effects of regulation. J Law Econ (April) 24:121–158

Seth R et al (1998) Do banks follow their customers abroad? Financ Mark Instrum Inst 7(4):1–25

Wagster JD (1996) Impact of the 1988 Basle accord on international banks. J Finance 51: 1321–1346

Chapter 5
Global Impact of the Gramm-Leach-Bliley Act: Evidence from Insurance Industries of Developed Countries

M. Kabir Hassan and Abdullah Mamun

Introduction

The Gramm-Leach-Bliley Act (GLBA) of 1999 is the most sweeping deregulation of the U.S. financial services industry in the last century. One would expect the impact of such extensive deregulation in the U.S. market would not be restricted only to its financial services industry. Thus, by analyzing the wealth effects of the GLBA on the insurance industries of other developed countries, especially on member countries of the European Union (E.U.), our study addresses three important questions that focus on opportunities created for non-U.S. insurance companies; the GLBA's impact on these companies; and, finally, the variable wealth effects on non-U.S. companies.

This study focuses on three important questions; first, does the GLBA create opportunities for non-U.S. insurance companies? Current research finds that the GLBA does not have a uniform effect on the financial services industry. However, these studies consistently find that the GLBA has positively affected shareholder value in the U.S. insurance industry. It should be noted that non-U.S. insurance companies control a substantial proportion of the U.S. insurance business. In 1990, only 9.8% of the market share in life insurance, and 7.1% of the market share in nonlife insurance on a gross premium basis in the United States, was written by non-U.S. companies,[1] or branches and agencies of non-U.S. insurance companies. However, by 1998 the market share controlled by non-U.S. insurance companies was 17.23% of life insurance and 8.67% of nonlife insurance business in the United States. Figure 5.1 shows the trend in non-U.S. insurance companies' market share

M.K. Hassan (✉)
Department of Economics and Finance, The University of New Orleans, 438 Kirschman Hall, 2000 Lakeshore Drive, New Orleans, LA 70148, USA
e-mail: mhassan@uno.edu

This chapter also appeared as Networks Financial Institute Working Paper 2009-WP-13.

[1]Companies in the United States whose equity is at least 10% owned by non-U.S. persons (before 1990). Thereafter, non-U.S. persons who own equity directly, or indirectly through a holding company system, 10% or more of the company.

J.A. Tatom (ed.), *Financial Market Regulation*, DOI 10.1007/978-1-4419-6637-7_5,

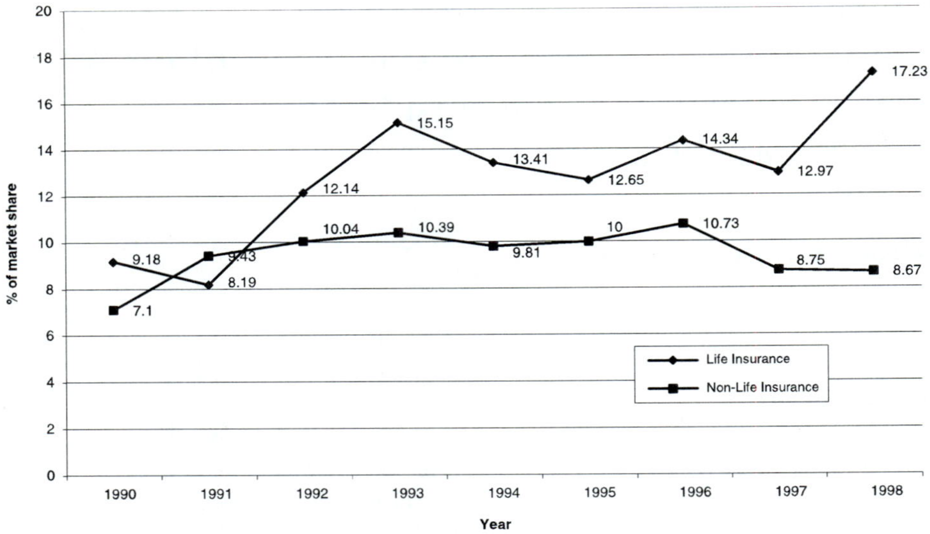

Fig. 5.1 Market share of non-U.S. controlled companies and branches and agencies of non-U.S. companies in the U.S. insurance market (Gross Premium Basis). Source: OECD Insurance Statistics Yearbook

in the U.S. insurance business since 1990. Historically, increases in the activity of non-U.S. financial firms in the United States have created political pressure on regulators to restrict their growth. For example, Goldberg and Saunders (1981) note that rapid growth in non-U.S. banks in the United States in the early 1970s led to restrictions in multi-state operations of all non-U.S. banks and subsequently led to the International Banking Act of 1978. So, it is interesting to investigate how a major regulatory change like the GLBA has impacted the non-U.S. insurance companies.

Second, we investigate whether the impact of the GLBA on non-U.S. insurance companies varies across countries. Specifically, we investigate whether the impact of the GLBA on E.U. insurers is different from non-E.U. insurers. Vaughan and Vaughan (1999), and Moshirian (1997) predict that U.S. insurance companies will face competition for European insurance companies in the domestic market. In addition, some of the largest insurance companies in the world are from Europe. For example, in 1998, eleven out of the top 25 insurance companies (on the basis of the revenue earned in 1998, as presented in Table 5.1) are from E.U. countries, 6 are from Japan, and the rest are from the United States

Previous studies that investigate the impact of the GLBA on the domestic insurance companies find that the firm specific characteristics such as size and profitability can explain the cross-sectional variation in abnormal returns from the events leading to the passage of the GLBA. We also examine whether these variables can explain the wealth effects of the non-U.S. insurance companies.

Table 5.1 World's largest insurance companies by revenues, 1998

Rank	Name	Country of domicile	1998 revenues ($ millions)
1.	AXA	France	78,729
2.	Nippon life	Japan	66,300
3.	Allianz	Germany	64,875
4.	ING group	Netherlands	56,469
5.	Assicurazioni generali	Italy	48,478
6.	State farm	USA	44,621
7.	Dai-ichi mutual life	Japan	44,486
8.	Sumitomo life	Japan	39,535
9.	Zurich financial	Switzerland	39,115
10.	CGNU	UK	37,589
11.	TIAA-CREF	USA	35,889
12.	Munich re group	Germany	35,465
13.	Prudential of America	USA	34,427
14.	Prudential (UK)	UK	33,677
15.	American int'l group	USA	33,296
16.	Meiji mutual group	Japan	28,476
17.	Metropolitan life	USA	26,735
18.	Allstate	USA	25,879
19.	Royal and sun alliance	UK	25,436
20.	CNP assurances	France	24,108
21.	Mitsui mutual life	Japan	22,226
22.	Loews	USA	20,713
23.	New York life	USA	19,849
24.	Asahi mutual life	Japan	19,418
25.	Aegon	Netherlands	18,727

Source: Jeremy Kahn, "The Fortune Global 500," *Fortune,* August 2, 1999

Our sample includes 83 non-U.S. insurance companies from eleven countries, including eight E.U. member countries (Austria, France, Germany, Greece, Ireland, Italy, Spain, and the United Kingdom) and 3 non-E.U. countries (Canada, Japan, and Switzerland). We include 31 U.S. insurance companies to compare the results of the impact of the GLBA on non-U.S. insurance companies. We find that insurance industries of Canada, France, Germany, Greece, Italy, and the United Kingdom (U.K.) are significantly and negatively affected by the GLBA. However, insurance industries of Austria, Ireland, Spain, and Switzerland are largely unaffected by this deregulation. In addition, the impact of this deregulation on any two countries is statistically different. We find no evidence that the impact of the GLBA is statistically different for firms that are from an E.U. member country versus those that are not. Furthermore, we find that profitability can explain the cross-sectional variation in the wealth effect after controlling for the country specific effects.

The rest of the study is organized as follows: section two briefly discusses the GLBA; the third section provides a literature review; section four introduces the major hypotheses; section five describes the methodology, data and lists the major events; section six presents the empirical results; and a final section concludes findings of our study.

Literature Review

Several studies examine the impact of the GLBA on the financial services industry; they consistently find that the GLBA positively affects shareholder value in the domestic insurance industry. Carow and Heron (2002) find that only the insurance industry gains from this deregulation. Akhigbe and Whyte (2001) and Mamun, Hassan, and Lai (2004) find that all the sectors of the financial services industry benefit from this deregulation, while Hendershott et al. (2002) conclude that this deregulation does not impact the banking industry. Most of these studies include size and profitability measures in their cross-sectional regression. Hendershott et al. (2002) find that only size can explain the cross-sectional variation in wealth effect in the insurance industry. Mamun et al. (2005) investigate the impact of the deregulation only on the insurance industry and find that size, profitability, and diversification benefit can explain the cross-sectional variation in wealth effect.

There is evidence in the literature that suggests the impact of GLBA may not be limited to the U.S. financial services industry. Bruner and Simms (1987) examine the reaction of U.S. banks to Mexico's loan crisis and find that U.S. banks reacted negatively to the news. Musumerci and Sinkey (1990) find that Brazil's announcement of a debt moratorium in 1987 had a negative impact on U.S. money center banks. Madura, Whyte, and McDaniel (1991) find that Citicorp's announcement of substantial increase in loan-loss reserves in 1987 had a significant negative impact on British banks. Carow and Heron (2002) document cross-border spillover effects from the GLBA. This study primarily focuses on the implications of the GLBA on domestic financial institutions but includes a sub-sample of 10 non-U.S. banks that are publicly traded in the United States. These banks experienced a negative wealth effect from the passage of the GLBA. Carow and Heron (2002) argue that the less favorable reaction of non-U.S. banks (compared to that of U.S. banks) is due to the requirement imposed by the GLBA that the entire non-U.S. banking organization has to be well capitalized. Although the sample size in this study is very small, it provides us with evidence of spillover effects of the GLBA on non-U.S. banks. In addition, Berger et al. (2000) predict that cross-border mergers and acquisitions may be motivated by the GLBA. In a more recent study Akhigbe et al. (2005) find that this deregulation only has a limited cross-border affect on non-U.S. banks. Their sample consists of Australian, Canadian, Dutch, German, Japanese, Swiss, and British banks.

There are several studies that investigate foreign direct investment (FDI) in the U.S. insurance industry. Moshirian (1997) finds that demand for insurance services in the United States, in addition to the relative rate of return, labor cost, exchange rate, size of the source country's insurance sector, bilateral relations, and trade between the United States and the host countries are the major determinants of FDI in the insurance industry in the United States. Grosse and Goldberg (1991) investigate foreign banking activity in the United States by country of origin. Their results show that foreign investment (FDI and foreign portfolio investment) in the United States, bilateral trade, and the size of each country's banking sector (demand deposits and time deposits) are positively related with the presence of that country's banks in the United States. Seth et al. (1998) show that one of the major determinants of financial institutions' growth abroad has been the parallel growth of FDI and foreign trade by globally oriented multinational corporations from the institution's home country.

GLBA and the Insurance Industry

Under the new regulation (GLBA), insurance remains a state-regulated business (the McCarran-Ferguson Act remains in place). The GLBA repeals sections of the Banking Act of 1933, including sections 20 and 32, which prohibit national banks from maintaining securities firms and bank officials from sitting on corporate boards of insurance companies. It also amends the Bank Holding Company Act of 1956 and creates a new entity known as a financial holding company (FHC). The FHC is the centerpiece of this financial modernization. FHCs may engage in activities that are financial in nature including banking, securities, insurance (underwriting as well as sales as an agent), and merchant banking. To qualify as an FHC, each subsidiary has to be well managed and well capitalized. In addition, the depository subsidiary of the FHC has to comply with the Community Reinvestment Act (CRA) rating requirement.

The GLBA also creates a new type of subsidiary, known as a financial subsidiary, through which banks can conduct many of the same activities as that of a subsidiary of a FHC.[2] However, to own such a financial subsidiary, the GLBA requires that the bank and each of its depository subsidiaries be well managed and well capitalized. A significant exception is that insurance underwriting may not be conducted in a financial subsidiary.

The GLBA also repeals Title VI of the Garn-St. Germain Act, which states that the sale or underwriting of insurance is "not closely related" to banking, which had effectively prevented bank holding companies from selling and underwriting insurance. The GLBA also preempts anti-affiliation laws. Any attempt by a state to deny a depository institution from trying to affiliate an insurer can be nullified since states are forbidden from discriminating against such entities. Hence, the GLBA allows cross-industry mergers that were not previously allowed under the previous Office of the Comptroller of the Currency rulings.

In order to engage in business in the U.S. financial services industry, a foreign financial intermediary must be well capitalized and well managed by the standards set by the Federal Reserve (Fed). The Fed will review worldwide operations of the financial intermediary to determine whether or not they can operate in the United States.

[2]Broome and Markham (2001).

Hypotheses

We test the following three hypotheses.

Hypothesis 1: The GLBA will have a significant negative spillover effect on the insurance industries of developed countries.

We expect that insurance industries of developed countries are going to have significant negative wealth effects from the passage of the GLBA for four reasons: first, Bruner and Simms (1987), Musumerci and Sinkey (1990) and Madura, Whyte, and McDaniel (1991) predict that if the financial sector of a country has exposure to any foreign market, then an event in that foreign market can have spillover effects on the financial sector of that country. In 1998, non-U.S. controlled insurance companies, branches or agencies controlled 17.23% of the U.S. life insurance market and 8.67% of the nonlife insurance market in the United States, and the major share of these non-U.S. companies are from developed countries. So, we expect that the GLBA will have spillover effect on non-U.S. insurance companies of the developed countries.

Second, the insurance industry depends upon diversification of risk for its survival.[3] Traditionally, the United States has been the largest insurance market in the world. In 1990, the market share of the U.S. insurance industry was 44.39% and in 1998 it was 45.14% (on gross premium basis) of all OECD countries combined.[4] In addition, the United States has the largest market share in both the life and nonlife insurance business. For example, in 1998 the U.S. insurance industry had 34.20% of the market share in life insurance and 57.23% of the market share in nonlife insurance of OECD countries.[5] The size of the market share makes the U.S. insurance market a natural target for the non-U.S. insurance companies to diversify their portfolio risk and also to expand their business. Due to the size of the U.S. market, any major regulatory change like the GLBA should have an impact on insurance industries of other countries.

Third, the GLBA will increase competition in the U.S. insurance industry. Under this regulation, a FHC is allowed to underwrite insurance and also work as an agent, which means that newly created FHCs will increase competition. One possible way holding companies may enter the insurance business is through acquisitions. Hendershott et al. (2002) predict that banks will acquire insurance firms and enter the insurance business. These new domestic participants in the insurance business will have a home field advantage[6] over non-U.S. firms; thus, we expect that non-U.S. insurance companies may have negative wealth effects from the passage of the GLBA.

---

[3] Pfeffer (1976) argues that no country has sufficient private insurance capacity to absorb all the insurable risk in its territory.

[4] OECD publications.

[5] OECD publications.

[6] See Berger et al. (2000) for details discussion of the Home Field Advantage hypothesis.

Furthermore, capital adequacy and management requirements by the Fed under the GLBA can also be a potential reason for negative wealth effects for non-U.S. insurance companies that are present in the United States. Carow and Heron (2002) argue that many countries impose lower capital requirements than the United States. These new eligibility requirements impose new costs for non-U.S. insurance companies that would like to participate in the U.S. insurance business, whether as an FHC or under any other structure.

Hypothesis 2: The economic impact of the GLBA on the insurance industries of any two countries will not be the same.

Studies find that country specific characteristics such as exchange rate, size of the source country's insurance sector, and trade with the source country may explain FDI in the United States. Since such characteristics, or the exposure to the U.S. insurance market, are not same for any two countries, the impact of the GLBA on any two countries' insurance industries will not be the same.

Hypothesis 3: Only the most profitable non-U.S. insurance companies will benefit from the GLBA.

The GLBA will create more competition in the U.S. insurance industry. Under the GLBA, banks can work as insurance agents and sell insurance. FHCs can underwrite insurance or work as insurance agents. These new participants in the U.S. insurance market have home field advantage over foreign insurance companies that are willing to participate in this market. As a result, we expect that the U.S. insurance market for foreign insurance companies will become more competitive. In addition, newly placed regulation will increase costs for participating in the U.S. market for the international insurance companies. Thus, the GLBA may eliminate some of the international competition and allow only the more efficient international insurance companies to enter, expand, and continue to participate in the U.S. insurance market. So we expect that only the more profit efficient international insurance companies will benefit from the GLBA.

Data and Methodology

Data and Events

We test the above hypotheses using daily common stock returns over the period of January 1998 to December 2000. Daily stock return and balance sheet information for major insurance companies from Austria, Canada, France, Germany, Greece, Ireland, Italy, Japan, Spain, Switzerland, and the U.K. are obtained from the DataStream database. The daily stock returns for 31 major U.S. insurance firms are obtained from the Center for Research in Security Prices database. The distribution of these firms across countries, along with some firm specific information and information regarding bilateral trade with the United States, is presented in Table 5.2. We

Table 5.2 Descriptive statistics of non-U.S. insurance firms

Country	No. of firms	Total asset in 1999[a,b]	ROA in 1999[b]	Export from USA 99[a,c]	Import to USA 99[a,c]
Austria	4	$7,361.03	5.85	$2,588.20	$2,909.30
Canada	8	$13,581.62	5.53	$166,600.00	$198,711.10
France	5	$121,844.71	19.00	$18,877.40	$25,708.60
Germany	10	$83,787.01	14.88	$26,800.20	$55,228.40
Greece	2	$788.53	12.85	$995.50	$563.10
Ireland	2	$21,395.57	7.82	$10,090.60	$22,356.50
Italy	7	$35,842.49	16.84	$19,436.60	$8,475.00
Netherlands	2	$356,892.93	13.18	$57,465.70	$130,863.90
Spain	3	$3,998.56	19.14	$6,133.40	$5,059.20
Switzerland	7	$48,517.03	9.82	$8,371.30	$9,538.60
UK	23	$60,554.09	20.33	$38,407.10	$39,237.20
USA	31	$91,216.92			

[a]In millions of U.S. dollars
[b]*Source*: Datastream
[c]*Source*: Board of Governors Federal Reserve System.

Table 5.3 Timeline of the Gramm-Leach-Bliley act

Date	Event
1/8/99	1. Financial Services Reform Bill is reintroduced in Congress
4/12/99	2. Senator Gramm meets with Senate minority leader to work on the bill
5/4/99	3. Clinton raises the privacy issue to be included in the bill
10/22/99	4. Gramm makes deal with White House on CRA
11/02/99	5. Joint House Conference Report signed by the majority of the conferees, clearing the way for the votes in both the House and the Senate

Note The first column 'Date' is the event date. If the event occurred after the trading closed for a day, then the next trading day is the event date. Event Window is defined as Event Date, –1 day and day 0. The second column 'Event' describes the main event

identify 5 major events from the *Wall Street Journal* and Lexis-Nexis wire service. In Table 5.3, we summarize the key dates related to the GLBA.

Portfolio Analysis

We first adapt the model used by Binder (1985) and then, following Wagster (1996), introduce long-term and short-term interest rates to control for interest rate risk. Returns on the exchange rate with the U.S. dollar are included because returns on foreign investment will depend not only on returns on the assets within each market but also changes in the exchange rate. Then, following the model of Cornett and Tehranian (1990), a lagged value of the market index is introduced to control for possible nonsynchronous trading effects. We use dummy variables to identify the major events that led to the passage of the GLBA. The dummy variable is equal to one over every event window (–1,0) and zero otherwise. The coefficient estimate associated with the dummy variable measures the impact of the event on the portfolio. The model we estimate is:

$$R_{it} = \alpha_i + \alpha_i{}'D + \sum_{j=1}^{2} \beta m_{ij} Rm_{i,t+j-2} + \sum_{j=1}^{2} \beta m_{ij}{}' DRm_{i,t+j-2} + \sum_{j=1}^{2} \beta w_{ij} Rw_{t+j-2} + \sum_{j=1}^{2} \beta w_{ij}{}' DRw_{t+j-2} + \delta l_i Rrl_{i,t} + \delta s_i Rrs_{i,t} + \kappa_i Rf_{i,t} + \sum_{j=1}^{5} \gamma_{ij} D_j + e_{it} \tag{5.1}$$

where, R_{it} is the return on portfolio i (i=12, each country has one equally weighted portfolio) at day t, $Rm_{i,t}$ is the return on the market index of country i at day t; Rw_t is the return on Morgan Stanley Composite Index (MSCI) world equity index at day t; D_j is a dummy variable that is equal to one over event window j and zero otherwise; γ_{ij} is the coefficient of a dummy variable that captures the impact of jth event on the insurance industry of the ith country. $Rf_{i,t}$ represents the return on the exchange rate between the U.S. dollar and the currency of the ith country at day t; $Rrs_{i,t}$ represents the return on the short term interest rate for country i at day t; and $Rrl_{i,t}$ represents the return on the long-term interest rate for country i at day t. D is a dummy variable that is equal to one after the enactment of the regulation and zero otherwise. Thus, $\beta m'_{i1}$-$\beta m'_{i2}$ captures the change in exposure to systematic risk between pre-act and post-act for country i with respect to its own country equity index, and $\beta w'_{i1} - \beta w'_{i2}$ captures the change in exposure to systematic risk between pre-act and post-act for country i with respect to its MSCI world equity index.

We estimate the model presented in Eq. (5.1) using seemingly unrelated regression (SUR). Schwert (1981) argues that individual asset returns of the firms in the same industry measured over a common time period are contemporaneously correlated since firms will react similarly to any unanticipated event. So in events such as regulatory changes the residuals will not be *iid*. If there is a contemporaneous correlation among the disturbances across equations but not correlated over time, SUR model estimates will be more efficient than ordinary least squares (OLS).

We use a likelihood ratio (LR) test to test the null hypothesis that the off-diagonal elements of the variance-covariance matrix is zero. We perform this test to check for contemporaneous correlation among the disturbances across equations. The result of the specification test for our portfolio model shows that the null hypothesis that the off-diagonal elements of the variance-covariance matrix are zero is rejected at the 1% level. Statistically that means that estimating the model with SUR is asymptotically more efficient as opposed to OLS.

The main advantage of using SUR is that it allows us to test interesting cross-country restrictions. In order to test for Hypothesis 2 we test the following null hypothesis:

$$H_0 : \sum_{i=1}^{5} \gamma_{i1} = \sum_{i=1}^{5} \gamma_{i2} = \sum_{i=1}^{5} \gamma_{i3} \ldots\ldots = \sum_{i=1}^{5} \gamma_{i11} \tag{5.2}$$

Cross-Sectional Analysis

In order to test whether size and profitability can explain the variation in abnormal return, we generate average abnormal returns, i.e. ϕ_i (i=1–83), for each firm using the model presented in Eq. (5.3).

$$R_{it} = \alpha_i + \alpha_i{}'D + \sum_{j=1}^{2} \beta m_{ij} Rm_{i,t+j-2} + \sum_{j=1}^{2} \beta m_{ij}{}' DRm_{i,t+j-2} + \sum_{j=1}^{2} \beta w_{ij} Rw_{t+j-2} + \sum_{j=1}^{2} \beta w_{ij}{}' DRw_{t+j-2} + \delta l_i Rrl_{i,t} + \delta s_i Rrs_{i,t} + \kappa_i Rf_{i,t} + \Phi_i DG_i + e_{it} \quad (5.3)$$

Here DG is a dummy variable that is equal to one on every event window and zero otherwise. All other parameters are same as the model presented in Eq. (5.1). We then estimate the following model using OLS, where ϕ_i is the dependent variable. The cross-sectional model is:

$$\Phi_{i,j} = \theta_{\text{aus}}\text{aus} + \theta_{\text{can}}\text{can} + \theta_{\text{fra}}\text{fra} + \theta_{\text{ger}}\text{ger} + \theta_{\text{gre}}\text{gre} + \theta_{\text{ire}}\text{ire} + \theta_{\text{ita}}\text{ita} + \theta_{\text{spa}}\text{spa} + \theta_{\text{swi}}\text{swi} + \theta_{\text{uk}}\text{uk} + \theta_{\text{size}}\text{size}_i + \theta_{\text{ROA}}\text{ROA}_i + \varepsilon_i \quad (5.4)$$

where, aus, can, fra, ger, gre, ire, ita, spa, swi, uk are country dummy variables, representing Austria, Canada, France, Germany, Greece, Ireland, Italy, Spain, Switzerland, and the U.K. respectively. These dummy variables are equal to one if a firm is from that country and zero otherwise. As mentioned in Hypothesis 2, these dummy variables shall control for country specific variations. Size$_i$ is defined as the log of total asset value (in U.S. dollar) in 1998 for firm i and ROA$_i$ is the return on asset of firm i in 1998.

Empirical Results

Portfolio Analysis

Estimates of model parameters of the portfolio model are presented in Table 5.4. We find that, for all the countries, their own country equity index is highly significant and positive while we find that MSCI world equity index is positive and significant only for Italy and the United States. Change in own country equity index after the enactment of the GLBA is negative and significant for most of the countries.

We find that in eight out of the twelve countries we analyzed, there are significant average abnormal returns from the events leading to the passage of the GLBA. The insurance industries of Canada, France, Germany, Greece, Italy, and the U.K. have been negatively affected from the passage of the GLBA. However, insurance industries of Austria, Ireland, Spain, and Switzerland do not experience any impact from the five major announcements that we analyze in this chapter. These results

Table 5.4 Estimation results of model parameters of the portfolio model (Eq. (5.1)

	Intercept	Change in intercept	Own country equity index (1 day lag)	Own country equity index	Change in own country equity index (1 day lag)	Change in own country equity index	MSCI World Equity Index (1 day lag)	MSCI World Equity Index	Change in MSCI World Equity Index (1 day lag)	Change in MSCI World Equity Index	Exchange rate with USA	Long-term interest rate	Short-term interest rate	Event 1	Event 2	Event 3	Event 4	Event 5	R^2
Austria	0.001	−0.001	0.145[a]	0.582[a]	−0.113	−0.190[c]	−0.068	0.046	0.060	−0.001	0.011	−0.005	−0.012	0.004	−0.002	−0.002	−0.001	−0.003	0.236
	1.103	−0.903	3.110	12.004	−1.160	−1.937	−1.174	0.842	0.662	−0.014	0.232	−0.120	−0.238	0.486	−0.231	−0.225	−0.108	−0.354	
Canada	−0.001	0.001	0.050	0.581[a]	−0.084	−0.239[b]	−0.010	0.056	0.175	−0.110	0.079	−0.006	−0.021	0.006	−0.019[b]	−0.003	−0.005	−0.019[b]	0.200
	−0.971	1.454	0.596	6.827	−0.768	−2.141	−0.110	0.578	1.179	−0.731	0.599	−0.122	−0.421	0.677	−2.113	−0.374	−0.550	−2.160	
France	0.001[c]	0.000	0.075	0.592[a]	−0.144[c]	−0.227[a]	0.151[b]	0.087	0.094	−0.158	−0.115[c]	0.004	0.028	−0.019[a]	−0.011	−0.010	−0.015[b]	−0.004	0.380
	1.656	−0.044	1.571	11.533	−1.912	−2.971	2.234	1.331	0.852	−1.505	−1.888	0.142	0.732	−2.661	−1.493	−1.347	−2.067	−0.543	
Germany	0.000	0.001	0.081[b]	0.570[a]	−0.050	−0.230[a]	0.081	−0.037	−0.122	−0.003	0.010	0.031	−0.005	0.002	−0.012[b]	0.003	−0.007	0.004	0.464
	0.581	1.034	2.551	17.128	−0.882	−4.034	1.572	−0.772	−1.425	−0.033	0.236	1.095	−0.155	0.306	−2.178	0.477	−1.211	0.676	
Greece	0.003[a]	−0.003	−0.010	0.717[a]	0.035	0.309[a]	0.003	−0.120	0.015	0.201	0.013	0.036	−0.040	0.004	−0.002	−0.032[a]	0.048[a]	−0.004	0.509
	3.306	−2.041	−0.280	18.012	0.539	4.442	0.031	−1.362	0.095	1.363	0.142	0.711	−1.145	0.275	−0.152	−2.474	3.702	−0.325	
Ireland	0.000	0.000	0.027	0.456[a]	−0.016	−0.126[c]	−0.040	0.047	0.132	−0.088	0.048	0.006	−0.027	0.010	−0.006	0.012	−0.010	0.010	0.231
	0.392	0.312	0.717	10.648	−0.227	−1.757	−0.650	0.880	1.335	−0.975	0.794	0.119	−1.174	1.279	−0.731	1.548	−1.366	1.333	
Italy	0.000	0.001[c]	0.058[c]	0.930[a]	−0.171[a]	−0.452[a]	0.068	0.119[b]	0.030	−0.100	−0.019	0.010	0.025	−0.013[c]	−0.001	0.000	−0.010	−0.002	0.652
	−0.357	1.880	1.724	26.141	−2.670	−7.079	1.136	2.040	0.311	−1.052	−0.332	0.268	0.593	−1.868	−0.198	0.044	−1.465	−0.309	
Japan	−0.001[c]	0.001	0.035	0.750[a]	−0.156[a]	−0.518[a]	−0.031	−0.012	−0.117	0.073	0.028	−0.002	0.000	−0.001	0.008	0.018[b]	0.010	0.003	0.369
	−1.764	1.411	0.842	17.685	−2.411	−7.350	−0.512	−0.210	−1.149	0.794	0.619	−0.142	0.472	−0.173	0.968	2.322	1.279	0.341	
Spain	−0.001	0.002[c]	0.105[b]	0.756[a]	−0.022	−0.584[a]	0.170[b]	0.022	−0.177	0.050	−0.047	−0.012	0.023	0.010	−0.003	−0.002	−0.004	−0.005	0.424
	−1.359	1.941	2.285	16.055	−0.261	−7.018	2.303	0.301	−1.474	0.428	−0.712	−0.251	0.687	1.148	−0.353	−0.225	−0.434	−0.621	
Switzerland	0.000	0.000	0.030	0.957[a]	0.028	−0.390[a]	0.064	0.005	−0.118[c]	0.023	−0.044	0.015	0.001	−0.007	0.006	0.007	0.001	−0.004	0.704
	0.792	0.402	0.940	28.957	0.419	−5.704	1.388	0.117	−1.698	0.335	−1.194	0.709	0.116	−1.417	1.254	1.363	0.183	−0.843	
UK	0.000	0.001	0.045	0.392[a]	−0.072	−0.064	0.120[a]	−0.048	−0.010	−0.068	−0.058	0.017	0.019	0.000	0.002	0.002	−0.009[c]	−0.008[c]	0.281
	1.218	1.336	1.216	10.146	−1.130	−0.992	2.711	−1.121	−0.143	−0.964	−1.309	0.729	0.571	−0.015	0.339	0.507	−1.810	−1.685	
USA	−0.003	0.012	−1.834[b]	4.690[a]	−0.153	−5.368[a]	0.435	7.523[a]	−2.382[c]	2.553[b]	2.463[a]	−1.287[a]	0.585	−0.033	−0.025	0.044	0.298[a]	0.009	0.494
	−0.757	1.527	−2.031	5.286	−0.124	−4.351	0.553	9.632	−1.859	1.980	2.481	−2.535	0.964	−0.449	−0.346	0.599	4.075	0.121	

[a,b,c]Denote significance at 1, 5, and 10% levels respectively

generally support our first hypothesis that the GLBA will have significant negative spillover effects on the insurance industries of other developed countries.

Our second hypothesis, that the information produced over these five events has the same impact on the insurance industry of any two countries, is rejected at 1%. This hypothesis is tested using a Wald test (presented in Eq. (5.2)) where the underlying distribution is χ^2 with eleven degrees of freedom.

Cross-Section Analysis

In order to identify the sources of the variation in wealth effects around the events that led to the GLBA, we performed a cross-sectional analysis. We estimate Eq. (5.4) using OLS. The results of the estimation are presented in Panel A of Table 5.5; the *t*-statistics are computed using the formulas suggested by MacKinnon and White (1985). We use country dummy variables to control for the country specific effects. The purpose of the test was to identify the source of cross-sectional variation in abnormal return. In particular, we want to test our third hypothesis that only the most

Table 5.5 Cross-sectional analysis of wealth effect on each firm in the insurance industries of selected developed countries

	Estimation method: OLS		Estimation method: bootstrap	
Variables	Coefficient estimates	*t*-statistics	Coefficient estimates	*t*-statistics
θ_{aus}	−0.265	−0.595	−0.341	−0.603
θ_{can}	−0.98[c]	−1.826	−1.074	−2.36
θ_{fra}	−1.592[a]	−2.746	−1.696	−3.353
θ_{ger}	−0.733	−1.487	−0.853	−1.703
θ_{ger}	0.192	0.524	0.092	0.222
θ_{ire}	−0.223	−0.521	−0.287	−0.468
θ_{ita}	−0.873[c]	−1.794	−0.982	−2.035
θ_{spa}	−0.411	−0.928	−0.483	−0.889
θ_{swi}	−0.121	−0.233	−0.229	−0.36
θ_{uk}	−0.364	−0.929	−0.437	−1.025
θ_{size}	0.017	0.602	0.023	0.772
θ_{ROA}	0.004[a]	2.89	0.004	1.853
R^2	0.386			
F-Statistics	3.257[a]			

We estimate the following model:

$$\gamma_{i,j} = \theta_{aus}aus + \theta_{can}can + \theta_{fra}fra + \theta_{ger}ger + \theta_{gre}gre + \theta_{ire}ire + \theta_{ita}ita + \theta_{spa}spa + \theta_{swi}swi$$
$$+\theta_{uk}uk + \theta_m\beta m'_{i,j} + \theta_w\beta w'_i + \theta_{size}Size_i + \theta_{ROA}ROA_i + \varepsilon_i$$

We estimate the model using OLS for 71 firms in the sample. Here $\gamma_{i,j}$ is the abnormal return of firm *i* of country *j*. *aus, can,....uk* are dummy variables for a particular country; these variables are equal to one for that country and zero otherwise. *Size* is log of book value of total assets and *ROA* is return on Asset. Bootstrap *p*-values are based on 1,000 replications.

[a,b,c]Denote significance at 1, 5, and 10 levels respectively

profit efficient international insurance companies may benefit from this deregulation. After controlling for the country effect, we find that profitability represented by ROA can explain cross-sectional variation of abnormal return of non-U.S. insurers.

We use the bootstrap method to test for the precision of our estimators due to the small number of observations. One may argue that asymptotic theory may provide a poor guide to the significance of the estimator. We can express Eq. (5.3) as follows:

$$y_i = X_i\theta + \varepsilon_i$$

We then use the following procedure:

1. We sample with replacement from the original (y, X) sample in pairs.
2. Then we estimate $\hat{\theta}_j$ and pseudo t-statistics for each $\hat{\theta}_j$, we also compute 95% confidence internal for $\hat{\theta}_j$ and pseudo t-statistics for each $\hat{\theta}_j$.
3. Repeat steps 1 and 2 for 1,000 times.
4. Then compare the estimates and statistical significance with the normal OLS regression.

The bootstrap results are presented in panel B of Table 5.5. It presents value of coefficient estimates and t-statistics from 1,000 bootstrap re-samples for all the country dummy variables, Size, and ROA. It also presents the average coefficient estimates and average t-statistics for all the independent variables. Using the bootstrap t-value, seven out of eleven country dummy variables are not significantly different from zero. The coefficient estimates for Size is also not significantly different from zero. The only variable that is significant at the cross-section regression is the profitability indicator ROA.

We also test whether E.U. firms experience a different impact from the GLBA than non-E.U. firms. We modify Eq. (5.3), and then replace all the country dummy variables with one dummy, which is one if the firm is from an E.U. country and zero otherwise. The modified model is presented in Eq. (5.5) as:

$$\gamma_{i,j} = \text{Intercept} + \theta_{\text{eu}}\text{eu} + \theta_{\text{size}}\text{Size}_i + \theta_{\text{ROE}}\text{ROA}_i + \varepsilon_i \qquad (5.4)$$

Here we test the hypothesis$H_0 : \theta_{\text{eu}} = 0$. The result, as presented in Table 5.6, shows that the null hypothesis is maintained; i.e. insurance companies from E.U. member countries are not affected differently from those in non-E.U. countries.

Conclusion

We have examined the impact of the GLBA, a major regulatory change in the U.S. financial services industry, on a sample of 83 non-U.S. insurance companies from 11 countries. In an era of globalization of financial markets, it is argued that deregulations like the GLBA or the single market program of the E.U. should have an

Table 5.6 Cross-sectional analysis of wealth effect on each firm in the insurance industries E.U. vs. Non-E.U. countries

Parameter	Estimate	t-statistic
Intercept	−0.173	−0.263
θ_{eu}	−0.003	−0.014
θ_{size}	−0.010	−0.265
θ_{ROA}	0.004[a]	3.370
R^2	0.035	
F-Statistics	0.784	

We estimate the following model: $\gamma_{i,j} = Intercept + \theta_{eu}eu + \theta_{size}Size_i + \theta_{ROE}ROA_i + \varepsilon_i$
We estimate the model using OLS for 83 firms in the sample. Here $\gamma_{i,j}$ is the abnormal return of firm i of country j, and *eu* is a dummy variable which is 1 if it is a E.U. member country and zero otherwise. *Size* is log of book value of total asset and *ROA* is return on Asset
[a,b,c]Denote significance at 1, 5, and 10% levels respectively

impact beyond the boundaries of the jurisdiction.[7] In this chapter we present further evidence of the globalization of financial institutions. In our portfolio analysis we find that the insurance industries of 7 out of 11 developed countries have significant negative spillover (wealth) effects from passage of the GLBA. We also find that the impact of the GLBA is not the same for insurance industries of any two foreign countries. Furthermore, the impact of the GLBA is statistically not different between firms from an E.U. member or non-member countries.

Most interestingly we find that a profitability indicator can explain the cross-sectional variation in wealth effect after controlling for the country effect. We predict that this is due to increased competition in the U.S. insurance market from the new domestic participants and increased cost imposed by the GLBA due to more strict capital adequacy and management requirement for foreign financial firms as argued by Carow and Heron (2002). As a result, the most efficient international insurance companies may continue to operate, enter or expand in the largest insurance market in the world.

References

Akhigbe A, Whyte AM (2001) The market's assessment of the financial services modernization act of 1999. Financ Rev 36:119–138

Akhigbe A, Frye MB, Whyte AM (2005) Financial modernization in the U.S. banking markets: a local or global event? J Bus Finance Account 37:1561–1585

Berger AN, DeYoung R, Genay H, Udell GF (2000) Globalization of financial institutions: evidence from cross-border banking performance. Brooking-Wharton Papers in Financial Services 3

Binder JJ (1985) Measuring the effects of regulation with stock price data. Rand J Econ 16: 167–183

Blander M (2000) Shrinking in the big apple. The Banker 150

[7]Berger et al. (2000).

Broome L, Markham J (2000) Banking and insurance: before and after the Gramm-Leach-Bliley act. J Corp Law 25:723–785
Bruner RF, Simms JM (1987) The international debt crisis and bank security returns in 1982. J Money Credit Bank 19:46–55
Carow KA, Heron R (2002) Capital market reactions to the passage of the financial services modernization act of 1999. Q Rev Econ Finance 42:465–485
Cornett MM, Tehranian H (1990) An examination of the impact of the Garn-St. germain depository institutions act of 1982 on commercial banks and savings and loans. J Finance 45:95–111
Goldberg LG, Saunders A (1981) The determinants of foreign banking activity in the United States. J Bank Finance 5:17–32
Grosse R, Goldberg LG (1991) Foreign bank activity in the United States an analysis by the country of origin. J Bank Finance 15:1093–1112
Lee DE, Tompkins JG (2002) Winners and losers as financial service providers converge: evidence from the financial modernization act of 1999. Financ Rev 37:53–72
MacKinnon JG, White H (1985) Some heteroskedasticity consistent covariance matrix estimators with improved finite sample properties. J Econ 29:305–325
Madura J, Whyte AM, McDaniel WR (1991) Reaction to the British bank share prices to Citicorp's announced $3 billion increase in loan loss reserves. J Bank Finance 15:151–163
Mamun A, Hassan MK, Lai VS (2004) The impact of the Gramm-Leach-Bliley act on the financial services industry. J Econ Finance 28:333–347
Mamun A, Hassan MK, Maroney N, Karels GV (2005) Financial services modernization act of 1999: market assessment of winners and losers in the insurance industry. J Ins Issues 28: 103–128
Moshirian F (1997) Foreign direct investment in insurance services in the United States. J Multinational Financ Manage 7:159–173
Musumeci JJ, Sinkey JF (1990) The international debt crisis, investor contagion, and bank security returns in 1987: the Brazilian experience. J Money Credit Bank 22:209–220
Pfeffer I (1976) Non-tariff barriers to alien insurance in United States. J Risk Insur 43(2):275–289
Schwert GW (1981) Using financial data to measure the effects of regulation. J Law Econ 25: 121–145
Seth R et al (1998) Do banks follow their customers abroad? Financ Mark Instrum Inst 7(4):1–25
Vaughan EJ, Vaughan T (1999) Fundamentals of risk and insurance, 8th edn. Wiley, New York, NY
Wagster, JD (1996) Impact of the 1988 Basel accord on international banks. J Finance 51: 1321–1346

Part III
Continuing Issues in Financial Regulation

Chapter 6
A Program for Minimizing the Private and Public Costs of Bank Failures

George G. Kaufman

Bank failures are often perceived to be more costly to the economy than the failure of other firms of comparable size and to generate widespread public fear. As a result, preventing bank failures is a major public policy concern in all countries. Unfortunately, most public policy strategies adopted in nearly all countries to achieve this objective have eventually failed to do so, at a large cost, not only in reduced income and wealth to many of the failed bank's customers and in the bank's market area through misallocation of financial resources, but also to the taxpayers of the country as a whole, who have frequently been asked to finance most or all of the losses to large bank depositors, other creditors, and, at times, even shareholders. The high cost of these policies has encouraged a search for more efficient ways of protecting the economy from bank failures, while permitting poorly managed or unlucky individual banks to exit but at no or little cost to either their customers or the economy. This chapter proposes a four-pillar program to achieve this objective efficiently.[1]

Four Pillar Program to Minimize Costs of Bank Failures

Bank failures generally involve direct losses to shareholders, depositors, other creditors, and borrowers. Because bank deposits serve as both money and liquid wealth and banks are typically closely interconnected through interbank deposits and loans, losses from failure may spill over to other banks and beyond. It is losses to bank stakeholders other than the shareholders that create the adverse externalities and are of primary public policy concern. Losses to depositors may be in two forms. One, credit losses, which occur if the recovery values of the assets fall short of the par value of the deposits. Two, liquidity losses, which occur when depositor access to the either insured or the asset recovery value of their uninsured deposits is delayed

G.G. Kaufman (✉)
Department of Finance, Loyola University, 1 East Pearson Street, Chicago, IL 60611, USA
e-mail: gkaufma@luc.edu

This chapter also appeared as Networks Financial Institute *Policy Brief* 2007-PB-11.

[1] Kaufman (2004a). Similar programs have been proposed by Mayes (2004) and Harrison (2005).

J.A. Tatom (ed.), *Financial Market Regulation*, DOI 10.1007/978-1-4419-6637-7_6,

until the assets are sold. The accounts are frozen for some length of time. Short-term deposits are effectively transformed into longer-term deposits or even bonds. Liquidity losses may also be experienced by borrowers, if performing loan customers cannot access their prearranged credit lines. Liquidity losses tend to receive less attention than credit losses, at least in the United States, even though they are as, if not more, damaging than credit losses. If there were no fear of either credit or liquidity losses, there would be no need either for depositors to run on their banks to withdraw funds in mass in anticipation of credit losses. Such runs could induce fire-sale losses from the resulting sale of assets and potentially drive a bank into insolvency or force banks to curtail access to legitimate credit lines and decrease the money supply, if depositors run into currency that is not redeposited in other banks. It follows that the cost of bank failures may be minimized by reducing, if not eliminating altogether, credit and liquidity losses.

Before discussing how this may be done, it is important to note that deposit insurance, which is the current policy of choice of most governments for minimizing the frequency and cost of bank failures, does not eliminate either credit or liquidity losses from bank failures. Rather, deposit insurance primarily shifts credit losses from depositors to the insurance agency and, if not priced correctly, may even actually increase these losses. If the insurance is underpriced, as is often the case, banks are likely to pursue excessive risk-taking moral hazard behavior. This is likely to increase the probability of failure. In addition, by reducing the urgency for explicitly or implicitly insured depositors to run, when banks encounter financial difficulties, insolvent banks may not lose funding and continue to operate for some time. As a result, regulators may not feel the urgency to take strong action to place financially troubled banks into receivership and thereby encounter the wrath of bankers, who would lose their institutions; of depositors, whose unbooked implicit losses would be transformed into booked and explicit painful losses; and of loan customers, whose access to ongoing bank credit lines would be curtailed. If so, as losses are likely to increase on average the longer insolvent banks are permitted to operate, the regulators would be poor agents for their healthy bank or taxpayer principals. Lastly, deposit insurance per se protects insured depositors against credit losses but not necessarily against liquidity losses, unless the powers of the insurance agency are augmented beyond those required to make depositors whole over time.

The proposed program to minimize or even eliminate credit and liquidity losses in bank failures include four pillars. All focus on the word "prompt" and assume that the legal and institutional frameworks, as well as the political will on the part of regulators and governments to permit the proposed remedial actions on a meaningful and timely basis, are in place.[2] Accordingly, the examples of such remedies used in this chapter are restricted primarily to the United States, where these prerequisites are most likely to exist. The four pillars are:

[2] An analysis of the current status of bank regulation and institutional arrangements across countries appears in Barth et al. (2006).

1. Prompt legal closure at positive capital to minimize credit losses,
2. Prompt estimates of credit losses (asset recovery values) and allocation of losses (haircuts) to ex-ante at-risk stakeholders,
3. Prompt reopening of most closed banks under new private or FDIC (bridge bank) ownership to minimize liquidity losses, and
4. Prompt reprivatization and recapitalization of reopened banks.

Pillar I: Prompt Legal Closure

To minimize if not eliminate credit losses, a bright line legal closure rule at positive capital needs to be incorporated in the statute and the bank's insurance and charter revoked and the bank placed in receivership as soon as or shortly after this line is breached. If successful, losses would be confined to shareholders. As assets are sufficient to cover the remaining liabilities, depositors and other creditors suffer no losses. It is important to differentiate between legal closure and physical closure. Legal closure refers to revoking the insolvent bank's charter and placing it in receivership or conservatorship when the capital of a bank declines below a prespecified positive capital-asset ratio. Generally this is done with the expectation of quickly selling, merging, or bridging all but the smallest banks or banks for which there is no demand to minimize liquidity losses. Physical closure denies customers temporary access to their accounts and creates liquidity losses. Thus, prompt legal closure of banks at the specified capital value is desirable, while physical closure is not.

A legal closure target at a positive value of capital rather than zero, which generally defines insolvency, is desirable as regulators may not always be successful in placing a bank in receivership before all of its capital is fully depleted, because of delays in obtaining and analyzing real-time accurate data, abrupt changes in asset and liability values, or outright fraud. Legally closing a bank quickly when the capital closure trigger is breached is more likely when both the authority and implementation to do so lie administratively with the bank regulatory agencies, with little if any provisions for ex-ante appeal by stakeholders, rather than lie judicially in the courts with provisions for ex-ante appeal. In the United States, these powers are granted the federal banking regulators in a separate bank bankruptcy code from the general corporate bankruptcy code.[3] Any positive capital remaining after legal closure and sale or liquidation is returned to the bank's shareholders at time of closure. Thus, there is no taking of private property.

To reduce the probability of the bank breaching the insolvency capital trigger either abruptly or without the awareness of the regulators, the legal closure rule

[3]The unique features of the bankruptcy code for banks are described in Bliss and Kaufman (2007). In addition, in many countries, the deposit insurance agencies differ greatly from the FDIC in the U.S. They are generally only cash boxes collecting premiums and paying depositors but without any regulatory or supervisory responsibilities or resolution authority. A description of a number of these agencies outside the U.S. appears in Eisenbeis and Kaufman (2007).

needs to be supplemented by an accompanying series of regulatory sanctions that become progressively harsher and more mandatory as the financial condition of an institution, as measured by, say, its capital-asset ratio, deteriorates. The purpose of these multi-tiered prompt corrective action (PCA) sanctions is not to punish troubled banks but to apply a carrot-stick approach to encourage them to reverse their downward direction and recapitalize to avoid insolvency. Only when these sanctions fail to turn a troubled institution around before insolvency is legal closure required. The regulatory sanctions are basically the same as those that the market would typically impose on troubled firms in nonregulated industries, such as limiting dividends, acquisitions, and growth, and preparing capital restoration plans. By making the sanctions progressively harsher as the financial performance of a bank deteriorates, the PCA structure attempts to constrain excessive moral hazard risk-taking behavior by the banks based on the existence of an underpriced safety net and reduce the moral hazard problem. By making the sanctions progressively more mandatory, the PCA structure attempts to reduce the ability of regulators to forbear in applying effective sanctions and reduce the principal-agent problem.[4]

In addition, by requiring regulators to intervene well before a bank's financial health deteriorates to the point where it is classified as regulatory, if not economically, insolvent, the PCA tranche structure buys the regulators time to become more knowledgeable about the bank, monitor it more carefully, and prepare for the possibility of legal closure while capital is still positive. (The structure of PCA in the United States is summarized in Table 6.1). Legal closure at regulatory insolvency is triggered when a bank's equity capital declines to a small but positive ratio of its assets. In the United States, for example, regulatory insolvency is triggered when the book value equity to total asset ratio declines below 2% and the bank is classified "critically undercapitalized." To achieve credibility and affect the ex-ante behavior of both banks and large ex-ante uninsured depositors, the sanctions and closure rule need to be developed by the regulators before crises occur, widely publicized, and applied without exception. However, the 2% book value equity to asset ratio is likely to be too low to prevent all credit losses in legal closures even if the regulatory agencies act quickly on timely and reliable data. But it should serve to minimize losses. The regulators may also legally close a bank for other reasons, such as not being operated in a safe and sound manner or unlikeliness to meet its deposit obligations, as specified in the statute.

Pillar II: Prompt Estimate and Allocation of Credit Losses

Both to minimize the cost of resolution to the deposit insurance agency or its stakeholders and to encourage effective market discipline by bank shareholders and ex-ante uninsured depositors and other creditors, it is necessary that they

[4]The development of the PCA structure in the U.S. enacted in the FDIC Improvement Act (FDICIA) of 1991 is described in Benston and Kaufman (1993).

Table 6.1 Summary of prompt corrective action provisions of the federal deposit insurance corporation improvement act of 1991

			Capital ratios (percent)		
			Risk based		Leverage
Zone	Mandatory provisions	Discretionary provisions	Total	Tier 1	Tier 1
1. Well capitalized			>10	>6	>5
2. Adequately capitalized	1. No brokered deposits, except with FDIC approval		>8	>4	>4
3. Undercapitalized	1. Suspend dividends and management fees 2. Require capital restoration plan 3. Restrict asset growth 4. Approval required for acquisitions, branching, and new activities 5. No brokered deposits	1. Order recapitalization 2. Restrict inter-affiliate transactions 3. Restrict deposit interest rates 4. Restrict certain other activities 5. Any other action that would better carry out prompt corrective action	<8	<4	<4
4. Significantly undercapitalized	1. Same as for Zone 3 2. Order recapitalization 3. Restrict inter-affiliate transactions 4. Restrict deposit interest rates 5. Pay of officers restricted	1. Any Zone 3 discretionary actions 2. Conservatorship or receivership if fails to submit or implement plan or recapitalize pursuant to order 3. Any other Zone 5 provision, if such action is necessary to carry out prompt corrective action	<6	<3	<3
5. Critically undercapitalized	1. Same as for Zone 4 2. Receiver/conservator within 90 days with two possible 90 day extensions. 3. Suspend payments on subordinated debt 4. Restrict certain other activities				<2

Source: Board of Governors of the Federal Reserve System.

share in losses according to their legal priority. Uninsured depositors, who in the United States have equal standing with the FDIC and higher standing than unsecured other creditors, need to share in losses with the FDIC only if the regulators are not able to legally close the bank before its capital turns negative or before it is sufficiently negative to exceed the bank's nondepositor unsecured creditors.[5] Shareholders are likely to lose their investments unless the actual recovery amounts exceed the combined par claims of the FDIC, uninsured depositors, and other creditors. By involving regulators well before regulatory insolvency, the multi-tiered PCA structure also provides time for the regulators to both determine the insurance status of individual deposit accounts and to make reasonable projections of expected asset losses when the bank is legally closed. (Additional time may be gained for identifying insured deposits, if necessary, by maintaining the original maturity dates of time deposits rather than accelerating all accounts to mature on the date of legal closure. This is proposed in the resolution plan developed by the Reserve Bank of New Zealand.[6])

Similar to the legal closure rule, the policy of imposing losses or "haircuts" on targeted at-risk (uninsured) depositors and other creditors needs to be widely publicized and strictly enforced in order to achieve credibility. Indeed, in the United States, insolvencies are required to be resolved at least cost to the FDIC by FDICIA of 1991. The Act also explicitly prohibits the FDIC from protecting uninsured claimants against losses in failure resolutions in which the FDIC incurs losses. But there is an exception to least-cost resolution, as is often the case in public policy rules—the Systemic Risk Exemption (SRE). In instances when policy-makers believe that failure to fully or partially protect these claimants would "have serious adverse effects on economic conditions or financial stability" and "any action or assistance ... would avoid or mitigate such adverse effects", the FDIC could provide protection and suffer larger losses than otherwise. By protecting the depositors and other creditors most able to monitor and discipline banks, invoking SRE is likely to reintroduce costly moral hazard behavior by large banks.

Fortunately, invoking SRE, formerly and inaccurately referred to as "too-big-to-fail" (TBTF), is not easy.[7] U.S. regulators must successfully hurdle five formidable barriers—three ex-ante and two ex-post. The exemption must first be recommended to the Secretary of the Treasury by two thirds of both the Board of Directors of the FDIC and the Board of Governors of the Federal Reserve System and approved by the Secretary of the Treasury after consultation with the President. If approved,

---

[5] In the U.S., depositor preference elevates both the FDIC and uninsured domestic depositors above unsecured other creditors. This provision was enacted in 1993, 2 years after FDICIA was enacted.

[6] See Harrison (2005)

[7] In the U.S., too-big-to-fail did not mean what it said. Insolvent banks were eventually failed, placed in receivership, and at least shareholder interests wiped out. What TBTF actually meant was that a bank was perceived to be too big to impose haircuts on uninsured depositors and possibly other creditors when the bank was legally closed. But even this practice was diminishing through time after the failure of the Continental Illinois Bank in Chicago in 1984. A history and analysis of TBTF in the U.S. appears in Kaufman (2004c).

this needs to be followed by written notification by the Secretary to both the House and Senate Banking Committees. Thereafter, an ex-post audit of the reasons for granting the exemption, the implementation process, and the effectiveness of the actions must be conducted by the Government Accountability Office (GAO) and reported to Congress. Lastly, any loss experienced by the FDIC in protecting uninsured claimants must be reimbursed to the FDIC expeditiously through a special assessment on all banks based on asset size. Losses to the FDIC from such operations may be expected, as otherwise there would be no need for the intervention. The threat of additional charges may be expected to encourage large bank competitors of the failed bank or banks to attempt to dissuade the FDIC and the other regulators from protecting the uninsured depositors at the insolvent banks and possibly permit these banks to continue to operate while insolvent and likely enlarge their losses further at the expense of the solvent banks.

Pillar III: Prompt Reopening of Legally Closed Institutions

As noted earlier, while deposit insurance protects insured depositors against credit losses, it does not automatically protect them against liquidity losses. To minimize the magnitude of adverse externalities from bank failures, it is important that liquidity losses are minimized through providing both insured and uninsured depositors speedy access to the appropriate value of their deposits and restoring borrowers to their pre-specified credit lines.[8] In the United States, currently, the FDIC pays insured depositors the par value of their deposits effectively the next business day after legal closure, generally by transferring the deposits to an acquiring or designated paying bank. This effectively involves two subpayments. One represents the estimated pro rata recovery value and the second the difference between this payment and the par value of the insured deposit.

At the same time, the FDIC gives uninsured depositors claims in the form of receivership certificates against the eventual pro rata recovery value of the bank's assets. These are paid by the FDIC from the proceeds received as the assets of the bank are liquidated. Because this typically requires some time, during which the depositors have at best only partial access to the total recovery value of the assets and a viable and deep secondary market for these certificates may not develop sufficiently quickly, these depositors suffer liquidity losses. As a result, the FDIC was provided with the authority to advance payments (dividends) to the depositors against the estimate of the recovery value.[9] But making payment to both insured and

---

[8]Liquidity losses are discussed at greater length in Kaufman and Seelig (2002) and Kaufman (2004b).

[9]For example, in the FDIC's recent resolution of the failure of NetBank, a $2.5 billion bank in Georgia, on Friday, September 29, 2007, insured deposits were assumed by another bank and available in full to depositors on Monday, October 1. Holders of uninsured deposits received receivership certificates also on Monday and an accompanying 50% payment of the par amount (FDIC 2007).

uninsured depositors in advance of the receipt of the proceeds from the sale of the bank or its assets requires that the deposit insurance agency either has a sufficient pool of funds available to it or has sufficient borrowing authority, generally at the Treasury.

Because it may be particularly difficult to resolve a large bank quickly by private sale or merger after it breaches the 2% critically undercapitalized trigger, and thus maintain seamless depositor and borrower access, the FDIC was authorized to charter a temporary FDIC-owned national bridge bank. The FDIC can maximize all aspects of liquidity by transferring to this bank the par value of the insured deposits, a conservative estimate of the pro rata recovery or market (after credit loss) value of the uninsured deposits, and the prearranged credit lines of performing loan customers. The bank is capitalized by the FDIC. The continuity of the services provided by the insolvent bank would be effectively maintained. Such bridging would also preserve any private information the bank may have on its loan and deposit customers, the loss of which is costly and disruptive. If liquidity losses along with credit losses could be successfully minimized, then both the fear of bank failures and the associated incentive to invoke SRE will be greatly diminished.

Unfortunately, outside the United States, most deposit insurance agencies do not have similar authority or follow similar practices. For example, most agencies do not have a pool of available funds or automatic borrowing authority to make payments to insured and uninsured depositors in advance of receiving proceeds from the sale of the insolvent bank or its assets. In addition, in most countries, the deposit insurance agencies are not required to either inform insured depositors of a bank's failure or to pay them quickly. Even insured depositors in many of these countries must file claims for payment, and payment may be delayed for months as the insurer collects the proceeds from the sale of the insolvent bank's assets. Thus, insured as well as uninsured depositors may suffer liquidity losses even if they avoid credit losses.[10]

[10]The importance of providing immediate access to deposits and lines of credit so as to minimize liquidity losses was demonstrated in the recent handling by the regulators in the United Kingdom of the insolvency or near-insolvency of the Northern Rock, a large mortgage specializing bank, in the summer of 2007. Questions about the financial health of the bank sparked a visible run by insured retail depositors. In large part, the run may be attributed to basic flaws in the U.K. deposit insurance system. The system provided insufficient full coverage for small depositors and had no provision for quick payment to either insured or uninsured depositors if the bank were failed. Deposit insurance protected fully only the first £2,000 (about $4,000) of deposits and only 90% of the next £33,000 (about $66,000) of deposits. Thus, most retail depositors realized they would suffer both credit and more severe liquidity losses if the institution failed and that these losses could be avoided by withdrawing funds before failure. Uninsured depositors and creditors both participated in a less visible "wholesale" run and shortened the maturities of their lending. To stop the run and keep the bank operating, the regulators were left with little option but to guarantee nearly all depositor and other creditor funds not only at Northern, but at all banks that threatened to suffer similar problems. To keep the bank operating beyond then, they later guaranteed new as well as old deposits. As a result, the probability of similar bank turmoil and the cost of its resolution are both likely to be considerably higher in the future. Also in response, effective October 1, 2007, the U.K. increased its insurance coverage to 100% of the first £35,000 of deposits. The Treasury

Pillar IV: Prompt Reprivatization and Recapitalization

State owned banks (SOBs) and state controlled banks (SCBs), including banks in government receivership or bridged, are notoriously inefficient and, as all deposits are effectively insured by the government, implicitly if not explicitly, frequently can operate for long period of time while insolvent, misallocating resources and increasing losses.[11] Thus, it is important to fully reprivatize government operated insolvent banks as quickly as can be done efficiently. All but the largest and most complex banks can be sold as a whole or in greater part at the time of legal closure. This is possible as the PCA structure again provides the regulators sufficient time to identify potential buyers and to circulate bidding materials, including estimates of the market value of assets, on a confidential basis to these parties before the date of legal closure. As noted above, to gain additional time to search out ultimate private buyers, large banks may need to be bridged in the U.S. under FDIC ownership. However, the potential 5 year maximum life of such bridge banks in the United States is far longer than necessary or desirable to reprivatize even the largest insolvent bank. To prevent the reprivatized banks from quickly following in the footsteps of their predecessors and return to insolvency, they should be required to be sufficiently recapitalized by the new owners, say, to levels, at minimum, consistent with the definition of adequately capitalized, if not well-capitalized, for purposes of PCA.

Summary and Conclusions

Healthy banks are by far the best protection against bank failure. Financially troubled banks should be turned around under provisions similar to PCA as quickly as possible after the adverse symptoms are first observed. Only if this fails should legal closure occur. But there is a strong incentive for regulators to delay legally closing insolvent banks. Legal closure would, among other things, be an official admission of the failure of the bank and a black mark on the regulators' record, reduce a regulator's chances of being employed by the industry after service as a regulator, and possibly ignite widespread public fear of substantial and costly adverse externalities beyond the insolvent bank. However, such regulatory forbearance is on average costly.

Costs associated with bank failures can be minimized by implementing a program that will minimize, if not eliminate altogether, both credit and liquidity losses. Such a four pillar program is proposed in this chapter. The program focuses on (1) prompt legal closure before a bank's capital is fully depleted to minimize credit losses, (2) prompt estimate of losses and assignment of haircuts to ex-ante uninsured depositors and other creditors as well as to the insurance agency to encourage

---

then issued a discussion paper on banking reform that attempts to correct these weaknesses in the existing depositor protection structure.

[11] See for example Barth et al. (2006) and Sapienza (2004).

market discipline and reduce costs to the agency, (3) prompt access of bank deposit and performing loan customers to the appropriate value of their eligible accounts or credit lines to minimize liquidity losses, and (4) prompt reprivatization of insolvent banks at minimum capital ratios to avoid misallocation of resources and possible quick returns to insolvency. By attempting to eliminate the costs associated with bank failure, this strategy permits inefficient or unlucky banks to exit at minimum or no cost and maintain efficiency in the banking system. It also is superior to deposit insurance. Insurance only shifts the losses from depositors to the insurer and in the process may actually increase the losses by encouraging both excessive moral hazard risk taking by banks and poor agency behavior by regulators that provides forbearance. Moreover, deposit insurance per se does not protect against liquidity losses. Explicit full deposit insurance on small deposits, however, should be retained to provide redundancy in instances that the proposed scheme fails to resolve insolvencies before a bank's capital is depleted so that credit losses may be incurred. This would protect against runs by insured depositors and remove them politically from the resolution process. It also follows that the magnitude of any credit losses is significantly under the control of the appropriate regulatory agency and if losses are minimized, insurance premiums will also be minimized and their structure less important.

But to be successful, the proposed program needs to be approved and in place in advance of bank insolvencies, widely publicly publicized, and implemented without exceptions in order to gain credibility and affect ex-ante behavior. Moreover, it requires an in-place institutional and legal infrastructure that permits and supports the proposed regulatory actions, including full and ex-ante nonappealable authority by regulators to legally close banks at some specified capital ratio greater than zero and rewards regulators with the political will to carry out the provisions of the program. Currently, the majority of the proposed program is probably feasible only in industrial countries that have much of the necessary infrastructure. But even these countries may still require changes in their institutional structure to implement most or all of the program. Other countries are likely to continue to experience higher than necessary costs of bank failures for some time. The United States, which has much of the necessary institutional and legal infrastructure in place, currently appears to have a resolution program in place that satisfies Pillars 1, 2, and 4 reasonably well, but satisfies Pillar 3 only partially at best. Federal regulators have only recently begun to seriously develop and simulate legal closure and resolution strategies and have not publicized those that they have developed.

The failure of U.S. regulators to focus more on processes for the efficient resolution of large bank insolvencies may be attributed to some extent, to their strong fascination with and devotion to Basel II. Basel II, which is scheduled to be implemented in the United States at the beginning of 2008 after a number of delays, is a highly complex three pillar structure to (1) compute minimum capital requirements in relation to a bank's risk exposure, (2) strengthen supervisory review and enforcement, and (3) enhance market discipline through increased disclosure. But all three pillars have been severely criticized as being ineffective, at least in the United States. This has required lengthy and detailed responses by the regulators

(Herring 2007; Kaufman 2004d). The recent turmoil in the financial markets in the summer of 2007 have also cast substantial doubt about the wisdom of relying heavily on rating agency credit ratings for small banks and on internal credit risk models for large banks to compute minimum regulatory capital requirements as is done in Basel II.

This point-counterpoint exchange between the regulators and their critics stretched over a number of years since Basel II was first proposed in 2001 and has absorbed considerable time and energy not only of the regulatory agencies but also of many large banks, consulting firms, policy makers, and academics. As a result, less time and energy remained for other projects at a high cost (Kaufman 2007). In the United States, many students of banking have concluded that Basel II is inferior to the in-place system of PCA for enforcing minimum capital requirements, whether risk-based or not (Kaufman 2005).[12] And unlike PCA, Basel II does not consider efficient resolution of bank insolvencies. Thus, there was little if any additional incentive for regulators to develop and test such contingency plans and even less to widely publicize any plans adopted before banks failures occurred.

But, secret plans to reduce the costs of bank failures are likely to be little more effective than no plans at all. The public is likely to act on a different set of expectations that were previously in place and will strongly oppose ex-post surprise or unexpected actions that may impose losses on it. When push comes to shove, as was evidenced in the summer of 2007 in Germany and the U.K. in 2008 in the U.S., bank regulators are likely to delay or abandon imposing their secret plans if they are tougher and give in to public pressure for protection as usual.

References

Barth J, Caprio G Jr, Levine R (2006) Rethinking bank regulation: till angels govern. Cambridge University Press, Cambridge, MA

Benston GJ, Kaufman GG (1988) Risk and solvency regulation of depository institutions: past policies and current options. Salomon Brothers Center for the Study of Financial Institutions, New York University, New York, NY

Benston GJ, Kaufman GG (1993) The intellectual history of the federal deposit insurance corporation improvement act of 1991. In: Kaufman GG (ed) Reforming financial institutions and markets in the United States. Kluwer, Boston, MA, pp 1–18

Bliss RR, Kaufman GG (2007) U.S. corporate and bank insolvency regimes: a comparison and evaluation. Virginia Law Bus Rev (Spring) 2:143–177

Eisenbeis RA, Kaufman GG (2007) Cross border banking: challenges for deposit insurance and financial stability in the European Union. In: Paper presented at Conference on Financial Instability, Supervision, and Central Banks, Helsinki, Bank of Finland, 7–8 June

Federal Deposit Insurance Corporation (2007) FDIC approves the assumption of the insured deposits of Netbank. Press Releases, Alpharetta, GA, 28 Sept

Harrison I (2005) The reserve bank of New Zealand's creditor recapitalization (BCR) project: an option for resolving large banks? In: Evanoff DD, Kaufman GG (eds) Systemic financial crises: resolving large bank insolvencies. World Scientific, Singapore, pp 397–406

[12]This was less true in many other industrial countries where PCA, if adopted, was considerably weaker in practice than in the U.S. (Mayes et al. 2007).

Herring RJ (2007) The rocky road to implementation of Basel II in the United States. Working Paper, University of Pennsylvania, Philadelphia, PA, September

Kaufman GG (2007) Basel II is a costly distraction on the road to minimizing the societal costs of bank failure. Working Paper, Loyola University Chicago, Chicago, IL, July

Kaufman GG (2005) Basel II vs. prompt corrective action: which is best for public policy? Financ Markets Inst Instrum (December) 14:349–357

Kaufman GG (2004a) Bank regulation and foreign-owned banks. Reserve Bank N Z Bull (June) 67:65–74

Kaufman GG (2004b) Depositor liquidity and loss sharing in bank failure resolutions. Contemp Econ Pol (April) 22:237–249

Kaufman GG (2004c) Too big to fail in U.S. banking: Quo Vadis? In: Gup B (ed) Too big to fail: policies and practices in government bailouts. Praeger, Westport, CT, pp 153–167

Kaufman GG (2004d) The roar that moused. In: Gup B (ed) The new Basel capital accord. Thomson, New York, NY, pp 39–52

Kaufman GG, Seelig S (2002) Post-resolution treatment of depositors at failed banks. Econ Perspect (Federal Reserve Bank of Chicago) (2nd Quarter):27–41

Mayes DG (2004) Who pays for bank insolvency? J Int Money Finance (April) 23:515–551

Mayes DG, Nieto MJ, Wall L (2007) Multiple safety-net regulators and agency problems in the EU: is prompt corrective action partly the solution? In: Benink H, Goodhart C, Lastra RM (eds) Prompt corrective action & cross-border supervisory issues in Europe. (Financial Markets Group Special Paper Series 171), London School of Economics, London, pp 62–88, Apr

Sapienza P (2004) The effects of government ownership on bank lending. J Financ Econ 72:357–384, May

Chapter 7
The Importance of Monitoring and Mitigating the Safety-Net Consequences of Regulation-Induced Innovation

Edward J. Kane

As officials seek to identify the events and circumstances that generated the 2007–2009 financial crisis, they are attracted to explanations that deflect blame from themselves and the organizations they serve. The resulting array of seemingly authoritative explanations creates forward-looking policy turbulence. Conflicts between alternative crisis stories make it hard for outsiders to understand whether and how various proposed reforms might or might not reduce the frequency or depth of future crises. A particularly important issue concerns how giant U.S. financial institutions and automobile companies made themselves too difficult to fail and unwind (TDFU).

To a greater or lesser extent, official narratives are self-serving cover stories designed to heap credit on their authors and the institutions they lead, while shifting the blame for financial and macroeconomic turmoil into someone else's territory. With respect to any crisis, accountability for top government officials is a negative function of their "ability" to sell their own sterilized "account" of the time line of crisis and recovery.

The plausibility of the key elements in a cover story is sustained by a combination of mischaracterization, distortion, and distraction. A common tool is post hoc ergo propter hoc storytelling. The narrator starts by connecting the absence of crisis in the past to something or someone that departed the scene shortly before the crisis emerged. For example, one might note that the United States didn't experience a full-fledged financial crisis until after Alan Greenspan or Paul Volcker had left the Federal Reserve (Fed) and then claim that the absence of their seasoned leadership explains both why the turmoil developed and why it degenerated into a disaster.

Obviously, this particular narrative would not serve the purposes of officials who held office during the crisis. By casting the nation's recent economic leaders as overmatched rookies, this story offers them no credit and considerable blame. Officials prefer stories that portray themselves as heroes who overcome odds as fearful as

E.J. Kane (✉)
Boston College, Chestnut Hill, MA 02467, USA
e-mail: edward.kane@bc.edu

This chapter was also published in the *Review of Social Economy*, Vol. 68, 2010 and appeared as Networks Financial Institute *Policy Brief* 2009-PB-08C.

J.A. Tatom (ed.), *Financial Market Regulation*, DOI 10.1007/978-1-4419-6637-7_7,

those faced by Horatius (and his brave colleagues Lartius and Herminius) at a bridge whose crossing would have allowed the most important country in the world (in their time, Rome) to be invaded by a deep depression. To avoid invidious comparisons with their predecessors, the story officials might choose could attribute the turmoil to weaknesses in the policy environment that previous officials (perhaps even Greenspan himself) might have mistakenly embraced.

The cover story that I perceive to be making the rounds among world leaders today traces the financial crisis to deregulation and to the Gramm-Leach-Bliley Act of 1999 (GLBA) in particular. The GLBA abandoned the regulatory strategy adopted after the Great Depression, which aimed at keeping banking, securities, and insurance firms from offering one another's traditional products. If this story were true and complete, repealing GLBA and simplifying the product lines of complex institutions would reduce the frequency and depth of future crises.

Almost every financial crisis is the product of overly aggressive leveraged risk taking. The GLBA did make it easier for institutions to expand and become more complex. But the GLBA did not arise in a vacuum and did not by itself make leveraged risk taking more attractive than it was before. To be complete, a theory of the crisis must explain why the GLBA was enacted, why so many loans were poorly underwritten, why counterparties failed to perform adequate due diligence along the chain of transactions traversed in securitizing and resecuritizing risky loans, and why borrowers and lenders chose to overleverage themselves.

In contrast, excessive risk taking, reduced due diligence, regulation-induced innovation, and the lobbying pressure that produced the GLBA can be explained by longstanding subsidies to risk taking that have been protected by the political and economic challenges of policing the safety-net consequences of regulation-induced innovation (Kane 2009a). These challenges, and the limited liability that their stockholders and counterparties enjoy, make it easy for financial managers to extract ex ante and ex post implicit subsidies to leveraged risk taking from national safety nets (Kane 2009b).

A complete story of the crisis must confront the economic and political difficulties of monitoring and controlling the production and distribution of safety-net subsidies. The next section of this chapter discusses exclusionary regulations and the extent to which their relaxation enabled large financial institutions to make themselves harder to fail and unwind. This section seeks to explain that, although Gramm-Leach-Bliley contributed to the crisis, the re-introduction of a compartmentalization strategy would not prevent future crises. The section "Strategies to Reduce Safety-Net Subsidies to TDFU Institutions" explains that to monitor and mitigate problems in controlling access to the federal safety net, government and private supervisory systems need doses of better information, better ethics, and better incentives. Meaningful reform requires that financial institutions be discouraged from abusing the benefits of safety-net support and that government supervisors be made specifically accountable for targeting and pricing safety-net benefits fairly and efficiently. Pursuit of safety-net subsidies can never be stopped, but it can be mitigated by changes in top officials' oath of office, changes in the ways officials are trained, recruited, and required to measure their performance, changes in financial-institution reporting responsibilities, changes in compensation structures, and changes in the kinds of securities TDFU institutions have to issue.

Original Purposes and Declining Effectiveness of Exclusionary Laws

The Glass-Steagall Act of 1933 and Bank Holding Company Act of 1956 are exclusionary laws intended to keep banks, securities, and insurance firms from poaching business from one another. Tailored to the less-complicated corporate structures that existed in the 1930s and 1950s, their stated purpose was to compartmentalize the activities of differently chartered firms so as to avoid potentially crippling concentrations of risk in individual financial firms and to constrain opportunities for multiproduct firms to take advantage of naïve customers.

Proponents of traditional compartmentalization policies had supposed that carefully restricting reciprocal entry into bank and nonbank financial activities could protect society from three kinds of potential harm (Benston 1990, pp. 13–14; Saunders and Walter 1994, pp. 134–135). Microeconomically, proponents sought to lessen incentive conflicts, to assure a wide range of financial-services competitors, and to lessen opportunities for banks to engage in imprudent, improper, or abusive business practices. Particular attention focused on the possibility that banks might coercively tie sales of financial products that could be purchased from a nonbank (such as securities underwriting) to sales of a product (such as loans) in which banks enjoy a degree of monopoly power. Macroeconomically, proponents sought to limit opportunities for banks to expand their risk taking into activities that might destabilize their earnings sufficiently to disrupt financial markets by increasing the risk of widespread bank failures. Distributionally, proponents sought to protect taxpayers from the possibility of suddenly being handed a large bill for resolving bank insolvencies. The current crisis amply demonstrates that outsized costs can be shifted to taxpayers when institutional risk taking is effectively subsidized by mispricing and undersupervising loss exposures booked by institutions able to count on safety-net support.

Decades of mining advances in information, communications, and financial-contracting technologies for opportunities to restyle traditional products and organizational structures allowed institutions to destroy the effectiveness of compartmentalized charters by booking risks in innovative and nontransparent ways. The *de jure* barriers between the banking, securities, and insurance industries that the GLBA repealed in 1999 had become loophole-riddled remnants of their original selves. They provided no more protection for contemporary citizens than the scattered fragments of ancient city walls that tourists admire in ancient European cities today. Fresh blasts of circumventive innovation will destroy these barriers again if Congress decides to resurrect them. The principal effect of re-erecting federal restrictions to cross-industry competition in the United States would be to influence the country or state in which particular risk exposures would be booked. It would also distract Congress, regulatory personnel, and the news media from addressing the need to repair the defects in supervisory incentives that fostered the shortcutting and outsourcing of due diligence at every stage of the derivatives design and securitization process.

Because the Bank Holding Company Act still constrains industry turf, the GLBA may be characterized as lowering and regularizing the cost of circumventing this law. GLBA removed the need to spend resources on bypassing legal restraints on what banks may do and extends the range of differently chartered (i.e., "nonbanking") financial corporations allowed to own a commercial bank.

The survival of compartmentalization strategies in the United States and the "desupervision" they engendered can be traced far more easily to the workings of money politics than to the conscientious pursuit of society-wide benefits. Theories of lobbying pressure portray the GLBA's enactment as a threshold effect. Such theories presume that, as loopholes expanded and proliferated in piecemeal fashion, the political contributions that supported the compartmentalized regulatory regime dwindled and finally fell below the value that opponents were prepared to offer to eliminate most of what was left of the scheme.

How Regulatory Competition Supports Regulation-Induced Innovation

Regulation-induced innovation accepts rules, but attacks mechanisms for enforcing them. The loopholes that innovation opened in compartmentalization laws not only reduced their value to the sectoral interests that sponsored them, but also increased the number and complexity of definitional issues that supervisory authorities had to investigate and defend.

As distance-related communications and transportation costs moved closer and closer to zero, financial activity became more and more footloose. The ease of undertaking jurisdiction-changing innovations in financial contracting and organizational form rendered laws designed to compartmentalize the banking, securities, and insurance industries increasingly irrelevant and difficult to enforce. In the years leading up to the enactment of the GLBA, U.S. courts became clogged with cases requiring judges to rule on whether or not an innovative contract, corporate structure, or cross-institutional delivery system had successfully moved a bank, securities firm, derivatives contract, or insurance company beyond the prescribed reach of a particular law or regulator (see, for example, Anderson 1993; Sivon 1992; Turner 1993).

Banking practices and market environments differ markedly over time and space. Much of this variation is driven by an irreconcilable tension between adjustments in regulation or supervision (on the one hand) and loophole-seeking avoidance activity undertaken to make regulatory interference less burdensome (on the other hand). Regulation begets avoidance activity, and avoidance eventually begets some form of reregulation. Regulatory problems, adjustments, and market events unfold and mutate as part of alternating sequences in which either regulation spawns new forms of avoidance (RA sequences) or the growing effectiveness of particular avoidance activities finally results in a threshold level of avoidance activity (A*) that calls forth innovative reregulation (A*R sequences). Adapting regulatory protocols to innovative avoidance activity is an endless task. Each and every piece of regulatory re-engineering kicks off a series of RAA*R sequences. Inevitably, the range, size, and speed of regulation-induced innovation outpace the vision and disciplinary powers that regulatory authorities can bring to bear. The current crisis tells us that, in recent years, across the chain of adjustments by regulators and regulated institutions, risk-taking incentives became more and more dangerously misaligned with societal interests. But this process began and gained momentum long before GLBA was enacted.

As national markets became highly connected and traditional products developed more and more potential substitutes, compartmentalization strategies were bound to become riddled with loopholes. Regulators and legislatures in different jurisdictions compete eagerly with one another for regulatory domain and seem all too willing to accept as tribute a mere fraction of the incremental value that the loopholes they create generate for the hard-lobbying firms that rely on them.

In the face of continuing foreign (especially European Union) regulatory competition, the ease of locating viable loopholes and the resource costs of adjudicating the permissibility of creative product-line and organizational transformations make it foolish to try to roll back the clock. A strategy of formally walling off the parts of a complex financial firm that formally enjoy safety-net support is unenforceable today. Realistically, the societal benefits compartmentalization could achieve in the 1930s have for years had to be pursued in other ways. Most other developed countries acted far earlier than the United States to allow domestic and foreign banks to sell insurance and securities products and permitted either direct or indirect cross-industry ownership of bank, securities, and insurance organizations (Borio and Filosa 1994; Hough 1991; Posner 2009). Rebuilding cross-industry barriers in the United States will make safety-net exposures less transparent and serve foreign interest by intensifying incentives for TDFU firms to undertake activities in competing countries through foreign subsidiaries. This means that to improve the operation of the U.S. safety net, one must also worry about improving the ways that the U.S. net links up with nets operated by other countries.

Large U.S. financial firms operate in a regime of multiple regulators. The absence of cross-country agreements for sharing resolution costs in the event of a multinational firm's insolvency encourages incentive-conflicted regulatory competition. Ambiguity about which country's taxpayers can be saddled with the bill for safety-net losses reduces accountability for supervisory and regulatory mistakes. It incentivizes politicians and regulators in different countries to compete aggressively for footloose financial-institution capital and employment. It also encourages officials to blame not themselves but foreign regulators if and when the risky business they have competed for falls into distress.

Strategies to Reduce Safety-Net Subsidies to TDFU Institutions

In a context where it pays multinational financial conglomerates and national champion banks to make themselves harder and harder to supervise, policymakers' root problem is not how to make TDFU firms smaller or less complicated.[1] Nor is it how to make financial firms more transparent and administratively easier to fail and unwind (although that would be helpful). The root problem is how to design and manage national safety nets so that they do not deliver subsidies to firms when they expand their political clout, organizational complexity, and/or risk taking in clever ways.

Plans to establish a systemic-risk regulator for U.S. firms will go awry unless proponents find a way to track and control the migration of insolvency risk to other jurisdictions. To be effective, programs of regulatory reform must address the sources of the agency costs that intensified problems in industry risk taking and in government insolvency detection and crisis management. To confront these issues squarely, Congress and the Obama Administration must focus beyond mere adjustments in form and bureaucratic structure to improve—within the United States and across countries—the information firms and authorities produce, the types of securities TDFU firms have to issue, and the incentives under which private financial managers and government safety-net officials operate.

Improving Incentives in the Private Sector

To help safety-net managers to serve taxpayers better, large institutions must be tasked with making safety-net loss exposures in their firms easier to detect and cheaper to resolve. Detection can be improved by developing explicit metrics for measuring the value of safety-net support at individual institutions and requiring safety-net beneficiaries to use these metrics to estimate the value of their safety-net support and report this value at regular intervals at least to their principal supervisor. Ideally the task of aggregating these estimates across firms and agencies should be assigned to a new federal entity specifically charged with measuring and monitoring safety-net costs and benefits (Lo 2009).

Although still provisional, researchers have developed a number of metrics for assessing the value of safety-net support. Carbo et al. (2009) estimate the value of safety-net support from data on a banking organization's stock price. Baker and McArthur (2009) extract estimates from a firm's credit spread. Hart and Zingales (2009) focus on the price of credit default swaps. Huang et al. (2009) use stock price, credit spreads, and credit default swap data simultaneously. If the analytical resources of the world's central banks and largest institutions can be incentivized to attack this estimation problem on a massive scale, the confidence intervals that practitioners have to build around different point estimates should decline rapidly in the future.

[1] This section makes use of ideas and material from Kane (2009a, c).

It would also be helpful to require financial firms to plan explicitly for the downside. To my knowledge, Herring and Carmassi (2009) were the first to propose that managers be required to prepare and file with their principal regulator a standby plan with which to handle their firm's bankruptcy and be obliged to test, update, and refile this plan on a regular basis. The existence of an up-to-date corporate "living will" would make the threat of putting an insolvent institution into receivership or conservatorship more credible because it would lower the costs of executing the threat. Unlike the chaotic haggling observed in addressing the insolvencies of Lehman Brothers and American International Group (AIG) in September 2008, having a benchmark winding-up scheme in place would make it much easier for authorities to wipe out the claims of stockholders and to negotiate prearranged haircuts for uninsured creditors as the threat of bankruptcy increased.

Types of Securities Issued

Explicitly planning for liquidation or breakup is one way of making insolvencies cheaper to handle. Another way is to re-establish extended liability for at least some owners of financial-institution stock. A mitigatable source of incentive conflict in industry risk taking and loss generation is the limited liability that stockholders enjoy. The less capital they have invested in the firm, the more valuable safety-net support becomes to them and their counterparties. Extended stockholder liability makes holders of assessable shares in a liquidating firm responsible for covering a layer of corporate losses beyond the value of the capital previously accumulated at the corporate level. Several now-industrialized countries (including the United Kingdom, the United States and Canada) imposed extended liability on bank shares when their safety nets and private contacting environments were less well developed.

Extended liability increases transparency, counterparty disciplinary rights, and regulatory accountability at the same time. It increases transparency by transforming movements in the stock price of publicly traded banks into a clearer signal of institutional strength or weakness. Extended liability means that a supervisor's right to liquidate an insolvent commercial or investment bank carries with it a right to collect specified amounts of additional funds from the personal or corporate assets of assessable stockholders. As compared to limited-liability shareholding, deterrence is enhanced by stockholders' duty to pony up additional funds if (but only if) managers and regulators allow the institution to become so insolvent that it passes into liquidation.

To create an opportunity to claw back compensation that personnel might earn from exploiting the safety net, bonuses and incentive compensation could be paid in slow-to-vest assessable stock. Stock markets would imbed the value of this contingency into the price of each TDFU firm's assessable shares and traders could fashion derivative instruments that capture various tranches of the loss exposure it entails. Like safety-net subsidies, the value of the contingency would be negligible for institutions that were performing well and adequately supporting their risk with paid-in corporate capital. However, the resolution authority's claim on off-balance-sheet stockholder resources would become increasingly valuable whenever a TDFU firm began to take poorly supported risks or to slide into financial distress. By increasing the sensitivity of TDFU stock prices to changes in earning power and earnings volatility, assessable shares would encourage information-revealing stockholder doubt about the viability of troubled institutions in advance of their final slide into complete economic insolvency. Because doubts would emerge gradually, "runs" on an institution's assessable stock would be far less catastrophic than the sudden meltdowns that inattentive regulators allowed Bear Stearns, Fannie Mae, Freddie Mac, AIG, and Lehman Brothers to experience in 2008.

A sustained sell-off by worried stockholders would increase the quality of counterparty and regulatory supervision by helping safety-net managers to identify institutions that deserve increased supervisory attention long before the enterprise-contributed capital of these institutions could become exhausted. The idea is to create a pool of contingent private capital that would be drawn inescapably onto an institution's balance sheet when and as it first falls into distress. Mark Flannery's proposal for contingent capital certificates (2009) would do this very well if an appropriate market-based trigger for forcing the debt-to-equity conversions can be found. Sharp declines in the price of a financial institution's stock could reinforce regulator-initiated triggers if large financial firms were required to issue extended-liability stock.

Improving Incentives in Government

Incentive conflict in government is rooted in three circumstances. First, no one is charged with measuring and monitoring safety-net subsides per se. Second, top government officials have horizons much shorter than the taxpayers they formally serve. Third, taxpayers are not their only principals. Different principals differ in at least four important ways: in their understanding of the duties officials owe them; in their ability to influence policy decisions as they are being made; in their ability to appreciate the consequences of alternative policy decisions; and in their ability to offer rewards for bending policy in the directions they prefer. The result is that officials feel disproportionately accountable to residents of sectors that make themselves particularly well-informed and politically powerful.

Requiring private institutions to prepare a regulator-certified unwinding plan and to estimate the value of their safety-net support would sharpen the missions of micro- and macro-prudential regulators. Besides verifying estimates of the value of safety-net support supplied by institutions under their purview, regulators could be further tasked with establishing, publicizing, and testing periodically a benchmark market-mimicking scheme for insolvency management.

While authorities would be free to deviate from their benchmark plan in an actual crisis, they would be obliged to explain why they are doing so. To help them to put crisis-management plans into operation more promptly, I would also require them to aggregate the estimates of safety-net subsidies that individual institutions produce. Each micro-prudential regulator would consolidate these estimates in ways that would track over time the aggregate value of safety-net benefits for firms they supervise. I would ask the Treasury, the Fed, the Office of the Comptroller, the Securities and Exchange Commission, the Commodities Futures Trading Commission, the Federal Deposit Insurance Corporation, credit union regulators, and the Office of Thrift Supervision (if it survives) to use these estimates and other relevant data to construct independent estimates of the evolving value of safety-net subsidies to the financial sector as a whole.

To discourage elected officials from trying to win special treatment for firms that contribute money to their campaigns, it would be useful to require that regulatory personnel report promptly and fully on interactions with elected officials that occur outside the public eye.

Obviously, these reforms would make the jobs and recruitment of top regulators more difficult. For this reason, Congress would be well advised to establish the equivalent of a West Point for financial regulators and admit students from around the world. Coupled with appropriate changes in regulators' oaths of office, such an academy would raise the prestige of this career path and instill a stronger and broader sense of communal duty in safety-net managers. In view of the damage crises can cause, it is hard to understand why regulators are not trained and incentivized as thoroughly as military, police, firefighting, and nuclear safety personnel.

It would also be appropriate to raise the salaries of top officials. However, to lengthen the horizons of safety-net managers, the raise should be framed as deferred compensation that would have to be forfeited if a crisis occurred within 3 or 5 years of their leaving office. While the incremental loss of income might seem trivial, the impact on a regulator's backbone could be considerable. If payouts were tied to measures of safety-net subsidies, deferred compensation would have the further benefit of making new appointees more cognizant of unresolved problems that his or her predecessor might be leaving behind.

In principle, supervisors should be willing to embrace the duties they owe society explicitly and be prepared to perform them selflessly and conscientiously. Ideally, oaths of office could be reworked to include five duties that conscientious supervisors ought to agree that they owe to the community that employs them:

1. A duty of vision: Supervisors should continually adapt their surveillance systems to discover and neutralize innovative regulatee efforts to disguise their rule breaking;
2. A duty of prompt corrective action: Supervisors should stand ready to propose new rules and to discipline regulatees whenever a problem is observed;
3. A duty of efficient operation: Supervisors should strive to produce their insurance, loss-detection, and loss-resolution services at minimum cost; and
4. A duty of conscientious representation: Supervisors should be prepared to put the interest of the community they serve ahead of their own.

5. A duty of accountability: Implicit in the other four duties is an obligation to make themselves politically accountable by bonding themselves to disclose enough information about their decision making to render themselves answerable for mishandling their responsibilities.

Legislatures could further sharpen monitoring and loss-control responsibilities by establishing schemes in which private and governmental monitors could hold one another financially responsible for the quality of their work. For example, Congress has proposed imposing product liability on credit-rating organizations and requiring safety-net managers to move trading in over-the-counter derivatives and other securities to clearinghouses or exchanges when and as their volume becomes large enough to pose material safety-net consequences. This duty would be strengthened if deposit insurers were made to reinsure with private parties the coverage they provide to over-the-counter market makers in derivative instruments. This could be done either by writing credit default swaps or by transacting directly in reinsurance markets.

Summary Implications

It is important to recognize that the current financial crisis is rooted in the economic—and especially the political—difficulties of monitoring and controlling the production and distribution of safety-net subsidies. Regulation-induced innovation by financial firms seeks relentlessly to outstrip the monitoring technology and the administrative focus that supervisory personnel use in controlling institutional risk taking. Exclusionary laws and rigid capital regulation encourage rather than control regulatory arbitrage over time.

Safety-net subsidies are easy to overlook in good times. To reduce the threat of future crises, the pressing task is not to rework bureaucratic patterns of financial regulation, but to repair defects in the information flow and incentive structure under which private and government supervisors manage the safety net. The mission of these managers is to balance the costs and benefits generated by: (1) protecting financial-institution customers from being blindsided by insolvencies; (2) limiting aggressive risk taking by financial firms; (3) preventing and controlling damage from runs; (4) detecting and resolving insolvent institutions; and (5) allocating across society whatever losses occur when an insolvent institution is closed (Kane 2001).

Proposals to reinstitute formal limits on the scope of a country's financial safety net can easily degenerate into cheap talk. In the United States and other countries, such limits have repeatedly melted away under the pressure of an actual crisis. Unless new rounds of limits on the safety net are backed up by incentive reform and solid crisis planning, they will create a false sense of security that is apt to foster new and more devastating crises and the continued extension of national nets. Crisis planning is important because the more effective a nation's safety net becomes, the less likely it is that regulatory personnel will have prior hands-on experience in coping with the severity of crisis pressures.

By themselves, redesigning regulatory instruments and relocating bureaucratic responsibilities for different features of the safety net will not do much to slow processes of regulatory arbitrage. Such steps can be made much more meaningful if they are accompanied by actions that make financial-institution managers and federal regulators accountable for estimating and controlling in a timely manner the safety-net consequences of transformative financial contracts and institutional structures.

7.1 Appendix: Tables on Financial Sector Lobbying Compiled by consumerwatchdog.org

Table 7.1 Contributions: senate banking committee financial sector. Contributions, 2005–2009

Senator	Raised from financial industry	Percentage of total funds raised (%)	Fundraising events hosted by financial sector[a]
Christopher J. Dodd (D-CT)[b]	$9,000,975	51	1
Mark Warner (D-VA)	$5,561,561	40	–
Charles E. Schumer (D-NY)	$4,086,349	31	4
Evan Bayh (D-IN)	$3,020,913	23	2
Bob Corker (R-TN)	$2,672,630	13	–
Robert Menendez (D-NJ)	$2,540,952	16	–
Richard C. Shelby (R-AL)	$2,461,009	28	1
Jack Reed (D-RI)	$1,732,958	33	–
Tim Johnson (D-SD)	$1,520,226	24	–
Mike Crapo (R-ID)	$1,419,555	33	7
Kay Bailey Hutchison (R-TX)	$1,380,399	14	–
Robert F. Bennett (R-UT)	$1,161,560	33	8
Sherrod Brown (D-OH)	$988,007	8	–
Jim DeMint (R-SC)	$940,856	14	7
David Vitter (R-LA)	$859,644	11	7
Jeff Merkley (D-OR)	$777,387	11	–
Jon Tester (D-MT)	$725,487	11	1
Michael Bennet (D-CO)	$617,676	17	3
Jim Bunning (R-KY)	$518,440	31	–
Mike Johanns (R-NE)	$462,440	11	2
Daniel K. Akaka (D-HI)	$242,750	8	–
Judd Gregg (R-NH)	$218,200	15	–
Herb Kohl (D-WI)	$9,400	0	–
Totals	$41,919,374	22	43

[a]As reported by Sunlight Foundations, http://www.politicalpartytime.org Center for Responsive Politics, http://www.opensecrets.org

[b]This figure may have been overstated by consumer watchdogs. A later double check of the opensecrets website indicated that even on the broadest possible definition of the financial sector, Dodd received only about $5.5 million.

Source: Center for Responsive Politics, http://www.opensecrets.org

The Sunlight Foundations obtain fundraiser invitations but neither receives invitations for all scheduled fundraisers, nor confirms if scheduled fundraisers have taken place.

Table 7.2 Contributions: financial sector contributions to eight senators tasked with re-drafting financial reform, 2009

Senator	Raised from financial industry ($)	Total raised ($)	% of Total
Mike Crapo (R-ID)	1, 419, 555	4, 302, 690	33
Charles E. Schumer (D-NY)	3, 086, 349	9, 895, 490	31
Bob Corker (R-TN)	2, 672, 630	20, 768, 188	13
Mark Warner (D-VA)	5, 561, 561	13, 985, 292	40
Christopher J. Dodd (D-CT)	9, 000, 975	17, 479, 197	51
Richard C. Shelby (R-AL)	2, 461, 009	8, 815, 915	28
Judd Gregg (R-NH)	218, 200	1, 437, 795	15
Jack Reed (D-RI)	1, 732, 958	5, 262, 977	33
Totals	26, 153, 237	81, 947, 544	32

Source: Center for Responsive Politics, http://www.opensecrets.org

Table 7.3 Contributions: industry breakdown of financial sector contributions to Senate Banking Committee, 2005–2009

Financial industries	Contributions to Senate Banking Committee Members ($)
Securities and Investment	13, 943, 320
Real Estate	8, 974, 423
Insurance	5, 580, 293
Misc. Finance	4, 300, 009
Commercial banks	3, 842, 799
Finance / credit Cos	3, 136, 806
Accountants	1, 823, 438
Savings and Loans	192, 986
Credit Unions	125, 300

Source: Center for Responsive Politics, http://www.opensecrets.org

Table 7.4 Contributions: top five bank and Wall Street contributors to Congress, 2009

	Contributor	Amount ($)
Commercial banks	American Bankers Assn	1,268,600
	Independent Community Bankers of America (ICBA)	513,050
	Citigroup Inc.	468,300
	Bank of America	326,125
	JPMorgan Chase & Co	308,261
Securities/investment	Investment Co Institute	487,875
	FMR Corp (Fidelity Investments)	470,350
	Morgan Stanley	450,453
	Paloma Partners	436,950
	Goldman Sachs	419,875

Source: Center for Responsive Politics, http://www.opensecrets.org
Note: ICBA is the trade association representing small banks and savings institutions. This sector's contribution to Congressional coffers in 2009 is exceeded by the combined contributions attributed to the nation's two largest zombie banking firms (Citigroup and Bank of America) and dwarfed by the amount of funding drawn from the securities industry.

Table 7.5 Lobbying: 2009

	No. of lobbyists	Expenditures ($)
Financial sector	2567	336,005,436
US Chamber of Commerce	127	52,256,000

Source: Center for Responsive Politics, http://www.opensecrets.org

References

Anderson WR (1993) The struggle between federal banking and state insurance laws. Life Assoc News 88:124–127, Dec

Baker D, McArthur T (2009) The value of the "too big to fail" big bank subsidy. Center for Economic and Policy Research Issue Brief, Washington, DC, Sept

Benston GJ (1990) The separation of commercial and investment banking: the Glass-Steagall act revisited and reconsidered. Oxford University Press, New York, NY

Borio C, Filosa R (1994) The changing borders of banking. Bank for International Settlements Monetary and Economic Department, Basel, Oct

Carbo-Valverde S, Kane E, Rodriguez-Fernandez F (2009) Evidence of regulatory arbitrage in cross-border mergers of banks in the EU. National Bureau of Economic Research Working Paper No. 15447

Flannery MJ (2009) Stabilizing large financial institutions with contingent capital certificates. Unpublished University of Florida Working Paper, September 18

Hart O, Zingales L (2009) A new capital regulation for large financial institutions. Chicago Booth Research Paper No. 09-36, 2 Oct

Herring R, Carmassi J (2009) The corporate structure of international financial conglomerates: complexity and its implications for safety and soundness. In: Berger AN, Molyneux P, Wilson JOS (eds) Oxford handbook of banking. Oxford University Press, New York, NY, pp 195–229
Hough V (1991) Banks and insurance: the lesson from abroad. Best's Rev 25–26:28, 30 Mar
Huang, X, Zhou H, Zhu H (2009) A framework for assessing the systemic risk of major financial institutions. Working Paper, University of Oklahoma, May
Kane EJ (2001) Financial safety nets: reconstructing and modeling a policymaking metaphor. J Int Trade Dev 3:237–273
Kane EJ (2009a) Incentive roots of the securitization crisis and its early mismanagement. Yale J Regul 26(Summer):405–416
Kane EJ (2009b) Extracting nontransparent safety net subsidies by strategically expanding and contracting a financial institution's accounting balance sheet. J Financ Serv Res (December) 35:1–31
Kane EJ (2009c) Discussion of 'an industrial organization approach to the too big to fail problem' by Jean-Charles Rochet. Prepared for Federal Reserve Bank of Boston 54th Economic Conference, Chatham, MA, Oct
Lo AW (2009) The feasibility of systemic risk measurement. Testimony Before the Financial Services Committee of the U.S. House of Representatives, 19 Oct
Posner E (2009) The origins of Europe's new stock markets. Harvard University Press, Cambridge, MA
Saunders A, Walter I (1994) Universal banking in the United States. Oxford University Press, New York, NY
Sivon JC (April 1992) Insurance activities permissible for banks and bank holding companies. American Bankers Association, Washington, DC
Turner R (1993) Bank sale of life insurance: the ideal solution. Banks in Insurance Report, pp 11–13

Chapter 8
Redefining and Containing Systemic Risk

Edward J. Kane

Government officials everywhere acknowledge a responsibility for overseeing systemic risk. But before one can begin to control a target variable (even something as straightforward as the temperature of a room), one must define the variable comprehensively and fashion from this definition one or more verifiable metrics for monitoring the target. Official definitions of systemic risk fail both of these tests.

Official definitions focus on a perceived potential for substantial spillovers of institutional defaults across important firms in the financial sector and from this sector to the real economy. These definitions are not comprehensive because they exclude a systemic phenomenon; this is that substantial spillovers of actual defaults have remained largely and predictably hypothetical.

Actual spillovers are minimal because authorities instinctively choose to intervene in the default process by characterizing firms that are politically or administratively difficult to fail and unwind (DFU) as "systemically important" (SI) and supporting DFU firms' credit when they allow themselves to become economically insolvent. In effect, authorities exercise a loss-shifting "taxpayer put" that allows insolvent DFU firms to operate as corporate zombies (Kane 1986; Eberlein and Madan 2010).

Official definitions of systemic risk lead to an incomplete diagnosis of its roots: that systemic risk is caused by defective risk management at DFU firms. The diagnosis is incomplete because it ignores the role of opportunism at DFU firms in exploiting gaps and incentive conflicts in policymaking and it undermines accountability for regulatory mistakes because it lacks a verifiable metric. The incomplete diagnosis supports an incomplete treatment plan, one that would: toughen capital requirements; reconfigure the boundaries of regulation; and extend new powers to

---

E.J. Kane (✉)
Boston College, Chestnut Hill, MA 02467, USA
e-mail: edward.kane@bc.edu

This chapter was published in the *Atlantic Economic Journal,* Vol. 38, September 2010, and is being reprinted with permission. It builds upon and extends the ethical arguments presented in the previous chapter and reproduces and condenses some key passages from that essay.

J.A. Tatom (ed.), *Financial Market Regulation*, DOI 10.1007/978-1-4419-6637-7_8,

regulators (e.g., over executive compensation, derivatives trading, and insolvency resolution) without addressing the fundamental incentive conflicts that persuade authorities to undersupervise innovative forms of risk taking at DFU firms and so-called "shadow" banking affiliates.

Economic policymaking is a balancing act, but one in which blame avoidance distorts the release and analysis of key information. It is no accident that the official diagnosis of the securitization bubble and the treatment plan it supports do not address the endogenous role that safety-net subsidies play in incentivizing firms to operate outside the boundaries of the regulatory system and to take political and economic action to attain and strengthen DFU status. Authorities do not wish to acknowledge that principled efforts to define and pursue the public interest are contested and repeatedly knocked off course by conflicting personal, bureaucratic, and political concerns that impinge inappropriately on government decision makers.

To understand why defects in insolvency detection and resolution persist, analysts must acknowledge that large financial institutions invest in disguising their risk taking and in building and exercising political clout. Mainstream models of safety-net management are just beginning to acknowledge that, even in good times, politically powerful financial firms shape and reshape their lobbying activity, product lines, accounting systems, and organizational forms to collect hard-to-document subsidies to leveraged risk taking from national safety nets (Kane 2009a; Acharya et al. 2010; Eberlein and Madan 2010).

Leveraged risk taking intensifies financial bubbles and increases the costs to taxpayers of repairing the damage that a bursting bubble entails. To minimize the extent and frequency of future bubbles and crises, reformers must understand that safety-net subsidies trace to the political clout, managerial opportunism, and organizational flexibility that aggressive firms exercise and not to a firm's size or complexity per se. Rulemaking that adjusts accounting standards or sets caps on size and complexity of selected categories of firms without introducing controls on clout, opportunism, or structural flexibility strongly incentivizes efforts to deconstruct and circumvent the changes introduced.

This chapter argues that, microeconomically and macroeconomically, the capitalized value of the safety-net subsidies that financial firms capture represents a cogent way to measure what authorities mean by "systemic risk" and that regulation-induced innovation is the vehicle through which subsidies to systemic risk taking are conveyed. This hypothesis implies that proposals for financial reform need to be judged by two criteria: (1) how much they promise to discourage financial institutions from abusing safety-net support and (2) how much they promise to improve the ways in which authorities measure, monitor, and restrain the flow of ex ante and ex post subsidies to creative forms of institutional risk taking.

Because they supply equity through the safety net, taxpayers ought to be empowered to monitor the value of their equity stake in the financial sector. Both within and across countries, financial systems can be made more stable by gathering and reporting this information on a regular basis. Regular disclosures would have the further benefit of making market signals more informative. Confidence intervals around each firm's estimates of its taxpayer put can be improved by reconfiguring the way that they keep their accounts and how they report to regulators and how regulators conceive of their responsibilities to taxpayers.

Reformers would do well to refocus their efforts on incentives. In government arenas, this means rewriting regulatory officials' oaths of office; changing the ways officials are recruited, trained, and compensated; and reworking the ways they measure and report regulatory performance. For the private sector, this means changing the character of the debt and equity securities that important financial institutions have to issue and requiring such firms to estimate and report the putative value of the safety-net benefits they receive and to file, negotiate, and update regularly a windup plan with their chartering authority and principal regulator.

When Do Risks Become Systemic?

Systemic risk may be likened to a disease. In medicine, comprehensive and verifiable definitions of disease lead to more accurate tests for its existence and more effective patterns of treatment. The primary characteristic of systemic risk is the emergence of widespread concerns about the potential for substantial "spillovers" of contagious defaults across counterparties in the financial sector and from these defaults to breakdowns in the real economy. This potential is traced either to individual firms' overexposure to common risk factors (underdiversification) or to a nexus of derivative contracts that result in an unobservable web of debt that highly leveraged institutions owe to one another (contagion).

These concerns cannot be the only symptom because, with the notable exception of the Lehman Brothers bankruptcy, in modern crises substantial spillovers of actual defaults have remained largely hypothetical. In country after country and sector after sector, monetary and fiscal authorities instinctively choose to intervene in the default process by supporting the credit of "systemically important" institutions that allow themselves to become economically insolvent. Such institutions are called "zombies" because the black magic of subsidized government loans and guarantees prevents their creditors from pulling the plug on their dangerous and unnaturally animated corporate corpse (Kane 1989).

The existence of this verifiable additional symptom suggests that an authentic definition of systemic risk ought to focus on a firm's or sector's ability to command or extract implicit and explicit life support from national safety nets. Eberlein and Madan (2010) portray zombies as being allowed to exercise what they term a taxpayer put. Highlighting this symptom links systemic risk not only to a condition of widespread financial weakness, but also to unhealthy forms of competition for regulatory clients (i.e., turf) and to other factors that make a firm or collection of firms politically or administratively DFU. Diagnosing these links makes it clear that, to be truly reliable, programs for reforming the regulation and supervision of DFU firms cannot ignore political and administrative issues. Systemic taxpayer loss exposures come not just from creative and aggressive risk taking by DFU firms, but from defects in micro- and macro-prudential supervision of the leverage and other risk exposures regulated and unregulated firms take on. This layering of blame makes it clear that meaningful reform must identify and remedy the incentive conflicts that tempted authorities to ignore the buildup of systemic risk in the shadow banking system during the securitization bubble and then led them to rush to aid zombie firms when the bubble burst without developing a program to confront and resolve the zombies' growing economic insolvency in a definitive way.

Adverse Consequences of Misdiagnosing the Policy Problem

Both in medicine and in crisis management, superficial diagnoses lead to ineffective treatment and deepening infirmity. Credit spreads faced by short-funded financial institutions surged in August 2007 and stayed high for months afterward. This surge lowered the value of these firms' risky assets and thereby reduced their capacity to replace their maturing debts. For months, Federal Reserve (Fed) officials refused to concede that higher credit spreads had pushed asset and collateral values down to levels that raised legitimate doubts about short-funded borrowers' solvency and that these doubts underlay the collateral calls stressed by Gorton (2008) that made it difficult for highly levered firms to roll over asset-backed debt. Without acknowledging the subsidy entailed in lending to insolvent institutions or how such lending turned monetary policy into tax-transfer policy, Fed officials repeatedly misframed the funding difficulties that DFU firms were experiencing as evidence of a shortfall in aggregate liquidity. Financing the deepening insolvency of zombie firms such as Bear Stearns, Lehman, and American International Group (AIG) allowed their managers not only to pay themselves undeserved bonuses, but to gamble improvidently for resurrection at taxpayer and creditor expense.

Despite being challenged by the persistence of funding difficulties and especially by the costs of the Bear Stearns rescue in March 2008, remnants of the liquidity-shortage hypothesis survived until mid-September 2008. Back-to-back policy decisions at that time consoled investors by effectively nationalizing Fannie Mae and Freddie Mac but surprised everyone by forcing creditors of Lehman to accept haircuts dictated by the bankruptcy process, and days later turned around and surprised them again by refusing to haircut the creditors and swap counterparties of the far more deeply insolvent AIG. The failure to offer a convincing rationale for shifting to and fro between contradictory insolvency-resolution strategies and resulting volatility in the value of DFU firms' taxpayer puts raised doubts about the diligence, integrity, and competence of Fed and Treasury officials. Consumer and investor concerns about regulatory diligence and competence were reinforced by a series of doomsday pronouncements about the extent of industry weakness that deepened the recession by frightening the populace into cutting back their spending (Kane 2009a).

The policy of explicitly supporting the creditors and counterparties of AIG and other zombie firms represented a new and seemingly desperate treatment plan. Its antiegalitarian effects on the distribution of income (which accorded top priority to bankers and other derivatives counterparties) were as obvious as they were hard to defend. Public justifications have mutated over time, but all have relied on the untestable (and insufficiently supported) claim that extravagant support of financial sector was a price that society had to pay to avoid another Great Depression.

Alternative Definitions of Systemic Risk Lead to Different Strategies of Regulatory Reform

Blame avoidance plays an unspoken role in any policy debate. Blame avoidance helps to explain why officials adopt definitions of systemic risk that lead to the self-serving hypothesis that systemic risk is caused by defective risk management at "systemically important firms" (SIFIs). Using our definition of systemic risk, SIFIs are private firms that have made themselves politically, economically, and administratively difficult to fail and unwind. By ignoring the process by which a firm attains and solidifies DFU status, the official diagnosis of safety-net risk exposure is distressingly shallow and leads to the incomplete treatment plan of trying to identify DFU firms by size and/or business plan and demanding that such firms monitor and support their risk exposures more effectively.

In the United States and Europe, the components of this incomplete plan are evolving along four principal dimensions:

1. Designing tougher and more comprehensive capital requirements for bank and nonbank financial firms (e.g., by measuring risk exposures in ever more granular ways);
2. Restricting the level and composition of executive compensation at financial firms (e.g., by limiting bonuses and incentive-based compensation at SIFIs);
3. Enhancing the powers that government regulators may exercise (e.g., with respect to taking over or liquidating a failing institution and intervening in how and where derivatives may trade);
4. Extending the boundaries of government regulation (e.g., to encompass hedge funds, derivatives trading, and credit-rating firms).

A financial crisis occurs when a sufficient amount of adversity hits a fragile system whose managers have concentrated and leveraged their portfolio enough to make their firms vulnerable to this amount and type of adversity. Our broader definition of systemic risk recognizes that regulatory enterprises are vulnerable SIFIs, too. Their managers determine how much of the deep downside of the risk exposures that DFU institutions pursue are transferred to taxpayers. Including regulators in the risk-generation process requires us to think about how political, bureaucratic, and administrative concerns are likely to influence the way in which new controls would be deployed under various circumstances.

The buildup of systemic risk in structured securitizations was generated by short-cutting and outsourcing due diligence in both the private and government sectors.

Until the securitization bubble burst in 2007, authorities failed to isolate and respond to the safety-net consequences of the risk transfers that were taking place along the chain of originating, valuing, selling, pooling, risk-rating, and insuring loans so that their risky cash flows could be engineered into highly rated, tradable securities. The durability of this neglect should warn us that, to reduce the depth and frequency of future crises, it is not enough to improve the mechanics of risk control. A parallel effort must be made to reframe the incentives of the system's operators. They must be encouraged to treat the interests of ordinary citizens less callously than they have in recent years.

Forward-looking policymakers must expect managers of financial firms to continue to mask leverage, credit, and interest-rate risk and to stall and subvert sensible reforms in order to protect their capacity to extract safety-net subsidies. To lessen their capacity to do this, officials and private managers must be tasked with estimating and controlling the effects that safety-net subsidies have on the stock price, credit spreads, and credit default swaps of the firms they oversee. The next two sections identify a few ways in which this might be done.

Why Incentive Defects Persist

Blame accrues to people who do "bad" (i.e., immoral, negligent, or incompetent) things. This means that assigning blame for government and market failures that led to the securitization crisis is both an economic and an ethical problem. Ethics seep into our definition of systemic risk to the extent that industry and government officials knowingly tolerate defective institutional arrangements[1] or fail to fulfill fiduciary duties that in principle they owe to one or more participants in the securitization process.

To be complete, reform strategies must address features of top officials' employment situation that encourage weakness in insolvency detection and dispose them to subsidize the financial sector massively in times of crisis. Table 8.1 lists six such

Table 8.1 Layers of incentive conflict that encourage weak enforcement

1. Asymmetric information (creates easy alibis and opportunities for coverup);
2. Uncertain hold on positions (shortens horizons);
3. Reputational and budgetary damage generated by industry criticism (dysfunctional accountability);
4. Post-government career opportunities (revolving door);
5. Attraction of passively waiting for a cyclical upswing (gambling for resurrection);
6. Administrative and staffing difficulties of trying to restructure complex firms.
   - A complete program of reform should mitigate these difficulties by improving compensation structures, performance measurement, and reporting responsibilities.

[1] I have in mind the push to adopt Basel II in the face of defects such as those uncovered by Kupiec (2009).

features. Top officials are exposed to scapegoating, and the reputational risk that scapegoating entails renders more tentative their ability to stay in office. Limited terms and relatively low salaries encourage top regulators to use their government service to nurture post-government career opportunities in the very industries they regulate. It is hard for an agency's leadership to balance: (1) the certain and immediate damage to their reputations that industry criticism is bound to visit on them if and when they resist strong lobbying pressure against (2) the less certain damage their reputations might or might not suffer from public-interested censure later. In most crises, it is not until long after an official has left office that careful investigations by Inspector Generals or other watchdogs can surface irrefutable and convincing evidence about the inappropriateness of safety-net policies. In any case, once insolvencies become deep and widespread, authorities are tempted to gamble that cycle-driven improvements in industry conditions will make insolvent institutions whole again (Kane 1989).

Their situation is further complicated by the existence of multiple principals and differences in the ability of different principals to defend their interests. Principals differ: in their understanding of the duties officials owe them, in their ex ante ability to influence official decisions in their favor, in their ability to appreciate the consequences of these decisions, and in their ex post ability to offer rewards for favorable and unfavorable decisions. The result is that de facto accountability to informed and politically powerful sectors routinely trumps the abstract duties that top regulators owe to society as a whole.

Changes in compensation structure, performance measurement, and reporting responsibilities can be designed to lessen these incentive conflicts (Kane 2010). But the current generation of politicians and other persons in authority is unlikely to benefit from pushing for such changes. As in a long-running poker game in which one player (here, the taxpayer) is a perennial and relatively clueless loser, other players see little reason to disturb the equilibrium.

Steps that Government and Industry Could Take Toward Genuine Reform

The essential problem of financial reform is how to incentivize safety-net managers and managers of protected institutions to serve more conscientiously the interests of the average taxpayer.[2] To make this possible, financial firms and their supervisors must agree to work together to design, implement, and staff an information system that can measure the flow of safety-net costs and benefits and a control system that can restrain the process of subsidy generation within and across major countries.

---

[2]This section draws heavily on Kane (2010). To make sure that readers understand the foundational arguments developed in Chapter 7, this chapter draws heavily on some key passages from that essay.

Joint Private Sector and Governmental Reforms

DFU institutions could simplify the task of safety-net management by making taxpayer stakes in these firms both more transparent and administratively easier to protect in times of duress.

One way to do this is to agree to separate the supervisory function of diagnosing systemic risk from that of treating it. Because the emergence of widespread insolvency inevitably embarrasses an agency's leaders, supervisory agencies have repeatedly succumbed to the temptation to understate or cover up surges in insolvency when they first occur. Insolvency detection can be improved by developing explicit metrics for measuring the value of safety-net support at individual institutions and requiring safety-net beneficiaries to use these metrics to estimate the value of their safety-net support and to report their estimates at regular intervals to their principal supervisor. For these estimates to be taken seriously, they must be challenged and vetted for accuracy by trained risk-management personnel at each supervisory agency.

Individual-institution data must then be aggregated across firms and across supervisory agencies. To minimize incentive conflict in staffing this function and processing politically sensitive information, the task of aggregating and publicizing the estimates should be assigned to a new federal entity (Levine 2009; Lo 2009) or to a special division of the Government Accountability Office specifically charged with measuring and monitoring safety-net costs and benefits. The idea is not only to separate accountability for mismonitoring safety-net subsidies from accountability for underpolicing them. It is also to make someone specifically responsible for identifying on an ongoing basis the ways in which regulation-induced innovation may be undermining existing turf.

Monitoring Systemic Risk

The layering of blame for the current crisis implies that private and government sources of systemic risk must be monitored and policed jointly. Although still at an early stage, econometric strategies for measuring safety-net subsidies already exist. Following the lead of Merton (1977, 1978), researchers have developed several promising metrics that a Safety-Net Accountability Office (SAF) could use to assess the value of safety-net support from balance-sheet and market data. Ronn and Verma (1986), Duan et al. (1992), Hovakimian and Kane (2000), and Carbo-Valverde et al. (2010) estimate the value of safety-net support from data on a banking organization's accounting leverage and stock price. These models show that the value of safety-net credit support increases dramatically as it stockholder-contributed capital begins to disappear. Baker and McArthur (2009) extract estimates from a firm's credit spread. Hart and Zingales (2009) show the usefulness of data on the prices of institutions' credit default swaps. Huang et al. (2009) use stock price, credit spreads, and credit default swap data simultaneously. Finally, Eberlein and Madan (2010) combine data on equity option prices with balance sheet data on the same dates to calculate values for the taxpayer put. At year-end 2008, they estimate loosely that, for six of the most important U.S. SIFIs, safety-net subsidies totaled over 860 billion dollars, with individual benefits ranging from a low of $3.37 billion (at Goldman Sachs) to $293.96 billion (at JPMorgan Chase).

Of course, the capitalized value of taxpayer costs for supporting safety-net benefits is generally less than the sum of the benefits that accrue to individual firms. But because correlations increase in crises and asset bubbles, it may not be much less. The costs of supporting the safety net may be analyzed as the return from a portfolio of perfectly correlated positions in the various firms the net protects. Research on correlations shows that the effects of crisis generating and other large common industry shocks are more highly correlated than smaller common shocks that industry capital is expected to absorb (see, e.g., Gropp and Moerman 2004).

To establish a better framework for analysis, I propose to divide responsibilities for collecting and processing data on safety-net benefits into at least three pieces. The first segment would task managers of financial firms with estimating and reporting to their primary regulators (on, say, a quarterly basis) interval estimates of the value of the safety-net benefits their firm receives. Especially for large or complicated firms, this task could (as discussed later) be streamlined by requiring financial institutions to issue securities that automatically convert to equity in troubled circumstances or carry extended liability. The second segment would task individual regulators with examining (i.e., conscientiously challenging the accuracy of) these estimates and undertaking correlation studies that would allow them to prepare interval estimates of the aggregate value of taxpayer support accruing to the firms they supervise. The third segment would task the regulators to report and justify their estimates and aggregation procedures to the Safety-Net Accountability Office and task the SAF with publically reporting interval estimates of the aggregate value of safety-net subsidies for different industry sectors. A fourth segment could eventually task SAFs in different nations with establishing arrangements for monitoring the quality of one another's work and preparing and publishing interval estimates of the value of bilateral and multilateral cross-country safety-net support.

If the analytical resources of the world's central banks and largest institutions can be incentivized to attack these estimation problems on a massive scale, the interval estimates emerging from different methods should converge over time. Each nation's SAF should also recognize that the confidence intervals that careful statisticians need to place around the different point estimates are apt to narrow with experience, but be sabotaged by regulation-induced innovation and to increase in times of financial turmoil.

Crisis Planning

To make insolvency resolution easier to initiate, supervisors and DFU firms must be made to plan and rehearse for crisis. Richard Herring was the first to propose that managers be required to prepare and file with their principal regulator a standby reorganization plan with which to handle their firm's demise and be obliged to test, update, and refile this plan on a regular basis. This proposal is explored and developed in Herring (2010) and Avgouleas et al. (2010).

The main value of an up-to-date corporate "living will" is as a starting point for planning divestitures that could reduce subsidies to creditors of declining firms. It promises to make the threat of putting an insolvent institution into receivership or conservatorship more credible as creditors and because it promises to lower the costs of executing the threat. Unlike the chaotic and ineffective haggling observed in addressing the insolvencies of Lehman Brothers and AIG in September 2008 (Ferguson and Johnson 2009), having a benchmark winding-up scheme in place would make it much easier for authorities to dilute the claims of zombie stockholders and to negotiate haircuts with uninsured creditors.

Security Design

Another way of making insolvencies easier to handle would be to re-establish extended liability for some or all classes of financial-institution stock. An important source of systemic risk is the limited liability that stockholders enjoy. Practically speaking, the less capital stockholders provide, the more safety-net support flows to them and their counterparties. Extended liability means that a supervisor's decision to liquidate an insolvent commercial or investment bank carries with it a right to collect specified amounts of additional funds from the personal or corporate assets of assessable stockholders. Holders of extended-liability stock (i.e., "assessable shares") in a liquidating firm accept the obligation to absorb to a specified degree the first waves of corporate losses that are found to exceed the value of the capital explicitly accumulated at the corporate level. Several now-industrialized countries (including the United Kingdom, the United States and Canada) imposed extended liability on bank shares when their safety nets and private contacting environments were less well developed.

Extending stockholder liability would increase transparency, strengthen private market discipline, and improve regulatory accountability at the same time. It would do this by encouraging holders of assessable shares to monitor the firm more closely. These well-informed investors' efforts to trade away from their extended liability would transform movements in the stock price of publicly traded institutions into a clearer and more timely signal of the strength or weakness of unfolding business plans.

To control compensation that risk managers might earn from promoting aggressive risk taking, bonuses and incentive compensation at any firm for which the value of estimated safety-net subsidies appears substantial could be paid exclusively in slow-to-vest assessable stock. Financial markets would imbed the value of the shareholder's contingent obligation into the price of the issuing firm's assessable shares. Like safety-net subsidies, the value of the contingency would be negligible for any institution that was adequately supporting its risk with paid-in corporate capital. However, safety-net managers' contingent claim on stockholder resources would become increasingly valuable whenever a firm began to take poorly supported risks or to slide into financial distress. By increasing the sensitivity of stock prices to changes in earning power and earnings volatility, assessable shares would reveal stockholder doubt about the viability of troubled institutions in advance of their final slide into zombie status.

Trading in extended-liability stock and what we might call "assessment derivatives" would improve the quality of counterparty and regulatory supervision because it would encourage insiders to identify institutions that deserve supervisory attention before stockholder-contributed capital at these institutions can evaporate. Contingent private capital resembles government safety-net support in that it is drawn onto an institution's balance sheet when and as its level of distress grows. Mark Flannery's proposal for contingent capital certificates (2009) works in a similar way and would work even better for firms that had assessable shares outstanding. This is because market-based, downward price movements in assessable shares promise to act as a more reliable trigger for forcing debt-to-equity conversions than self-interestedly overstated accounting measures of a troubled firm's net worth.

Strictly Governmental Reforms

In government supervision, incentive conflict is rooted in three circumstances. First, no one is charged with measuring and monitoring safety-net subsides per se. Second, top government officials have horizons much shorter than the taxpayers they formally serve. Third, taxpayers are not an official's only principal, and ordinary citizens are poorly positioned to defend their stake in financial regulation.

Under the assumption that private institutions prepare a regulator-certified unwinding plan and estimate the value of the safety-net support they enjoy, it becomes easy to define the missions of micro- and macro-prudential regulators sharply and independently of the particular bureaucratic structure of regulation a country might establish. The first task would be for agencies to test and verify the estimates of the value of safety-net support that would be supplied to them by institutions under their purview. To do this, they would use robust modeling techniques of solvency assessment and onsite and electronic methods of data collection. They would also be expected to communicate to the SAF the estimates of safety-net subsidies that they and individual institutions they supervise produce. Each micro-prudential regulator would also prepare consolidated estimates of the aggregate value of safety-net benefits at the firms they supervise and report their methods of aggregation and estimates to the SAF for further analysis.

A second task would be to establish, publicize, and rehearse periodically a prepackaged bankruptcy-like scheme for allocating losses incurred in insolvency and crisis management. Authorities would be free to deviate from their benchmark plan during an actual crisis, but they would be obliged to explain why they are doing so.

A desirable third task would be to discourage elected officials from trying to win special treatment for firms that contribute money to their campaigns. One way to do this would be to oblige regulatory personnel and elected officials to report to the

SAF promptly, fully, and separately on interactions with elected officials that occur outside the public eye.

These three reforms would make the jobs and recruitment of top regulators more difficult. For this reason, the United States and other countries would be well advised to establish the equivalent of a publicly funded West Point for financial regulators and welcome cadets from anywhere in the world. Reinforced by appropriate changes in regulators' oaths of office, such an academy would raise the prestige of this form of public service and instill a stronger and broader sense of communal duty in safety-net managers than the current generation of officials has shown during the current crisis. In view of the damage crises can cause, it is unfortunate that regulators are not trained and incentivized as carefully as military, police, firefighting, and nuclear-safety personnel.

In principle, supervisors should be recruited from a population of individuals who are willing to embrace explicitly the fiduciary duties their agency owes to society and be prepared to perform these duties selflessly and conscientiously. Ideally, oaths of office could be reworked to include five duties that conscientious supervisors ought to agree that they owe to the community that employs them:

1. *A duty of vision*: Supervisors should continually adapt their surveillance systems to discover and neutralize innovative regulatee efforts to disguise their rule breaking;
2. *A duty of prompt corrective action*: Supervisors should stand ready to propose new rules and to discipline regulatees whenever a problem is observed;
3. *A duty of efficient operation*: Supervisors should strive to produce their insurance, loss-detection, and loss-resolution services at minimum cost;
4. *A duty of conscientious representation*: Supervisors should be prepared to put the interests of the community they serve ahead of their own;
5. *A duty of accountability*: Implicit in the first four duties is an obligation for safety-net managers embrace political accountability by bonding themselves to disclose enough information about their decision making to render themselves answerable for mishandling their responsibilities.

Legislatures around the world could extend loss-control responsibilities beyond national borders by establishing schemes in which private and governmental monitoring organizations would be able to hold one another financially responsible for the quality of their supervisory work. In the United States, Congress has proposed imposing product liability on credit-rating organizations and requiring safety-net managers to move trading in over-the-counter derivatives and other securities to clearinghouses or exchanges when and as their volume becomes large enough to pose material safety-net consequences. This duty affects other countries and would be strengthened if national deposit insurers were made to reinsure in private markets the coverages they provide to market makers in derivative instruments. This could be done either by writing credit default swaps or by transacting directly in reinsurance markets.

To offset their enhanced accountability, it would be appropriate to raise the salaries of top officials. However, to lengthen the horizons of safety-net managers, the raise should be framed as deferred compensation that would have to be forfeited if a crisis occurred within 3 or 5 years of their leaving office. While the incremental loss of income might seem trivial, the impact on a regulator's reputation and ability to resist lobbying pressure could be considerable. If payouts were tied to measures of safety-net subsidies, deferred compensation would have the further benefit of making incoming appointees more cognizant of unresolved problems that his or her predecessor might be leaving behind.

Summary Implications

In good times, systemic risk and safety-net subsidies are easy to overlook. Systemic risk is rooted in the economic and political difficulties of monitoring and controlling the production and distribution of safety-net subsidies. Regulation-induced innovation by financial firms is designed to outstrip the monitoring technology and to circumvent the tools and administrative focus that supervisory personnel use in controlling institutional risk taking.

To reduce the threat of future crises, the pressing task is not to rework bureaucratic patterns of financial regulation, but to repair defects in the information flow and incentive structure under which private and government supervisors manage the safety net.

Without appropriate reforms in incentives, redesigning capital requirements, introducing a few new regulatory instruments, and relocating bureaucratic responsibilities for particular components of national safety nets will change the form, but not the substance of safety-net arbitrage. To build a robust and reliable system of financial regulation, financial-institution managers and national regulators must accept responsibility for estimating and controlling in a timely, proactive, and accountable manner the safety-net consequences of transformative financial contracts and institutional structures.

References

Acharya V, Schnabl P, Suarez G (2010) Securitization without risk transfer. NBER Working Paper No. 15730, Cambridge, MA, Feb

Avgouleas E, Goodhart C, Schoenmaker D (2010) Living wills as a catalyst for action. DSF Policy Paper No. 4, 1 May. Available at: http://ssrn.com/abstract:1533808

Baker D, McArthur T (2009) The value of the "too big to fail" big bank subsidy. Center for Economic and Policy Research Issue Brief, Washington, DC, Sept. Available at http://www.cepr.net/documents/publications/too-big-to-fail-2009-09.pdf

Carbo-Valverde S, Kane E, Rodriguez-Fernandez F (2010) Regulatory arbitrage in cross-border mergers of banks in the EU. Journal of Money, Credit and Banking (forthcoming)

Duan J-C, Moreau AF, Sealey CW (1992) Fixed-rate deposit insurance and risk-shifting behavior at commercial banks. J Bank Finance 16:715–742

Eberlein E, Madan D (2010) Unlimited liabilities, reserve capital requirements, and the taxpayer put option. Unpublished Working Paper. University of Maryland, College Park, MD (March 20). Available at SSRN: http://ssrn.com/abstract=1540813

Ferguson T, Johnson R (2009) Too big to bail: the "paulson put," presidential politics, and the global financial meltdown. Int J Polit Econ 38(1):3–34 and 2:5–43

Flannery MJ (2009) Stabilizing large financial institutions with contingent capital certificates. Unpublished University of Florida Working Paper, 18 Sept. Available at SSRN: http://ssrn.com/abstract=1485689

Gorton G (2008) The panic of 2007. Federal Reserve Bank of Kansas City, Jackson Hole Conference, Aug. Available at http://www.kc.frb.org/publicat/sympos/2008/gorton.08.04.08.pdf

Gropp R, Moerman G (2004) Measurement of contagion in banks' equity prices. J Int Money Finance 23(3):405–459

Hart O, Zingales L (2009) A new capital regulation for large financial institutions. Chicago Booth Research Paper No. 09-36, 2 Oct. Available at SSRN: http://ssrn.com/abstract=1533274

Herring RJ (2010) Wind-down plans as an alternative to bailouts: the cross-border challenges. In: Scott K, Shultz G, Taylor J (eds) Ending government bailouts as we know them. Hoover Press, Palo Alto, CA

Hovakimian A, Kane EJ (2000) Effectiveness of capital regulation at U.S. commercial banks, 1985–1994. J Finance 55:451–469, Mar

Huang X, Zhou H, Zhu H (2009) A framework for assessing the systemic risk of major financial institutions. Bank for International Settlements Working Paper No. 281, Apr. Available at: http://www.bis.org/publ/work281.pdf?noframes=1

Kane EJ (1986) Appearance and reality in deposit insurance: the case for reform. J Bank Finance 10:175–188, June

Kane EJ (1989) The S&L insurance mess: how did it happen? Urban Institute Press, Washington, DC

Kane EJ (2009a) Incentive roots of the securitization crisis and its early mismanagement. Yale J Regul 21(Winter):28–33

Kane EJ (December 2009b) Extracting nontransparent subsidies by strategically expanding and contracting a financial institution's balance sheet. J Financ Serv Res 35:161–68

Kane EJ (2010) The importance of monitoring and mitigating the safety-net consequences of regulation-induced innovation. Rev Soc Econ 68(2):145–161

Kupiec P (2009) How well does the Vasicek Basel model fit the data? Evidence from a long time series of corporate credit rating data. Federal Deposit Insurance Corporation Working Paper. Available at SSRN: http://ssrn.com/abstract=1523246

Levine R (2009) The sentinel: an auxiliary precaution for governing financial regulations. Presented at Federal Reserve Bank of Chicago's Twelfth Annual International Conference, Sept. Available at: http://www.chicagofed.org/digital_assets/others/events/2009/twelfth_annual_international_conference/2009_international_levine.pdf

Lo AW (2009) The feasibility of systemic risk measurement. Testimony before the financial services committee of the U.S. house of representatives, 19 Oct

Merton RC (1977) An analytic derivation of the cost of deposit insurance and loan guarantees. J Bank Finance 1:3–11

Merton RC (1978) On the cost of deposit insurance when there are surveillance costs. J Bus 51:439–452

Ronn E, Verma AR (1986) Pricing risk-adjusted deposit insurance: an option-based model. J Finance 41:871–895

Chapter 9
I Am Superman: The Federal Reserve Board and the Neverending Crisis

Christopher Whalen

I am I am I am Superman and I know what's happening.
I am I am I am Superman and I can do anything.
"I am Superman" R.E.M. (1986)

This article asserts that, in dealing with the 2007–2009 financial crisis, the Federal Reserve Bank (Fed) has placed its role as monetary agency and de facto steward of the market for U.S. Treasury debt ahead of its statutory responsibility for ensuring the soundness of the private banks. This is not to say that the Fed supplies whatever credit the government wants—at least not yet—but in terms of both the provision of credit to the private financial system and the price of this credit, the growing fiscal imbalances of the U.S. government seem to be playing an increasing role in Fed policy decisions. This chapter explores some of the issues involved in recent Fed policy decisions and draws some preliminary conclusions as to the conflicts between the Fed's role as central bank and also as prudential supervisor.

During the 2007–2009 financial markets crisis, the Fed seemingly left behind the mandate to conduct monetary policy in such as way as to achieve price stability and full employment. Specifically, the decisions taken during the financial crisis seem to be an effort to placate political constituencies by bailing out private sector banks and, earlier, by not exercising appropriate prudential supervision of Fed members banks and bank holding companies (BHCs). It needs to be said that nowhere in the Federal Reserve Act (FRA) or the various employment acts passed by Congress over the past half century is the central bank charged with maintaining sound money. Enlightened self interest, however, suggests that a central bank that overtly embraces the use of inflation through mechanisms such a quantitative easing to subsidize the

C. Whalen (✉)
Institutional Risk Analytics, 371 Van Ness Way, Suite 110 Torrance, CA 90501, USA
e-mail: chris@rcwhalen.com

This chapter also appeared as Networks Financial Institute *Policy Brief* 2010-PB-03. This essay reflects research by the author for an upcoming book, *Inflated: How Money and Debt Built the American Dream*, scheduled for release by John Wiley & Sons in December 2010, and is used with permission.

J.A. Tatom (ed.), *Financial Market Regulation*, DOI 10.1007/978-1-4419-6637-7_9,

issuance public debt by the Treasury and various government sponsored entities (GSEs) is in political terms signing its own death warrant.

Far from being an objective and fair prudential regulator, over the past several decades the Fed has shown a willingness to bend the rules or even launch into new, speculative areas of public policy, all in the name of appeasing the short-term political agenda of the Congress and the largest U.S. financial institutions. Maintaining access to cheap credit for the private sector as well as the stability of the largest banks, which include several of the most significant underwriters and dealers in government securities, may be seen as a means to larger ends, namely: (1) maintaining the appearance of positive levels of economic output and (2) preserving the ability of the Treasury to refinance existing debt and also issue debt.[1] This essay discusses the ability of the Fed to act as an effective prudential regulator, especially in the context of the accommodation of deteriorating fiscal and governance structures of the United States, and suggests some possible means of improving the current system.[2]

Bank Regulator or Monetary Authority?

As the bank of issue and the provider of credit to the financial system, the Fed has the leading role among U.S. prudential regulators with respect to providing market and liquidity risk management, and general market oversight and surveillance. It is debatable as to whether the central bank has done a satisfactory job of its market surveillance function. Until the most recent crisis, market surveillance activities by the Fed have been limited. This self-imposed incapacity goes back to the early 1990s and the sudden end of the tenure of E. Gerald Corrigan as the President of the Federal Reserve Bank of New York.[3]

After 1986, when regulatory responsibility for the government bond market had been explicitly given to the Securities and Exchange Commission (SEC), the Fed of New York (FRBNY), at Corrigan's instruction, had largely curtailed its surveillance of the market for Treasury debt, particularly the informal "when-issued" market in Treasury paper before each auction. As Martin Mayer noted in his book, *Nightmare on Wall Street: Salomon Brothers and the Corruption of the Marketplace*:

---

[1] The average maturity of the $11 trillion in U.S. federal debt is only about 5 years, meaning that the entire corpus of debt must be refinanced each decade or so, this in addition to the new incremental debt issued each year. This precarious position for the Treasury was created by Undersecretary Peter Fisher, who in October of 2001 announced that the Treasury would suspend issuing 30-year Treasury bonds. Fisher's decision, made at a time when receipts to the Social Security system were masking the overall federal deficit, has gradually shortened the duration of the outstanding public debt of the United States.

[2] The Fed's quantitative easing policy and various bank rescues since 2007 amount to direct monetization of what are arguably fiscal expenditures. As in the 1930s, Congress has ratified many actions by the Fed and Treasury in 2008 and 2009 after the fact.

[3] Whalen (1993).

> Neither in Washington nor in New York did the Fed seem aware that the dangers of failure to supervise this market had grown exponentially in 1991. Like the Federal Home Loan Bank Board in its pursuit of making the S&Ls look solvent in 1981–1982, the Fed had adopted tunnel-vision policies to save the nation's banks. And just as excessive kindness to S&Ls in the early 1980s had drawn to the trough people who should not have been in the thrift business, Fed monetary policies in the early 1990s created a carnival in the government bond business.[4]

The Fed's chief area of competency, after all, is supposed to be monetary policy, but surveillance of the government debt markets has also been an important activity—and one that has been handled unevenly. For the reasons discussed below, giving the Fed direct responsibility for financial institution supervision and consumer protection has been a disaster, at least in the view of this author.[5] There are several reasons for this view:

- First, because of chronic U.S. fiscal and external deficits, the U.S. central bank already has its hands very full with monetary policy and does not give adequate attention to prudential regulation. The focus by the Fed on credit expansion, as opposed to price stability and interest rates, and a lack of attention to choices being made with respect to market structure and the regulation of Fed member banks served to make the crisis of 2007–2009 far more difficult than ought to have been the case.
- Second and as an outgrowth of the first point, there is what we shall call the "superman complex" operating at the Fed, thus this essay's epigraph. Because of the growing fiscal imbalances in the U.S. economy and the need to compensate for these imbalances by expanding credit, the Fed is called upon more and more to rescue the private economy from the resulting market volatility. Fed officials fall into the trap of believing that direct intervention in the financial markets is actually helpful, instead of an act of interference in the political process of American democracy. The rescue of Bear, Stearns, American International Group (AIG), and Merrill Lynch are three cases in point. The Fed should have declined to act directly to bail out these institutions, but instead offered to finance a rescue operation led by the Treasury. The Treasury would have then needed to obtain the fiscal authority from the Congress.
- Central banks, by definition, seem to tend to be authoritarian and regressive in their thinking and not open to contradiction, a behavior usually evidenced by concern over maintaining "confidence" in the financial system. This overarching concern with public perception and confidence is an outgrowth of a currency system that, in fact, has no backing independent of government. In the fiat currency

---

[4]Mayer (1993).

[5]The author has worked as a bank analyst and investment banker for almost three decades. He was a management trainee at the Federal Reserve Bank of New York and worked in the bank supervision and foreign currency functions of that institution. His firm, Institutional Risk Analytics, is a rating agency and consulting firm that publishes quarterly performance benchmarks and stress indicators for all U.S. banks.

system that has existed in the United States since the 1930s and especially since President Richard Nixon formally broke the link between the dollar and gold in 1971, international confidence in the dollar has become a function of the political credibility of the Fed and the entire U.S. government.
- Finally, there appears to be something about central banks and the study of macroeconomic policy in general that seems to make the inhabitants of the given agency concerned believe in the possibility of an all-encompassing "God's eye view" of markets and agents. The key priorities in risk management and prudential regulation, however, are quite the opposite. In the surveillance of financial institutions and markets, attention to the particular and idiosyncratic factors is absolutely essential to managing risk or identifying potential systemic issues. The top down view that may seem useful to economists for monetary policy is useless for assessing credit and market risk.

In short, there seems to be operating at the Fed, on the one hand, a belief that financial institutions can be managed from on high, in the same top–down fashion as is used in the execution of monetary policy. On the other hand, there is also unwillingness among the leadership of the central bank to admit when they are wrong, especially when it comes to the development or recognition of systemic risks in the financial system and for the reasons discussed. Consider some examples.

- In 2005, an economist named Raghuram Rajan questioned the value of financial innovation in a speech at the Fed's annual Jackson Hole retreat. "Mr. Rajan quickly came under attack as an anti-market Luddite, wistful for old days of regulation. Today, however, few are dismissing his ideas. The financial crisis has savaged the reputation of Mr. Greenspan and others now seen as having turned a blind eye," reported Justin Lahart of the *Wall Street Journal*.[6]
- In 2008, Tobias Adrian and Hyun Song Shin published an excellent analysis of the link between monetary policy and the balance sheets of financial institutions. The paper, "Money, Liquidity and Monetary Policy," is part of a larger body of work by the authors and asserted that the monetary policy transmission mechanism runs through the balance sheets of financial institutions. This implies that monetary policy and regulatory policy are intertwined. Yet the Fed continues to this day to view monetary policy and bank supervision as entirely separate silos with zero real rates having no implication for the stability and soundness of banks and BHCs.[7]
- In a 2008 interview, Roger Kubarych described how officials of the Federal Reserve Bank of New York were told by a respected market participant as early as February 2007 that the failure of New Century Financial was the start of a larger contagion in the private market for subprime asset-backed securities (ABS), yet

[6]Lahart (2009).

[7]Adrian et al. (2008).

> the warnings were ignored.[8] More, this author has personally interviewed scores of bank supervisory personnel over the past eight years who knew that subprime originators such as Washington Mutual (WaMu) and Countrywide were in trouble as early as 2006. Indeed, WaMu had begun to shrink assets and show signs of distress as early as the end of 2005.

There are many other instances in the 2005–2007 period when experts from the world of banking, housing, loan servicing and investment banking told Fed officials that there was a problem brewing in the financial markets. Yet the central bank discounted these reports and instead remained focused on monetary policy. Despite claims by Fed officials of success in dealing with the most recent crisis, the fact is that the Fed was so focused on fighting the perceived risk of deflation earlier in the decade that the central bank actually created the circumstances for the subprime crisis that resulted in the failure of a number of large banks and primary dealers.

In 2001, when the U.S. economy experienced a "mini" recession, Fed Chairman Alan Greenspan and the Federal Open Markets Committee (FOMC) responded by dropping interest rates to very low levels. Critics of Chairman Greenspan have subsequently criticized the Fed for keeping rates too low for too long and thereby causing the bubble in real estate later in the decade. But what many observers fail to appreciate is that the Fed, operating in real time, was mostly concerned with deflation a la Japan.

"During the period after 2001, people in the Fed were worried about repeating the deflationary experience of Japan," David Kotok, CEO of Cumberland Advisers said in a June 2010 interview with the author.[9] "They chose policies that were designed to blunt the risk of deflation, but they failed to appreciate the other risk, namely encouraging a bubble in the domestic real estate market. It is easy to criticize the Fed in hindsight, but the central bank operates in real time. In this case the perceived solution to one problem created another."

Based upon the work done by the author's firm in analyzing and rating U.S. banks, it appears that the Fed's motivation in the early 2000s was not to create a bubble in the housing market, but to keep the level of nominal economic growth and employment above some acceptable minimum level. Large subprime lenders such as Citigroup, a bellwether of an economy where the average borrower is subprime, experienced significant increases in credit losses during the 2001–2003 period, credit losses far above the bank's peers and also higher than many market analysts thought possible. The FOMC took the federal funds rate from 5% at the end of 2000 down to just above zero by the end of 2003, causing officials at the central bank to consider new policy alternatives for operating in an environment of very low nominal interest rates.[10]

---

[8] Whalen (2008).

[9] Unpublished June 2010 interview with the author.

[10] Federal Open Market Committee (2003).

Had Chairman Greenspan and the FOMC raised interest rates sooner, the bubble in the housing market might not have been nearly as large, but the U.S. economy might well have weakened rapidly because of a basic lack of economic strength, a problem that continues to the present day. Henry Kaufman, among others, has warned for decades about the connection between monetary "gradualism" and instability in financial markets. Given the dramatic increase in Fed monetary intervention in the most recent crisis, the warnings of Kaufman that a low rate environment allows "credit creation to flourish, and its deflationary and destabilizing impact on the system is only recognizable with a delay" seem more important than ever.[11]

By, on the one hand, encouraging extreme swings in economic performance through overly accommodative monetary policies, while on the other encouraging the expansion of unregulated over-the-counter (OTC) markets for complex assets and derivatives, the Fed orchestrated many of the factors that contributed to the financial crisis.

As discussed in greater detail below, the fiscal priority of maintaining at least nominal economic growth seems to directly conflict with the duty to maintain the safety and soundness of regulated financial institutions.[12]

Monetary Policy and Prudential Regulation: Conflict of Visions

Most major industrial nations in the world do not give the central bank paramount responsibility for bank safety and soundness, and for good reason. The monetary agency typically is charged with the currency system, price stability and economic growth generally, although it must be said that there are no hard and fast rules. Interestingly, if the new British Chancellor of the Exchequer George Osborne has his way, the United Kingdom (UK) may go back to its previous situation with the Bank of England having bank supervision authority.

It seems that every country that separated bank supervision from central banking now, post crisis, wants to combine them, while every country where they had been joined wants to separate them. In fact there is no clear-cut model that is convincing either way, arguing in favor of those who have called for a flexible, evolving approach to the regulation of markets and institutions.

The author believes that, consistent with the models of checks and balances in America's governance structures, separation of the monetary and prudential functions is a good point of departure for any nation. This does not mean that these two agencies should not work in harmony, but the monetary and prudential regulatory tasks should have separate owners in a bureaucratic sense and each should be held

[11]Kaufman (2009).

[12]The maintenance of low inflation and sound money, even of a fiat variety, are certainly necessary conditions for bank safety and soundness. Banks which hold worthless fiat currency as assets obviously have no economic or social utility, no matter how well run.

separately accountable to the public. Being both a monetary authority and a prudential regulator creates political conflicts of interest and of personalities that arguably make it impossible to do a good job of either task when these responsibilities are put under one roof. Robert Eisenbeis and George Kaufman (2007) and Gillian Garcia (2007) all describe the conflicts that can arise with respect to bank resolutions and market crises that involve different governmental agencies and jurisdictions, both among agencies within the same country and among different nations.[13]

In addition to the political conflicts that arise between the Fed's role as monetary authority and prudential regulator, the more narrow issue of regulation must be considered. While some people claim that the Glass-Steagall Act law dividing banking and commerce has been repealed, the Bank Holding Company Act of 1956 and, in particular, the 1970s amendments to that law that truly separated banking from commerce, particularly insurance, are still extant.[14] This law makes the Fed the protector of a cartel of semi-monopolies known as bank holding companies and with particular emphasis on the largest banks, financial houses which are dealers in U.S. Treasury and agency debt.

The Fed's enforcement of the cartel among the largest U.S. banks is illustrated by the fact that, subsequent to the crisis, the top four BHCs and broker-dealers, such as Merrill Lynch, Bear Stearns, Countrywide, and Washington Mutual, were merged with other large BHCs, instead of being sold to other entities. The financial reform legislation that was pending in the Congress as this chapter was written provides the Fed more authority over financial institutions than ever before, but with no accountability for its increasingly destructive behavior. Specifically, merging large troubled banks and dealers is hardly a way to enhance the safety and soundness of the financial system and arguably works against ending "too big to fail." Yet the Fed seems incapable of liquidating large banks for fear that it will undermine confidence in the Treasury's debt markets and the dollar. Fed officials will no doubt find such comments distasteful. The fact remains, however, that the Fed, by placing systemic priorities ahead of enforcing prudential rules, is the enabler for many of the problems affecting the American political economy. This particularly applies to the increasingly unstable financial behavior of the largest banks. But it must be said that the same is true of the other regulators, especially in the European Union (EU).

The Europeans, in their collective obsession with Basel II capital standards, also were enablers of financial innovation along with the Fed and other U.S. regulators. EU regulators allowed dealers in London and Paris to participate in the subprime phenomenon in New York. Private banks and state-sponsored entities in the EU then bought some of the worst of the subprime originations. The EU is in the process of subsidizing the losses on these subprime exposures as well as buying the debt of insolvent nations such as Greece from EU banks. One of the biggest examples of EU regulatory incompetence was the treatment of guarantees provided to EU banks by AIG as part of the capital standards regulatory avoidance program. There is plenty

---

[13]Benink et al. eds. (2007).

[14]Whalen (2008).

of blame to go around. The point of this chapter is not to insult anyone personally or in particular, but instead to illustrate the conflicts inherent in the current system that make it difficult for the Fed to be both an effective prudential regulator and monetary authority.

Among the fallacies motivating the current legislative reform proposals in the Congress is the idea that the Fed would ever willingly stand by and liquidate one of the top banks in the United States. Until the Fed is willing to support the liquidation of a large banking institution for failure to manage risk, the central bank will have no credibility as a prudential regulator. But when push comes to shove, monetary policy and the Fed's duty to preserve market access for the Treasury will override any other consideration. And the funny part is the Fed is defending an anachronism in the primary dealer system.

Veteran observers such as Robert Eisenbeis of Cumberland Advisors, who worked for many years as a researcher at the Fed focused on the dealer4 community, have argued that the Fed should go to continuous intraday trading of Fed funds, which would eliminate the primary dealer system. Indeed, the rise of noncompetitive bids in Treasury auctions by significant Buy Side firms may be an indicator that the dealer system is going the way of the trading floor. But the Fed is loath to end the primary dealer system, even though a majority of the dealers are now foreign owned.

Since the 2007 fiscal crisis, the Fed has taken extraordinary and extra-legal power over the U.S. economy, and assumed a de facto fiscal role a la the Reconstruction Finance Corporation of the 1930s and 1940s. Using the emission of trillions of dollars in new fiat dollars to bail out the Treasury and the banking system, the Fed has become the chief fiscal authority in the United States. There are a couple of related issues here:

- First, the Fed's loans to AIG and other entities during the crisis seem to be a violation of the FRA. The act envisions the Fed making fully secured loans that are collateralized with marketable securities. Instead, in the case of AIG and perhaps other assets financed by the central bank in the wake of the collapse of Lehman Brothers, the central bank has ended up holding an equity position—and an illiquid one at that. As Alan Meltzer said in testimony before Congress earlier this year: "During the Great Depression Congress authorized section 13(3) that told the Federal Reserve to lend directly to small- and medium-sized firms that could not get accommodation from the banks. In this crisis, Section 13(3) was used to lend to AIG. This stretched the original purpose beyond any reasonable interpretation. Congress should remove this authority."[15]
- The second issue is the use of quantitative easing to absorb all of the inventory of mortgage-backed securities, agency debt and Treasury securities that the Sell Side firms on Wall Street could not or would not finance in the wake of the Lehman collapse. In a market that was "financed rather than funded,"

[15]Meltzer (2010).

in the absence of confidence the Fed became the only source of liquidity. In the wake of the subprime crisis, researchers have begun to quantify and define the difference between funding an asset with core deposits and "hot money" in the form of repurchase agreements, but such distinctions have been obvious for years. In 2004–2005, for example, the Corrigan group explicitly discussed the risks involved in using short-term market sources to fund long-term assets. As discussed in detail below, the bilateral OTC market structure that made this all possible was encouraged by the Fed and other agencies as part of "financial innovation."

- Third, and related to the first point, is the aggressive moves by the Fed to prop up the remaining primary dealers and essentially buy the debt issuance of the Treasury during periods of late 2008 and 2009 when the markets were dysfunctional. The merger of Merrill Lynch into Bank of America and the acquisition of Bear Stearns by JPMorgan both represented overt attempts to preserve the infrastructure of the primary dealer community, in the view of the author, more than efforts to fight perceived systemic risk.

In each case, the Fed interposed its balance sheet and credit to save the financial markets from a liquidation and orchestrated mergers among some of the largest banks, arguing in essence that bailing out these private firms was necessary to save civilization from complete collapse. Yet the fact remains that Lehman Brothers did fail, it did go through bankruptcy and the world did not end. As Peter Wallison of the American Enterprise Institute wrote in a recent commentary:

> Unlike Bear, Lehman was likely not solvent, and it had certainly become illiquid by the time it filed for bankruptcy. Nevertheless, despite all the market turmoil that followed Lehman's bankruptcy filing, there was only one case of a Lehman counterparty or creditor failing because of Lehman's inability to meet its financial obligations. That case was the Reserve Fund, a money-market fund that held a substantial amount of Lehman's commercial paper. The Reserve Fund's losses caused it to "break the buck"—in other words, it failed to maintain a $1 per share redemption value—and triggered runs at other money-market funds where investors felt they might be at risk of a similar loss. The threat to "thousands of counterparties" that Bernanke envisioned occurring if Bear had not been rescued never materialized after Lehman filed for bankruptcy.[16]

The instability of financial institutions and heightened volatility observed in the financial markets is merely a symptom of a far greater fiscal disorder in Washington and one that is deliberately perpetuated by the central bank. While critics of Chairman Greenspan like to blame him for the subprime bubble, not nearly enough attention is paid to the fact that American presidents from Bill Clinton forward allowed the Fed Board to become very narrowly focused on monetary policy. Only very recently has the Obama Administration made a deliberate attempt to nominate Fed governors who are not primarily economists—yet another legacy of the tenure of Chairman Greenspan. It is interesting to note that of the recent appointments by President Barrack Obama, Dan Tarullo is a lawyer, Peter Diamond is an expert in

[16]Wallison (2010).

Social Security and fiscal policy, Janet Yellen is an economist, Elizabeth Duke is community banker and Sarah Bloom Raskin, Maryland's commissioner of financial regulation.

Chairman Greenspan may not have been a particularly good economic prognosticator, but he was and is an exceptional politician. In 1992, when President-elect Bill Clinton invited Alan Greenspan to Little Rock, Greenspan jumped at the chance and reintegrated himself back into the White House policy loop he knew so well.[17] By accommodating the political concerns of the White House, Greenspan gained effective control over the Fed's Board of Governors through his entire term and thus the Board and its staff tended to be focused almost entirely on monetary policy.

What Fed Independence?

We should recall the political battle between the Fed and Treasury from the late 1940s to 1951 over maintaining the artificially low interest rates prevailing during World War II, a struggle that restored the nominal independence of the central bank. In the Fed-Treasury Accord of 1951, the two agencies agreed on a set of rules with respect to their respective operations whereby the Fed would seek to maintain the Treasury's ability to issue debt while limiting the degree of monetization of federal obligations.[18] In the intervening years, however, the political independence of the central bank has been steadily eroded by the fiscal excesses of the Treasury. Today the Fed can neither conduct credible monetary policy nor act as a good steward of the banking industry because of the enormous conflicts between monetary policy and prudential supervision.

Compared with the capitulation by Chairman Bernanke and the FOMC during the 2008–2009 market collapse, when the central bank subordinated itself to the Treasury in order to bail out banks and whole markets, the posture of the Fed in 1950 was remarkable. By refusing to cave in to pressure from President Truman, Fed Governors such as Mariner Eccles and Chairman Tom McCabe, and FRBNY President Allan Sproul were heroes in the American story of money and debt. Truman had refused to re-appoint Eccles as Fed Chairman because of the dispute over interest rates, but Eccles remained on the Board to support McCabe for the balance of his tenure as governor. Even when Chinese troops attacked American troops in Korea, the Fed refused to change its plans to restore market interest rates to the U.S. markets.

In a telling lesson for today's policy makers, only when the Fed regained control of monetary policy in 1951 were market rates really reflective of investor sentiment and risk instead of the carefully controlled market that reflected the wartime fiscal priorities of the Treasury. More important, inflation started to subside, at least prior to the Korean War. The Fed now faces precisely that same choice between

[17]Woodward (2001).

[18]Hetzel et al. (2001).

political expedience and the soundness of the financial system and the dollar. Today maintaining the short-term stability of the U.S. economy by targeting private credit creation is the Fed's new "wartime" task. Since many senior Fed officials tend to hold beliefs regarding economic policy ranging from neo-Keynsian socialism to various variations of the Taylor Rule, credit targeting and direct intervention to bail out failed banks is hardly a great leap of faith. In a speech to Humboldt University in Berlin in June 2010, George Soros illustrated the basic dilemma facing the Fed and all global central banks:

> In the week following September 15, 2008 global financial markets actually broke down and by the end of the week they had to be put on artificial life support. The life support consisted of substituting sovereign credit for the credit of financial institutions which ceased to be acceptable to counterparties. As Mervyn King of the Bank of England explained, the authorities had to do in the short-term the exact opposite of what was needed in the long-term: they had to pump in a lot of credit, to replace the credit that had disappeared, and thereby reinforce the excess credit and leverage that had caused the crisis in the first place. Only in the longer term, when the crisis had subsided, could they drain the credit and reestablish macro-economic balance.[19]

The increasingly visible schizophrenia in Fed policy roughly parallels the compromises in terms of monetary policy that the Fed has been forced to make since the 1970s. Not since Fed Chairman Paul Volker (1979–1987) has a Fed chairman been willing to confront a President and the Congress over inflation and fiscal excess. But since the departure of Paul Volcker and the arrival of Alan Greenspan, the Fed has entered a period of increased accommodation and virtually no conflict with either the Congress or the Executive branch. John Taylor refers to this period as being "From Great Moderation to Great Deviation to Great Recession." He observes:

> Why did the Great Moderation end? In my view, the answer is simple. The Great Moderation ended because of a "Great Deviation," in which economic policy deviated from what was working well during the Great Moderation. Compared with the Great Moderation, policy became more interventionist, less rules-based, and less predictable. When policy deviated from what was working well, economic performance deteriorated. And lo and behold, we had the Great Recession.[20]

The compromises made by the Fed to fulfill the twin legal mandates of (1) full employment and (2) price stability have made it increasingly difficult if not impossible for the Fed to also function as an effective prudential regulator. Simply put, the Fed is so busy keeping the U.S. economy growing at some minimal, politically acceptable level of growth and at the same time working to prevent the over-indebted U.S. government from sliding into monetary collapse that managing the nation's banks has at best taken a back seat. The real problem in the U.S. over the past decade was that Bernanke and the other members of the Fed Board were so committed to targeting a minimum level of private credit expansion that they ignored other indications that something was seriously amiss in the financial system.

---

[19] Soros (2010).

[20] Taylor (2010).

It needs to be said that whole generations of Fed officials have been groomed to act (if not believe) that current U.S. fiscal policy is sustainable, thus the agency has an abrasive self-confidence about all of its policy prognostications. Yet the central bank almost never says no to demands for liquidity from either the financial markets or the Treasury. It can be argued that coming out of the 1990s, when Treasury ran a primary surplus including receipts for Social Security, Fed policy was too accommodative because of a false sense of confidence regarding the fiscal outlook. Many economists actually talked about the Treasury paying down most of the public sector debt during this period, this even though the surplus was transitory. Studies were performed on how to conduct monetary policy in a market where there was no significant public sector debt. To his credit Chairman Greenspan raised the very medium and long term fiscal issues regarding Social Security and other unfunded mandates that have since driven federal budget deficits into the stratosphere. It is interesting to note that 2010 marked the inflection point when contributions to the Social Security trust fund are now smaller than benefit payments.

A Culture of Innovation

In the same way that the Fed gradually has been forced to accommodate monetary policy to the increasingly dissolute fiscal behavior of the Congress and the U.S. Treasury, it has likewise been forced by political pressure from the Congress and the Executive Branch to essentially allow the largest banks to do everything and anything in search of profit. The Fed's lack of leadership in terms of market structure in the United States makes arguing over distinctions about the solvency of supposedly private banks seem a little absurd. Martin Mayer told Gretchen Morgenson of the *New York Times*: "This insistence that you mustn't slow the pace of innovation is just childish," Mayer said. "Innovation has now cost us $7 trillion," he added, referring to the loss in household wealth that has resulted from the crisis. "That's a pretty high price to pay for innovation."[21]

The Fed's abandonment of the decades of success in using leverage ratios to define well capitalized banks, which kept down the number of failures, seems to be a direct contributor to the scale of the financial crisis. The entire framework of the Basel II capital accord was a celebration of efficient market theory and the OTC marketplace. Contemporary risk measurement concepts such as "Value at Risk" were substituted for traditional, consistent and deterministic measures of solvency. In many cases, the valuation models and solvency measures were generated by the banks themselves and were thus made peer comparisons impossible. One of the greatest and least remarked upon failures of the Fed and other global regulators during this period was allowing the banks, in effect, to set their own rules.

The era of financial innovation under Chairman Greenspan was a time when the Fed Board and their counterparts at the Bank for International Settlements loosed

---

[21] Morgenson (2010).

themselves from the bounds of earth and embraced relativity in assessing bank safety and soundness. When you add the opacity of the financial products in the OTC markets and the poor methods for managers or regulators to gauge the credit and market risks of these securities, the scenario for the 2007–2009 market disaster was perfect.

If you really examine the collapse of Lehman Brothers and Bear, Stearns & Co., in both cases the firms had more than adequate capital, at least as governed by the marketplace. While it might be argued that more capital would have made these organizations more stable, especially given their true risk profiles, this author believes that the issue of market structure was the determining factor in these failures. Citigroup too had levels of capital that, while below peer, were still in the right neighborhood. But in each case, it was the risk-taking activities of these banks that made whatever capital they had in place irrelevant—often by an order of magnitude or more. If you doubled the capital of Lehman or Bear Stearns or WaMu, for example, would it make the financial system less risky? Would these institutions have survived? Since they held sufficient capital, at least according to regulations, and did not survive, the answer must be no.

"Our system evolved from one funded by intermediaries, to one largely financed by markets," noted FRBNY Executive Vice President Terrence Checki in a December 2009 speech to the Foreign Policy Association. "The traditional ties between borrower and creditor were weakened as credit risk became just another commodity to be traded and distributed."[22] The same wave of selling and collateral demands would have destroyed the largest commercial banks too. Were it not for the extraordinary actions by the Fed to essentially float the entire rancid corpus of private label residential mortgage securitizations on the rising tide of liquidity in the form of quantitative easing, many more institutions likely would have failed.

One of the key issues that global regulators and their political leaders still don't seem to understand is that while the crisis that began in 2007 did start in the market for nonbank finance, much of the market for ABS and derivatives was sponsored by the banks themselves and/or the Buy Side clients of the largest banks. In the world of off-balance sheet or "OBS" vehicles and OTC derivatives, the effective leverage on the capital of banks and nonbank dealers was infinite and still remains today far higher than official capital ratios suggest. In a risk adjusted and economic sense, the total assets and liabilities of a financial institution includes all securitizations, variable interest entities (VIEs), and derivatives exposures.

For example, Wells Fargo's market "footprint" includes $1.7 trillion in securitizations and VIEs that are not consolidated under Financial Accounting Standards Board (FASB) 166/167. These off-balance sheet vehicles were "financed rather than funded," to again borrow the quotation by Checki. The apparent liquidity for these vehicles collapsed as soon as concern about counterparty credit risk became pronounced. The Fed and other regulators actively encouraged banks to increase their leverage via OBS securitizations, VIEs and OTC derivatives. The regulators

[22]Checki (2009).

accommodated these activities to increase effective leverage in order to enhance the appearance of nominal profitability of the large banks.

The True Nature of Credit Default Swaps

In order to understand the negative impact of the OTC markets and especially the market for credit default swaps (CDSs) and similar instruments on prudential regulation, both from an institution and systemic perspective, it is important to review some key issues that many regulators and policy makers still do not fully appreciate:

- Symmetry vs. Asymmetry: While OTC contracts for interest rates, currencies and even energy tend to be symmetrical and thus self-regulating in terms of balancing risk positions, the OTC credit markets are not. CDSs and similar derivatives are contingent or "barrier" options to use the insurance industry term. Thus while OTC "swaps" in interest rates or energy tend to help diversify and balance risk, CDSs can be used to create highly toxic concentrations of risk on one side of a given trade. Since there is cash settlement for these CDS contracts and no credit or market oversight, as is found in a multilateral exchange, these concentrations go unnoticed. In the case of AIG, this factor became fatal and caused the collapse of the entire company.[23]
- Back Office vs. Front: Starting in 2007, then FRBNY President Tim Geithner and other members of the OTC dealer community began to focus on the back office problems in this unregulated market. While much of the attention focused on the issue of clearing these bespoke, nonstandardized contracts, Fed officials missed the fact that much of the volume in the market was still not being reported to the clearinghouse. Specifically, AIG was not reporting its sales of CDS contracts to Fiserv or the New York clearing house. Thus neither the Fed nor the other regulatory agencies were aware of the exposures being created in the front office of AIG. Meanwhile, Goldman Sachs, Deutsche Bank, JPMorgan, and other dealers essentially looted AIG and then forced the Fed to bail out their client![24]

Ironically one often cited explanation for the crisis of 2007–2010 is that because Bear Stearns and Lehman were not part of the "bank" club, these firms failed. Goldman Sachs and Morgan Stanley were saved only via extraordinary efforts by the Fed and conversion of these broker-dealers into ersatz commercial banks. But the wave of selling and demands for cash and collateral that almost destroyed all of the nonbank dealers was a function of confidence, not capital. All of the major banks in the United States, whether a commercial bank or broker dealer, were effected equally in the collapse of the OTC marketplace.

[23]Morgenson et al. (2010).

[24]Ibid. See also Morgenson et al. (2010), "In U.S. Bailout of A.I.G., Forgiveness for Big Banks," *New York Times*, June 29, 2010 A1

Toward A Rules-Based Regulatory System

By deliberately encouraging and tolerating the growth of complex OTC instruments inside banks, Fed officials have been sowing the seeds of our collective destruction—but the arrogance of Fed officials makes them believe that they are capable of managing such a financial system. One of the great paradoxes of our time is the insistence of intelligent, well-educated economics professionals who model the likely outcomes in our economy without understanding many of the details. As long as behavior is expected to be rational, actual outcomes will follow the models.

David Colander of Middlebury College testified before the House Science and Technology Committee in September 2009 on the difficulty of applying the tools of the hard sciences to social sciences such as economics or quantitative modeling:

> Using models within economics or within any other social science, is especially treacherous. That's because social science involves a higher degree of complexity than the natural sciences. The reason why social science is so complex is that the basic unit in social science, which economists call agents, are strategic, whereas the basic unit of the natural sciences are not. Economics can be thought of the physics with strategic atoms, who keep trying to foil any efforts to understand them and bring them under control. Strategic agents complicate modeling enormously; they make it impossible to have a perfect model since they increase the number of calculations one would have to make in order to solve the model beyond the calculations the fastest computer one can hypothesize could process in a finite amount of time. Put simply, the formal study of complex systems is really, really, hard. Inevitably, complex systems exhibit path dependence, nested systems, multiple speed variables, sensitive dependence on initial conditions, and other nonlinear dynamical properties. This means that at any moment in time, right when you thought you had a result, all hell can break loose.[25]

Unfortunately, few of the people who work for the Federal Reserve Board and other prudential regulators in Washington have apparently heard this news. Classical economists such as John Stuart Mill "recognized the economy's complexity and were very modest in their claims about the usefulness of their models," Colander continues. But at the Fed's Board of Governors in Washington, the belief in possibility of a God's eye view of the global markets and even the inner workings of institutions and complex securities remains intact. Despite public comments by the Fed regarding the need to reduce systemic risks, the Fed's support for highly destabilizing asset classes such as OTC derivatives remains unchanged. At a March 20, 2010 speech to the Independent Community Bankers, Chairman Bernanke said:

> It is unconscionable that the fate of the world economy should be so closely tied to the fortunes of a relatively small number of giant financial firms. If we achieve nothing else in the wake of the crisis, we must ensure that we never again face such a situation.[26]

And yet in the maneuvering and lobbying over financial reform legislation during the past year and more, the Fed has gone out of its way not only to preserve its regulatory turf, but to defend and keep as unaffected as possible the activities of the

---

[25] Colander (2009).

[26] Bernanke (2010).

largest dealer banks in instruments such as OTC derivatives, instruments for which there is no real market nor any connection to the real economy. Keep in mind that when you explicitly depend upon efficient market theory to identify risk or manage prudential soundness of banks, you are flying blind. That is precisely the situation with OTC credit derivatives. Rajiv Sethi Professor of Economics, Barnard College, Columbia University, argues that:

> Generally speaking, stability in financial markets depends on the extent to which trading is based on fundamental information about the securities that are changing hands. If too great a proportion of total volume is driven by strategies that try to extract information from market data, the data itself becomes less informative over time and severe disruptions can arise.[27]

The Fed's fierce opposition to efforts by former Fed Chairman Paul Volcker to force banks out of OTC derivatives for their own account illustrates the degree of capture by the banks over their supposed prudential regulator. The sad fact is that OTC derivatives increase systemic risk far beyond the native risk that exists in the real economy. Some current and former regulators contend that these instruments are a fact of life and proposing some systematic means of managing their risk is unacceptable. But OTC derivatives may be impossible to risk manage and are thus impossible to regulate, particularly in times of market stress. As already discussed, the key flaws of the OTC markets, including dependence upon a bilateral credit and collateral relationship, and the lack of symmetry in CDSs, are issues that a central clearing facility only partly address. Liquidity risk, as the author had learned as a risk practitioner over several decades, exists only in particular transactions and cannot be measured or managed in aggregate.

An Objective Basis for Finance and Regulation

One of the core fallacies of the Fed as a prudential regulator is the notion that models can effectively manage risks inside large financial institutions. The term "model" as it applies to finance or regulatory structures such as Basel II can be described as a simulation of reality in terms of predicting future financial outcomes or events. The author Nassim Taleb says the term "VaR" or value at risk describes a statistical estimate of "the expected maximum loss (or worst loss) over a target horizon within a given confidence interval."[28]

VaR models and similar statistical methods pretend to estimate the largest possible loss that an investor might experience over a given period of time to a given degree of certainty. The use of VaR type models, including the version imbedded in the Basel II agreement, involves a number of assumptions about risk and outcomes that cannot be effectively hedged, yet public officials such as Chairman Bernanke and other Fed official pretend otherwise. More important, the widespread use of

---

[27] Sethi (2010).

[28] Taleb (1997).

these statistical models for risk management and the regulation of financial markets suggests that large financial institutions, especially those active in OTC derivatives markets, are subject to periodic "Black Swans" in the form of risk events that cannot be anticipated.[29]

But this author takes a different view. There is no such a thing as a "Black Swan." A more likely explanation is that leaders at the Fed, in finance and in politics, simply made the mistake of, again, believing in what were in fact flawed models and blinded themselves to what should have been plainly calculable risks created by deviations from established prudential norms. When John Taylor talks about the Great Deviation in terms of Fed monetary policy in the 2000s, we should also speak of the deviation in terms of what was acceptable in the financial markets and in terms of prudential regulation.[30]

As early as 2004 with the publication of the policy statement on "Interagency Statement on Sound Practices Concerning Complex Structured Finance Activities," the Fed, prudential regulators and SEC all publicly recognized that there were legal and reputational risks to banks dealing in OTC derivatives. Yet nothing was done to rein in this activity. If financial markets and the models used to describe them are limited to those instruments that can be verified objectively, then we no longer need to fear the ravages of Black Swans or systemic risk. The source of systemic risk in the financial markets is fear born from the complexity of opaque securities for which there is no underlying basis. And yet the Fed's Washington staff, in their arrogance, believe that OTC derivatives, which have no observable cash markets, may be substituted for cash securities and that to do so is consistent with safe and sound banks.

The real sea change that is required by the Fed and other prudential regulators to recover credibility is to insist that most OTC transactions be standardized and migrated to public, multilateral exchanges. Nonstandard OTC products should be subject to rigorous reserving and disclosure, as proposed in pending reform legislation. If we accept that the sudden change in market conditions or the "Black Swan" event that Taleb and other theorists have so elegantly described arises from a breakdown in prudential regulation and basic common sense, and not from some unknowable market mechanism, then we no longer need to fear surprises or systemic risk. To avoid systemic risk, we need to simply ensure that all of the financial instruments in our marketplace have an objective basis, including a visible, cash basis market that is visible to all market participants.

If investors cannot price a security without reference to subjective models, then the security should be banned from the U.S. markets as a matter of law and regulation. Simply saying that we must accept the existence of OTC markets because they

[29] For an excellent discussion of the misuse of mathematics and other quantitative tools expropriated from the physical sciences by economists, regulators, and investment professionals, see Whalen (2008).

[30] See Taylor (2010).

enhance bank profits, even though we know that these instruments also increase systemic risks, is an act of intellectual cowardice. The Fed needs to develop the courage to say no to the banking industry and, in so doing, might be surprised by the level of public support for greater sanity in the world of finance.

As Graham and Dodd wrote nearly a century ago, the more speculative the inputs, the less the analysis matters.[31] Models only have real value to society when their workings are disciplined by the real world. When investors, legislators and regulators all mistook models for markets, and even accepted such speculations as a basis for regulating banks and governing the OTC markets for all types of securities, we as a nation were gambling with our patrimony. Were the failures of Bear Stearns, Lehman Brothers, WaMu or the other "rare" events really anomalous? Or are we just making excuses for our collective failure to identify and manage risk?

Supporting "Financial Innovation"

While the leadership of the Federal Reserve Board is largely drawn from the world of monetary economists, historically there were virtually no economists in the Board's Division of Supervision and Regulation (DS&R). It is especially relevant that during the key time of the tenure of Alan Greenspan leading up to the crisis, a noneconomist named Rich Spillenkothen headed the DS&R for many years. During this time, when some Fed officials set records for tenure at any federal agency, the DS&R was regarded by some close observers of the Fed as being behind the curve on financial innovations.

When JPMorgan Chase, Citibank and some of the other large, internationally active banks began to expand into OTC securities and derivatives, and lobby in Washington for even greater powers and exemptions, the Fed Board and other agencies were either caught unaware or actively assisted in the process of liberalization of prudential rules. Though Chairman Greenspan relegated both DS&R and Consumer Affairs to nonpriority status, this did not prevent many Fed governors and staffers from actively supporting the expansion of the OTC market for subprime debt and derivatives, a posture that continues to this day.

In October of 2009, Fed Chairman Ben Bernanke and Governor Dan Tarullo promoted Patrick M. Parkinson as director of the Division of Banking Supervision and Regulation. Parkinson had formerly worked as a senior official in the DS&R at the Fed, where he was known as a brilliant researcher and also a tireless advocate for bank participation in OTC derivatives and other forms of "financial innovation." As already noted, OTC products were enshrined in the Basel II framework, so Parkinson's support for OTC was typical of many Fed officials and is used as a general illustration.

[31] Benjamin Graham and David Dodd, *Security Analysis: The Classic 1940 Edition*, McGraw-Hill Professional (2002), Pg 343

The Fed press release announcing Parkinson's appointment noted that as an economist and senior adviser in the Board's Division of Research and Statistics, Parkinson served as the division's deputy director. Of note, Parkinson served as the Chairman's principal staff adviser on issues considered by the President's Working Group (aka the "Plunge Protection Team") on Financial Markets from 1993 to 2008.

In addition, at the time of his promotion, the *Wall Street Journal* reported that Parkinson "recently took a leave from the Fed to work at the Treasury, where he was an architect of the Obama administration's proposed overhaul of financial regulation. The administration's financial-revamp plan, now pending in Congress, would give the Fed more authority over systematically important financial institutions and move consumer regulation to a separate agency."[32]

Notice, too, the stint by Parkinson working for the President's Working Group, a semi-public entity which lobbies regulators on public policy, and even distributes white papers and other documents to federal and state prudential regulators, but is completely unaccountable to the Congress or the public. Keep in mind too that when Alan Greenspan, Robert Rubin, Phil Gramm, and Larry Summers were attacking U.S. Commodity Futures Trading Commission head Brooksley Born more than a decade ago for suggesting that OTC derivatives ought to be better regulated, Fed staffers such as Parkinson were on Capitol Hill laying down a supporting barrage of barnyard debris for the big banks. And instead of being disciplined for his more than decade long role in encouraging this fiasco, Parkinson was promoted to head the Fed's key DS&R by Chairman Bernanke.

In May of 1999, for example, Parkinson testified on modernization of the Commodity Exchange Act (CEA) before the Subcommittee on Risk Management, Research, and Specialty Crops, Committee on Agriculture, U.S. House of Representatives. In that testimony, he said that the Congress did not need to extend the CEA to OTC derivatives. Parkinson also warned that regulation of OTC derivatives might make U.S. banks uncompetitive:

> [I]f the United States continues to impose what market participants perceive as unnecessary regulatory burdens, such systems could instead develop abroad. In particular, much of the existing activity in financial derivatives consists of transactions between large global financial institutions, all of which already have substantial operations in London.[33]

In 2005, when Parkinson appeared before the Committee on Banking, Housing, and Urban Affairs, U.S. Senate, he was still singing the Greenspan song of free market discipline and how the OTC derivatives markets did not need to be subjected to prudential oversight and regulation. Indeed, Parkinson's comments on behalf of the Fed Board of Governors were explicitly linked to the work of the President's Working Group and their efforts to stymie regulation of OTC derivatives:

> The Federal Reserve Board believes that the [Commodities Futures Modernization Act of 2000] CFMA has unquestionably been a successful piece of legislation. Most important, as recommended by the President's Working Group on Financial Markets in its 1999 report,

---

[32] Reddy and Paletta (2009). See also Harwood (2010).

[33] Board of Governors of the Federal Reserve (1999).

> it excluded transactions between institutions and other eligible counterparties in over-the-counter financial derivatives and foreign currency from regulation under the Commodity Exchange Act (CEA). As the Working Group argued, regulation of such transactions under the CEA was unnecessary to achieve the act's principal objectives of deterring market manipulation and protecting investors. Such transactions are not readily susceptible to manipulation and eligible counterparties can and should be expected to protect themselves against fraud and counterparty credit losses... Consequently, the Board believes that major amendments to the regulatory framework established by the CFMA are unnecessary and unwise.[34]

By November 2008, when Parkinson again appeared before the Congress, he was singing a new tune—yet only an incremental change. The basic Fed line was to advance "reforms" to the OTC derivatives markets, but to continue supporting the use of OTC derivatives by the largest banks. He testified on credit derivatives:

> As noted in my earlier statement, supervisors have worked with market participants since 2005 to strengthen the infrastructure of credit derivatives markets through such steps as greater use of electronic confirmation platforms, adoption of a protocol that requires participants to request counterparty consent before assigning trades to a third party, and creation of a contract repository, which maintains an electronic record of CDS trades. Looking forward, the most important potential change in the infrastructure for credit derivatives is the creation of one or more central counterparties (CCPs) for CDS.[35]

And this basic policy by the Fed continues to this day. Yet notice that none of the reforms that are summarized above by Mr. Parkinson really address the fundamental problem of valuation and liquidity in the OTC markets for CDSs. Yes, having a central counterparty for all OTC CDS trades is a fine idea. But the fact that it took Fed officials the better part of a decade to reach this conclusion is incredible. The fact is that the multilateral exchanges have had central counterparties since the 1930s and even before, yet for some reason the Fed thought that OTC markets could function without this basic and well-accepted risk management feature.

Despite their belated and only partial demonstrations of contrition, many Fed officials apparently do still believe that trading in OTC derivative contracts on a bilateral basis is consistent with bank safety and soundness. As already noted, the same Fed economists believe that big is better in the banking industry, even though the overwhelming data of historical data on the net losses of large banks and statistical evidence regarding risk suggests otherwise.[36] The more conservative bank supervision personnel in the DS&R in Washington, at the 12 regional Federal Reserve banks and within agencies such as the Office of the Comptroller of the Currency, Office of Thrift Supervision and Federal Deposit Insurance Corporation (FDIC), often opposed ill-considered liberalization efforts such as OTC derivatives and the abortive Basel II accord. But the Fed's powerful but isolated Washington

---

[34] Board of Governors of the Federal Reserve (2005).

[35] Board of Governors of the Federal Reserve (2008).

[36] I recommend Martin Mayer's 2001 book, *The Fed: The Inside Story of How the World's Most Powerful Financial Institution Drives the Markets*, particularly Chapter 13, "Supervisions," on the Fed's role in bank regulation.

staff of academic economists almost always had its way. And the Congress supports and encourages the Fed even as that agency's policies undermine the safety and soundness of our financial markets.

The result of our overly generous tolerance for economists dabbling in the real world of banking and finance is a marketplace where some of the largest U.S. banks are in danger of insolvency, because their balance sheets are laden with illiquid, opaque, and thus toxic OTC instruments which nobody can value or trade. Comments by Fed officials made over the years to the Congress lauding the very same OTC cash and derivative instruments which caused the financial crisis are a matter of public record, yet none of the Fed officials in question have been censured or held accountable with the exception of some perfunctory public hearings before Congress.

Proposals for Improving Financial Regulation

Making financial regulation effective again must start with a discussion of limits on risk taking activities by banks, particularly the use of OTC instruments and off-balance sheet securitizations and VIEs, the very toxic waste that now pollutes the Fed's balance sheet. The FASB rule requiring the repatriation of all OBS vehicles back onto the balance sheets of the sponsor banks at the end of last year started that process, but it will also illustrate that the problem is the effective leverage employed by banks, not static measures of capital, assets, and liabilities.

For example, former Chairman Greenspan is dead wrong when he calls the 2007–2009 financial crisis a "once in a century" event. If you as Fed chairman allow banks to continue to traffic in OTC derivatives and structured assets, then the only certainty is that the present systemic crisis will become the norm, not a "rare event" as Chairman Greenspan asserts. But these behaviors must be seen in the context of financial and fiscal actions by the Treasury and the Congress that are equally reckless. The banks on Wall Street merely mimic what they see in Washington.

The second aspect of this discussion about the regulation of markets and financial institutions that the leaders of the U.S. regulatory community must recognize is that risk-adjusted returns for larger commercial banks have been falling in the United States for almost a decade. Even with the supra-normal nominal returns earned by some larger banks from OTC and the mortgage bubble, the overall trend measured via the return on risk-adjusted return on capital (RAROC) calculated by The Institutional Risk Analytics (IRA) Bank Monitor in our Economic Capital model has been down, with less and less diversity observed among bank business models. The chart below shows RAROCs for the top 100 U.S. banks by assets for the period 1989 through 2009 (Fig. 9.1).

Despite the observable decline in risk-adjusted returns by large U.S. banks, the economists who populate the Fed continue to believe that current policies of supporting OTC cash and derivatives markets and other "innovations" are helping bank profitability and soundness, in nominal if not real terms. In fact, the banking industry

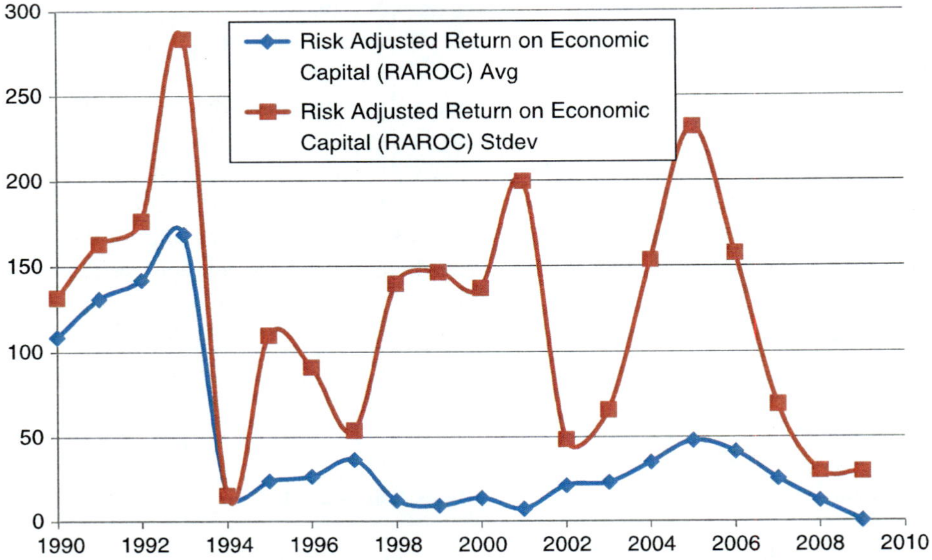

Fig. 9.1 Risk adjusted return on capital (%). Source: FDIC/The IRA Bank Monitor

and investors are responding to changes in the financial markets and the competitive environment that are largely caused by the Fed and Treasury. Unfortunately, with the growth in government debt and mandates, no amount of new prudential regulation will suffice to make the markets more stable. But you will never hear anyone at the Fed talk about such things, at least not in public, because doing so would hurt confidence.

We can place considerable blame on the Fed for the subprime crisis, but it must be said that an equally important factor was the tendency of Congress to use financial regulatory and housing policy to raise money and win elections. Members of Congress in both parties have freely used the threat of new regulation to extort contributions from the banking and other financial industries, often with little pretense as to their true agenda. Likewise, the Congress has been generous in providing the banking industry with new loopholes and opportunities for regulatory arbitrage, enabling the very unsafe and unsound practices in terms of mortgage lending, securitization, and the derivatives markets that have pushed the global economy into a deflationary spiral. But during most of the past decade or more when the Congress was creating new opportunities for "innovation," Fed officials were either supportive of such liberalization efforts or silent as to the risks.

The subprime housing bubble that began the present crisis came about with the active support of the Congress, two different political administrations, the GSEs, the mortgage, real estate, banking, securities and homebuilding industries, and many other state and local organizations. It should also be recalled that the 1991 amendment to the Federal Reserve Act which allowed the Fed of New York to make the ill-advised bailout loans to AIG and other companies was added to the FDIC

Improvement Act (FDICIA) legislation in the eleventh hour, with no debate by the Congress. The provision was added by members of the Senate Banking Committee and at the behest of officials of the Federal Reserve. The FDICIA legislation, let's recall, was intended to protect the taxpayer from loss due to bailouts for large financial institutions.[37]

The Neverending Crisis

It is important to understand that the same mindset of Fed officials that views speculative instruments such as OTC derivatives as an acceptable part of the financial markets is an outgrowth of the distorted worldview of the Fed more generally regarding the American political economy. Since President Richard Nixon took the U.S. Treasury off of the gold standard in 1971 and Washington embraced a policy of using deficit spending to maintain full employment, the Fed has been forced to rationalize a series of increasingly inconsistent policies pursued by the Congress and successive inhabitants of the White House. It is interesting to observe that the financial crisis of 2007–2009 so badly damaged the credibility of America's political establishment that elements of the military and intelligence communities have begun to actively monitor and assess developments in the financial markets.[38]

The idea of "financial innovation" is a canard adopted by the Fed and other central banks to maintain the appearance of profitability at some of the world's largest banks. As already discussed, Fed officials have known for more than a decade that the largest money center banks are not truly profitable without the supra-normal profits generated by OTC derivatives. An analyst for JP Morgan estimated that if the money center banks were required to exit OTC dealing activities as was threatened during the financial reform process, equity returns for these banks could fall by as much as one-third and reduce global investment bank return on equity to 11% from almost 20% today.[39] Yet on a risk adjusted basis, many of the largest U.S. banks often display negative returns even with the OTC derivatives flows factored into the mix, suggesting that, on net, the operation of the OTC derivatives markets is actually a drain on the real economy.

Benjamin M. Friedman, writing in *The New York Review of Books* on May 28, 2009, "The Failure of the Economy & the Economists," describes the market for credit defaults swaps in a very concise way and in layman's terms.

---

[37]When the amendment to Section 13 of the FRA was adopted by the Senate, Fed Vice Chairman Don Kohn, then a senior Federal Reserve Board staffer, reportedly was present and approved the amendment for the Fed, with the knowledge and support of Gerry Corrigan, who was then President of the Federal Reserve Bank of New York and Vice Chairman of the FOMC. See also Whalen (2009).

[38]During the past three months, the author has been contacted by no less than three agencies in the U.S. intelligence community under the pretext of studying risks in the U.S. financial system.

[39]Dawn Kopecki, "U.S. Bank Profits May Suffer on Senate Bill, JPMorgan Says," *Bloomberg News*, May 27, 2010.

> The most telling example, and the most important in accounting for today's financial crisis, is the market for credit default swaps. A CDS is, in effect, a bet on whether a specific company will default on its debt. This may sound like a form of insurance that also helps spread actual losses of wealth. If a business goes bankrupt, the loss of what used to be its value as a going concern is borne not just by its stockholders but by its creditors too. If some of those creditors have bought a CDS to protect themselves, the covered portion of their loss is borne by whoever issued the swap. But what makes credit default swaps like betting on the temperature is that, in the case of many if not most of these contracts, the volume of swaps outstanding far exceeds the amount of debt the specified company owes. Most of these swaps therefore have nothing to do with allocating genuine losses of wealth. Instead, they are creating additional losses for whoever bet incorrectly, exactly matched by gains for the corresponding winners. And, ironically, if those firms that bet incorrectly fail to pay what they owe—as would have happened if the government had not bailed out the insurance company AIG—the consequences might impose billions of dollars' worth of economic costs that would not have occurred otherwise.[40]

The dirty little secret that the Fed does not want to reveal is that the market for OTC derivatives is a tax, a form of gaming such as a lottery that effective subsidizes the largest banks in the world. The Fed accepts and even encourages this situation because it knows that without the excess profits from OTC derivatives, many of the largest U.S. banks would wither and gradually die, as has been the case with the banking sector in Europe. The hollowing out of the real economy in the United States has forced the banking system to focus more and more on speculative activities for survival. The Fed knows that it is only one fiscal crisis away from the same situation that prevails today in the UK, France, and Germany, where decapitalized banking systems are collapsing back into the arms of equally enfeebled, heavily indebted states. But it is interesting to note that, unlike the United States, the EU member states seem to be determined to aggressively attack these fiscal deficits.

By subsidizing and protecting the U.S. banking system, the Fed seemingly believes that it is ultimately supporting its primary objective of keeping America's wobbly ship of state on an even keel. By encouraging and facilitating the fiscal excesses of Washington, the Fed has not only set a bad example for the banks and companies that make up the real economy, but it has poisoned the proverbial pond for all of the citizens of the world economy with a consistent policy tolerating growing inflation and debt. In such an environment, talking about sound banks or stable financial markets is absurd.

Richard Alford, who worked in the foreign exchange function of the Federal Reserve Bank of New York at the same time as the author, commented in the crisis of 2007–2009 from a risk management and public policy perspective:

> Policymakers would like everyone to believe that the recent crises were random unpredictable Black Swan events. How can they be blamed for failing to anticipate a low probability, random, and unpredictable event? If on the other hand, the crises had observable antecedents, e.g. increased use of leverage, maturity mismatches, near zero default rates, and spikes in housing price to rental rates and housing price to income ratios, then one must ask: why policymakers did not connect the dots, attach significant higher than normal probabilities to the occurrence of severe financial disturbances, and fashion policies

[40]Friedman (2007).

accordingly? Ultimately, that is a question that Ben Bernanke and the rest of the federal financial regulatory community still have yet to answer.[41]

The monetary policies blessed by the Fed over the past forty years have ensured greater financial instability for banks and financial markets in the years ahead, not because the Fed is a bad regulator per se, but because its first job will always be keeping the U.S. Treasury floating on an ever expanding sea of dollars—even if this means destroying the private capital in banks and nonfinancial companies as a consequence. To really be "superlative" in this challenging time, Fed Chairman Bernanke, Governor Tarullo, and their colleagues on the Federal Reserve Board need to start reclaiming the independence of the central bank, as their predecessors did in the 1950s and the 1970s, by learning how to say no. Then Chairman Bernanke can take his place next to predecessors such as Eccles, McCabe, and Volcker and say "I am superman."

References

Adrian T, Shin HS (2008) Money, liquidity and financial cycles. Princeton University, Princeton, NJ, June. http://www.princeton.edu/~hsshin/www/CImoney2.pdf

Alford R (2009) Systemic risk: is it black swans or market innovations? Inst Risk Anal 18 Aug

Benink H, Goodhart CAE, Lastra RM (eds) (2007) Prompt corrective action and cross-border supervisory issues in Europe. The Financial Markets Group Special Paper 171, The London School of Economics and Political Science, Apr. http://feweb.uvt.nl/pdf/2009/LSE_Special_Paper_PCA.pdf

Bernanke B (2010) Preserving a central role for community banking. Independent Community Bankers of America National Convention, 20 Mar. http://www.federalreserve.gov/newsevents/speech/bernanke20100320a.htm

Board of Governors of the Federal Reserve (1999) Testimony of Patrick Parkinson, Associate Director, Division of Research and Statistics, on Modernization of the commodity exchange act, before the subcommittee on risk management, research, and specialty crops. Committee on Agriculture, U.S. House of Representatives, 18 May. http://www.federalreserve.gov/boarddocs/testimony/1999/19990518.htm

Board of Governors of the Federal Reserve (2008) Testimony of Patrick M. Parkinson, Deputy Director, Division of Research and Statistics, on Credit Derivatives, before the committee on agriculture, U. S. house of representatives, 20 Nov. http://www.federalreserve.gov/newsevents/testimony/parkinson20081120a.htm

Board of Governors of the Federal Reserve (2005) Testimony of Patrick M. Parkinson, Deputy Director, Division of Research and Statistics, on the commodity futures modernization act of 2000, before the committee on banking, housing, and urban affairs, U.S. house of representatives, 8 Sept. http://www.federalreserve.gov/boarddocs/testimony/2005/20050908/default.htm

Checki TJ (2009) Keynote Address, Foreign Policy Association Corporate Dinner, St. Regis Hotel, New York, NY, December 2, 2009. Transcript available at http://www.fpa.org/usr_doc/2009_Corporate_Dinner_Checki.pdf

Colander D (2009) The risks of financial modeling: VaR and the economic meltdown. Testimony submitted to the Congress of the United States, House Science and Technology Committee, 10 Sept. http://democrats.science.house.gov/Media/file/Commdocs/hearings/2009/Oversight/10sep/Colander_Testimony.pdf

[41] Alford (2009).

Eisenbeis R, Kaufman G (2007) Prompt corrective action and cross-border supervisory issues in Europe. The Financial Markets Group, The London School of Economics and Political Science, pp 5–62, Apr. http://www2.lse.ac.uk/fmg/documents/specialPapers/2007/sp171.pdf

Federal Open Market Committee (2003) Briefing on monetary policy alternatives. 28 Oct. http://www.federalreserve.gov/monetarypolicy/files/FOMC20031028bluebook20031023.pdf

Friedman BM (2007) The failure of the economy & the economists. The New York Review of Books, 28 May. http://www.nybooks.com/articles/archives/2009/may/28/the-failure-of-the-economy-the-economists/

Garcia G (2007) Prompt corrective action and cross-border supervisory issues in Europe. The Financial Markets Group, The London School of Economics and Political Science, pp 137–150, Apr. http://www2.lse.ac.uk/fmg/documents/specialPapers/2007/sp171.pdf

Harwood J (2010) Obama looks to close sale on financial reform. New York Times, 22 Apr. http://dealbook.blogs.nytimes.com/2010/04/22/obama-looks-to-close-sale-on-financial-reform/?scp=1&sq=Obama%20looks%20to%20close%20sale%20on%20financial%20reform&st=cse

Hetzel RL, Leach RF (2001) The treasury-fed accord: a new narrative account. Federal Reserve Bank of Richmond. Q Econ 87(Winter):33–34

Kaufman H (2009) The road to financial reformation: warnings, consequences, reforms. Wiley, Hoboken, NJ, p 186

Kopecki D (2010) U.S. bank profits may suffer on senate bill, JPMorgan says. Bloomberg News, 27 May. http://www.bloomberg.com/apps/news?pid=21072065&tkr=CMC:GR&sid=aVAIJVfagzys

Lahart J (2009) Mr. Rajan was unpopular (but prescient) at greenspan party. Wall Street Journal, Eastern Edition, 1/2/2009, Vol. 253, Issue 1, p. A7.

Mayer M (1993) Nightmare on wall street: Salomon brothers and the corruption of the marketplace. Simon & Schuster, New York, NY

Mayer M (2001) The fed: the inside story of how the world's most powerful financial institution drives the markets. Free Press, New York, NY

Meltzer AH (2010) Testimony, house financial services committee (March 17). http://www.house.gov/apps/list/hearing/financialsvcs_dem/meltzer.pdf

Morgenson G (2010) It's time for swaps to lose their swagger. New York Times, 27 Feb. http://www.nytimes.com/2010/02/28/business/economy/28gret.html?pagewanted=al

Morgenson G, Story L (2010) How Goldman pressed A.I.G. for cash. New York Times, B1, 1 Jul

Reddy S, Paletta D (2009) Wall Street Journal, Eastern Edition. 10/21/2009, Vol. 254, Issue 95, p. A2.

Sethi R (2010) The new market makers. 4 June. http://rajivsethi.blogspot.com/2010/06/new-market-makers.html

Soros G (2010) George Soros speech at Humboldt University. 23 June. http://www.georgesoros.com/interviews-speeches/entry/george_soros_speech_at_humboldt_university/

Taleb N (1997) Against value-at-risk: Nassim Taleb replies to Philippe Jorion. http://www.fooledbyrandomness.com/jorion.html

Taylor JB (2010) Getting back on track: macroeconomic policy lessons from the financial crisis. Federal Reserve Bank of St. Louis, Review, May/June. http://research.stlouisfed.org/publications/review/10/05/Taylor.pdf

Wallison PJ (2010) Ideas have consequences: the importance of a narrative. Financial Services Outlook, May. http://www.aei.org/outlook/100960

Whalen C (1993) Gone fishing: E. Gerald corrigan and the era of managed markets. Herbert Gold Soc. http://www.rcwhalen.com/pdf/fishing.pdf

Whalen C (2008) A change in bank control: interview with Ernest Patrikis. Inst Risk Anal 9 July
Whalen C (2008) Fed chairmen and presidents: roundtable with Roger Kubarych and Richard Whalen. Inst Risk Anal 30 Oct
Whalen C (2008) New hope for financial economics: interview with Bill Janeway. Inst Risk Anal 17 Nov
Whalen C (2009) IndyMac, FDICIA and the mirrors of wall street. Inst Risk Anal 6 Jan
Woodward B (2001) Maestro: Greenspan's fed and the American boom. Simon & Schuster, New York, NY

Chapter 10
How to Avoid the Next Taxpayer Bailout of the Financial System: The Narrow Banking Proposal

Ronnie J. Phillips and Alessandro Roselli

As recovery from the present economic crisis begins, policymakers must address what reforms will be made in the financial system in order to prevent the reoccurrence of a similar crisis in the future. In formulating these reforms, policymakers will also have to address the heightened moral hazard and broadened too big to fail doctrine associated with the bailouts of financial firms. These policies to deal with the impact of the crisis have resulted in large federal government deficits, a monetary base expansion with the potential for future inflation, and the depletion of the Federal Deposit Insurance Corporation's (FDIC) Deposit Insurance Fund (DIF). What will Congress do in response? In terms of long-term financial reform, what is to be expected from Congress is passage of legislation that increases oversight and regulation by the federal financial regulatory agencies. Will the Federal Reserve System (Fed), or some other new or existing federal agency, be given additional regulatory and supervisory power to manage system risk? Will these reforms invite regulatory avoidance behavior by financial institutions or will financial innovation be stifled? These are the important questions that must be answered by any proposal to reform our financial system.

The purpose of this policy brief is to explain and evaluate one proposal for reform of the financial system that would help mitigate the policy conundrum that often results from conflicting short- and long-run policies. This proposal, known as narrow banking, would regulate and supervise the role of banks in providing a safe and stable means of payment separately from the system of credit creation by financial institutions. The heart of the proposal is to make checkable deposits as safe a means of payment as currency presently issued by the Fed, but without the need for the elaborate supervisory and regulatory structure required when federal deposit insurance and the discount window are part of the financial safety net. The proposal is intended to provide a safe payments system and reduce the economic need, and therefore the political pressure, to bail out large financial holding companies.

R.J. Phillips (✉)
Networks Financial Institute, Indianapolis, IN 46208, USA; American Institute for Economic Research, PO Box 1000, Great Barrington, MA 01230, USA
e-mail: rphillip@me.com

This chapter also appeared as Networks Financial Institute *Policy Brief* 2009-PB-05.

J.A. Tatom (ed.), *Financial Market Regulation*, DOI 10.1007/978-1-4419-6637-7_10,

What Caused the Present Crisis?

Before presenting the proposal, a brief review of how we got into the present crisis will highlight the kinds of reforms that would reduce the likelihood of a similar crisis in the future. The present crisis began with the surge in delinquency in subprime mortgages that began in early 2007. This led to losses at large financial institutions and ultimately the failure of Lehman Brothers. As the problems spread to the mortgage market in general, and more institutions found themselves with bad loans, Congress responded in Fall 2008 with a $700 billion capital purchase program to aid the financial institutions. After President Obama took office, Congress passed a nearly $800 billion economic stimulus program. The Fed, blamed by some for the low interest rate policies during the period 2001–2004, responded to the financial difficulties by expanding the size and type of securities that are eligible for purchase by the central bank. As bank failures rose, the FDIC saw its DIF reduced from $53 billion in January 2008 to $6.5 billion in mid-2009. The FDIC also insured additional noninterest bearing transactions accounts, and created a Temporary Liquidity Guarantee Program (TLGP).

A low interest rate policy by the Fed is not the sole culprit in the financial crisis. Lax banking regulation and accounting standards and China's growing balance of payments surplus are also often mentioned as contributing to the global nature of the financial crisis. Banking has undergone an extraordinary evolution in the past decade as banks became aggressive in wholesale markets and securities trading. Various factors have affected the on-balance sheet and the off-balance sheet activities of financial institutions. On the assets side, banks shifted from an originate and hold model—where the bank generates loans and holds them to maturity—to an originate and distribute, or credit distribution model—where the bank generates loans but securitizes and transfers risk to other entities. These other entities include other financial intermediaries and institutional investors and this has a deep influence on the structure and growth of the credit market.

The financial system became characterized by both a blurring between credit (loans) and securities and the less perceptible differences between bank and nonbank financial intermediaries. Banks remain crucial as deposit-takers with access to the central bank's liquidity, but their involvement in the process of credit creation, as a transaction-oriented activity, has notably changed. More and more, the traditional distinction between commercial banking and investment banking has given way to another distinction, between retail banks and banks as corporate finance providers, where any activity of business financing (loans, securities, derivatives) is carried out in a kind of universal banking scheme that may differ from country to country but is essentially the same.

The loan participation market, where a loan originated by a bank could be sold, with or without recourse, to other banks, has evolved into a new connection between retail and wholesale banking through the pooling of loans into securities, especially mortgage and consumer loans. Asset-backed securitization (ABS) involves the pooling of similar assets into a special purpose vehicle (SPV). These are legal, bankruptcy-remote entities, created for bookkeeping purposes to exploit regulatory capital and tax advantages. They have permitted an enormous expansion of private debt. Their use by commercial banks, or other mortgage lenders, represents an important link between retail banking and financial markets. The extensive use of derivatives, based on these securities, has added complexity and risk.

On the liabilities side, deposits, which in previous decades were the almost exclusive source of funds, have had a diminishing role in bank funding. Banks, therefore, appear to be exposed to unexpected changes in conditions in the volatile wholesale market, increasing the possibility of bank runs by depositors. International connections on the wholesale market only enhance the fragility of this business model. The gap between bank lending funded by deposits and total lending by banks has increasingly been funded in the wholesale market.

Investment banks have further expanded their asset share in the financial industry due to a little noticed decision of the U.S. Securities and Exchange Commission (SEC) (Appendix E to Rule 15c31 in 2004) that deregulated investment banks by permitting a substantially higher leverage through the use of private risk management techniques. Just two of the five biggest broker/dealers who benefitted from the SEC decision survived by restructuring themselves as financial holding companies and being funded by government money.

In the United States, the financial assets of the security broker/dealers increased in the period 2000–2007 by 153%, or as a percentage of the commercial banks assets, by more than 30%. The share of credit market instruments in the portfolio of the broker/dealers grew in the same period from 18 to 26%. The ratio of total assets to equity (leverage) increased greatly at the independent investment banks (i.e., those not belonging to financial holding groups), thanks to the SEC amendment concerning their capital gearing, as mentioned above. The sudden decline of the ratio of broker/dealers assets to banks' assets in the most recent period is due to the precipitous deleverage of the broker/dealers. Mortgages climbed above 30% of commercial banks' total assets. Deposits, which in previous decades were the most important source of funding for banks, declined to 40–50% of their total liabilities. (Source: Federal Reserve, Flow of Funds Accounts of the United States, Tables F.109, F. 110, F. 129, L. 109, L.110, L. 129; June 11, 2009).

In the current turmoil, what seems to be emerging is that the system cannot avoid bank runs without a substantial expansion of the government guarantee and a huge potential cost to the taxpayer, and that even nonbank institutions can be too big, or too interconnected, to fail. The wholesale market in a global financial system has assumed a paramount importance for maintaining stability.

Perhaps the most striking development occurred in the assets held by issuers of ABS or SPVs, as mentioned above. These assets, according to the originate and distribute model, are transferred from the balance sheets of banks to the balance sheets of SPVs (mostly, mortgage pool securities and other types of loans, such as student and business loans, and consumer credit). The obligations issued by the SPVs are claims against the above mentioned assets and are serviced by the bank that originates the loans for a fee. These SPVs now equal nearly 40% of commercial banks' on-balance sheet assets. The peak year of SPVs activity was 2007. In that year, just 29.7% of SPV assets and commercial banks' assets were backed by demand and time deposits, while the rest were funded by wholesale, often volatile, funding. It's a very different picture even from that of the 1990s, when ABSs were a very minor segment of the market and remained so until the early 2000s.

What will be the likely long-run policy response from Congress to these problems? There is little doubt that Congress will pass legislation to more closely regulate the activities of financial intermediaries and further empower the federal regulatory agencies to take actions when they believe financial stability is threatened. The Fed will also come under more scrutiny in its conduct of monetary policy and may face increased difficulty in reducing the high level of bank reserves that have resulted from Fed actions during the crisis. Congress will also have to evaluate the success of the system of federal deposit insurance. The FDIC will undoubtedly need to raise insurance premiums and alter the guidelines for the minimum size of the deposit insurance fund. If history is a guide, we will increase the regulatory burden on financial institutions in an attempt to avoid the problems that led to this crisis. There will be some marginal changes in policy and some substantial reforms as well. The next section will examine one recommendation for policy change that would address both the long-term reforms and improve the policy response whenever a crisis erupts.

An Alternative Way to Deal with the Problems: Narrow Banking

Do we need special financial institutions, such as banks, to serve both a depository and lending function? If so, then there will continue to be extensive government regulation and supervision to mitigate the effects on the economy of their illiquidity or insolvency, as well as economic and political pressure to bailout those institutions. However, if other kinds of financial institutions could safely separate both depository and lending services, why would we need the extensive regulatory structure for banks with the large resource costs to the economy? The policy question is whether there is a way to assure a safe and stable payment system without the danger of another large taxpayer bailout. At the same time, we do not want to lose the benefits of innovation in the financial system in terms of better allocation of resources, lower cost of credit, widened credit availability, and higher economic growth. The best policy option would be to strike a balance between these two goals—safety and innovation—in order to save both of them (Spong 1996).

During the savings and loan debacle in the 1980s, Robert Litan of the Brookings Institution put forward a proposal which he labeled narrow banking as a solution to the moral hazard problem of banking. A kindred proposal was put forward in the 1930s but ultimately lost out to the New Deal proposals for deposit insurance and reform of the Fed (Phillips 1995a). Litan proposed to create monetary service companies—institutions that would serve strictly a payments function and would hold only safe assets such as cash, government securities, and high-grade commercial paper. Previously, Nobel Prize winning economists Milton Friedman, James Tobin, and Maurice Allais supported the idea of narrow banking. Tobin proposed the creation of deposited currency, which would combine the convenience of a checking account with the safety of currency. Also during the 1980s, the late L. William Seidman, then head of the FDIC, proposed what he termed "two-window banking." A two-window banking firm would allow savers to choose between "insured" and "uninsured" windows in which to deposit their funds.

The safe banking proposal, or narrow banking, would require that the money supply, M–1 = Currency + Checkable Deposits, be backed by safe assets, most likely government securities. This is the same principle used in the National Banking Act in 1863 and, previously, in the Peel Act regarding the Bank of England in 1844. Until the present crisis, the Federal Reserve Banks were effectively narrow banks because their liabilities (Federal Reserve Notes or currency and commercial bank reserves) were backed almost 100% by holdings of federal government debt. Under the narrow banking proposal, private sector financing would be funded either by a separate window of the bank, where noninsured deposits would be collected, or through separate affiliates of the same holding company that would control the narrow bank, that may be called finance houses. It would also be possible for such safe accounts to be held directly at the Federal Reserve Banks, perhaps with commercial banks as agents just as there once existed a postal savings system in the United States. (Jessup and Bochnak 1992). Narrow banks could come about either through mandatory legislation or voluntary change. Deposit insurance for these institutions could be maintained, but since it is redundant (short-term government securities are safe assets), it would be mainly for fraud purposes, and therefore at a minimal cost and risk. The separate window of the bank or the separate section of the holding company (the finance house) could be allowed to engage in any activities, as long as there is a clear distinction between insured deposits and uninsured deposits or other financial instruments. The result would be a reduction in the regulatory burden for narrow banks while maintaining a safe and stable deposit function.

The narrow bank can keep safe the core deposits of the banking system. Because bank deposits are commonly used as substitutes for currency, and governments have sought to protect currency, there is a rationale for protecting bank deposits in a similar manner to the way currency is protected, namely, backing by safe assets. Deposit insurance, or an implicit government guarantee of all deposits for large banks (too big to fail policy), is an ex post remedy. It is based on the assumption that systemic instability consequent to a lack of government intervention in a crisis would impose a cost higher than the cost involved in the public bailing out of the institution. The idea of narrow banking would radically reverse this point of view: bank deposits must have ex ante the same level of government protection as currency. The basic money supply is currency issued by the Fed and checkable deposits. Not to assure the same level of protection given currency to money deposited in an insured account would potentially encourage bank runs, loss of trust in the currency, capital flights in search of safe havens, and a destabilization not only of the banking system, but of the monetary system as well. Any form of deposit insurance aims at partially preventing these risks at a cost to the banking industry and, as we are seeing now, ultimately for the taxpayer. Narrow banking aims at the full prevention of the same risks at almost no direct cost, thus shrinking the scope of the public safety net.

There is also a social component in this approach that was stressed by James Tobin through the above-mentioned idea of a deposited currency. Stressing the similarity of currency and deposits, as components of the money stock, he said:

> Currency and coins are the basic money and legal tender of the United states. They are generally acceptable in transactions without question. But they have obvious inconveniences – insecurity against loss or theft, indivisibility of denomination – that limit their use except in small transactions (or in illegal or tax-evading transactions.) These disadvantages, along with zero nominal interest, lead to the substitution of bank deposits for currency... assuming statutory limits on insurance of other deposits are made effective, depositors who wish safety and liquidity on larger sums would be protected. (Tobin 1987, pp. 172–173).

This kind of narrow bank, limited to just safe assets, and funded exclusively by checkable, demand deposits, would be the core of the payments system. The remuneration of these deposits would be quite low or nonexistent, but the depositors, both less affluent and risk-adverse people, would be willing to accept it in exchange for total safety. The comparative advantage over the Treasury bills in which the bank is invested would be represented by the right to transfer funds by checks and by a higher liquidity.

In summary, the implications of narrow banking are as follows:

1. A narrow bank is more like a public utility and would be akin to the postal savings system that operated in the United States. before the Great Depression and continues to exist in some countries today such as Japan;
2. The impact of monetary policy on credit to the private sector would be altered and likely reduced, though this depends upon whether the narrow banks invest in safe short-term government securities or are required to hold 100% in central bank liabilities. If the banks hold reserves in central bank liabilities, then the M-1 money multiplier would be one. The monetary base and the basic money supply would be the same. This is the meaning of putting checkable deposits on the same level as currency. Under this version of the narrow banking plan, the central bank would have the same degree of control over the basic money supply that they presently have over the monetary base. However, if banks are able to hold government securities, then obviously credit could be affected by monetization of the money supply. The Fed's control over the basic money supply would not be much different than the present institutional arrangement whereby bank deposits are backed by central bank liabilities, government securities and private sector loans, except that private loans would no longer make up any of that backing. This is the situation today since changes in monetary policy through open market operations impact financial institutions whose liabilities are backed by government debt (Phillips 1995a, b);
3. Capital requirements for a narrow bank will be reduced assuming government securities backing the narrow bank have near zero maturity;
4. There will be less of a need for federal deposit insurance because the solvency of the bank would rarely be challenged. Within the narrow bank, given the safety of the deposits, the current discrimination in favor of the depositors at banks too

big to fail and against depositors who wish safety and liquidity on large sums, would be phased out (Burnham 1991; Tobin 1987);

5. The need for the lender of last resort facility of the Fed comes into question. In the most extreme view, this safety net would disappear since it is not needed in the narrow bank scheme because of the safeness and liquidity of the narrow bank's assets. Since the finance houses would not be supplying a means of payment, the Fed need not be a lender of last resort to the finance houses because this would be inconsistent with a policy of allowing market discipline for such institutions. If narrow banks are permitted a limited exposure to the nongovernment assets or longer-term government assets, then the need for a public safety net resurfaces to a certain extent, especially if it is believed that there is a systemic risk problem with the narrow banks. The present problem with banks serving a dual deposit and lending function resurfaces in a somewhat different and perhaps less virulent form. However, there may be those who believe that because the finance houses may generate systemic risk, it would be necessary to provide access to the discount window of the central bank for those institutions (see 7 below);
6. Regulation of the narrow bank would be fairly simple, given its streamlined structure, though supervision of its compliance with its very strict limits of activity would be more delicate, because of the strong incentives to gamble in order to get higher returns, and because of the firewalls to be erected between the narrow bank and the finance house authorized to engage in a much broader range of activities, if both are affiliates of the same holding company (Padou 2004). More supervision, less regulation would characterize the narrow bank, but the overall regulatory burden to institutions would be reduced (Phillips 1995a, b);
7. The regulation of the finance house, however, would be a very different matter. Friedman and the monetarist school argued in favor of a totally unregulated system. Pierce (1991) and Pollock (1993) supported, without explicit reference, this view, however admitting that finance houses should have a limited access, under stressful circumstances, to the Fed discount window. Even today, a skeptical view of the regulator's ability to check the bankers' moral hazard through "hammering" the financial system by "intrusive" regulation and supervision, proposes the narrow bank as a way to eliminate moral hazard, while the finance house would be subject to the market discipline imposed by its shareholders, without any need for intrusive supervision (James 2007).

Objections to the Narrow Banking Proposal

Numerous writers have put forth objections to the narrow banking proposal. Critics argue that the credit to the economy would shrink and be therefore more costly, and that rather than eliminating systemic risks, embedded in the scheme is a potential systemic instability. In simple terms the problem arises because the ability of narrow banks to create money would be constrained. Though as noted, this depends upon whether bank deposits are backed by government debt or central bank liabilities.

However, the finance houses, in order to extend an equal amount of credit as a conventional bank, would need to attract more customers' funds by a higher remuneration than that paid by a conventional bank on insured deposits (Bossone 2001). Finance houses could create financial assets that are close substitutes for money, but the important point is that they would not have deposit insurance. Private lending rates may go up as a result. At the same time, prices of Treasuries—as eligible assets of the narrow bank—would swell, and their yield would go down. However, the finance houses would not be subject to regulatory costs that either raise the cost of funds or lower the rate of return on the assets of conventional banks (Litan 1987, pp. 180–181).

In an experimental setting, Bossone has shown that the restriction of credit would not be dynamically offset through alternative supplies of funds and that, as narrow banking increases its dimension, no alternative forms of credit on the financial markets emerge to counterbalance the reduction of bank credit (Bossone 2001). A more elaborate view has been expressed, based on the observation that depositors with uncertain liquidity needs, who are totally risk-adverse, in the current system have to place their money with banks that are exposed to credit risk, investment risk, and bank runs: they are unable to find riskless, even if no-return, banks. According to this view, a substantial welfare loss occurs when banks bundle together deposit accounts with risk-taking. In the context of a well-developed securities market, if a narrow bank policy is adopted, the severe lending restrictions associated with total safety will expand consumers' saving and investment opportunities (Shy 2008). A risk-free, zero-return opportunity is an additional choice. However, other theoretical models suggest that imposing narrow banking is an inferior solution to allowing the mixing of payments and lending (Cao and Illing 2009).

By leaving the safe harbor of the deposit-taking institution, the consumer should be well aware of the relative riskiness of other available retail financial products. But we know how this awareness is difficult to achieve in the absence of a full financial education, therefore a simple caveat emptor is unfair and impractical. For example, in the increasing number of countries where the state pension is in retrenchment, people have to rely on private—occupational or personal—schemes. If small savers have to invest their savings in view of, or during, their retirement in vehicles, trusts, funds other than bank deposits, the political pressure to a government protection actually increases.

Regarding the availability of permissible assets in relation to the size of deposits at the narrow bank, and the sudden swings between safe deposits and other financial instruments in case of financial distress, there is the question of the overall stability of the financial system with narrow banks and finance houses. We would probably have an optimal balance if the supply of permissible assets matched the demand for them by the narrow bank, fuelled by its deposits, and if the demand for credit by the private sector were matched by the finance house in a variety of technical forms. Most probably, neither condition would be met.

Wallace (1996) noted that, in the United States, "the magnitude of short-term safe assets outside the banking system exceeds the magnitude of bank demand deposits," but, for instance, in Italy, Treasury bills (if they are considered as the typical, or exclusive, permissible asset) have been in the last 3 years well below 20% of the demand deposits at Italian banks. Therefore, the classes of permissible activities should be necessarily extended. The existence, size and composition by maturity of the government debt are important; at the same time, it would be inappropriate to adjust debt management policies to narrow banking objectives (Bossone 2001).

If we counterbalance safe deposits at the narrow bank to less protected financial instruments at the finance house, letting the finance house fail would raise concerns when its situation deteriorates, possibly causing a flight to safety into the narrow bank. The deposit/other credit instruments ratio would increase abruptly (a concern strongly signaled in the past by Friedman). Another key goal of the narrow bank concept—to shrink the scope of the taxpayer safety net—would be defeated, if the government were obliged, because of systemic preoccupations, to open the discount window to stabilize the outflow from the finance house (Ely 1991).

More importantly, we are accustomed to associate systemic risk with the typical commercial bank structure: not by chance, the U.S. federal safety net, or similar institutional arrangements in other countries, was restricted to that structure, in the belief that other, riskier financial activities could well deal with their problems, while the government intervention was mostly confined to the conduct-of-business/transparency supervision, enacted by a separate authority (the SEC, in the United States). Recent events are evidence that, with the blurring of boundaries between institutions, the widespread financial innovation, the enormous size taken by some investment companies, and the new players of the shadow banking system, a systemic problem could come from any segment of the financial system, insurance firms included, particularly if involved in derivatives transactions as credit default swaps. The recent extension, in the United States, of the lender of last resort support to investment banks and to insurance companies makes it hard to believe that a kind of prudentially unregulated financial activity can be unleashed outside the territory of the narrow bank. The problem of reconciling government intervention with new forms of moral hazard would resurface in other areas of the financial industry.

The size of a flight to quality in times of financial turmoil, one of the most mentioned arguments against narrow banking, that would generate increases in the ratio of checkable bank deposits/other financial products, should be empirically tested in reference to previous phases of financial turbulence. The supply of checkable bank deposits is relatively inelastic so the adjustment outside the narrow bank would be larger.

The opposite situation might also occur: a flow from deposits at the narrow bank, to riskier assets, in case of a benign financial environment. In advanced countries, deposits have lost their pre-eminence as a percentage of financial assets. In general, the likelihood that the narrow bank would retain the same volume of deposits as conventional banks currently have is small, because bank customers would be willing to exchange some portion of their deposits for higher yielding securities issued by nondepository institutions (Litan 1987). In a narrow bank system, depositors should have to reassess their views about a trade-off of yield for safety. It is possible that the above mentioned ratio proves to be stickier, also in times of financial stress, than one could think in terms of purely rational behavior.

A Tripartite System

If we rule out the idea of a totally unregulated finance house, a question must be raised about how to regulate activities that are fairly different. In particular, what we might call the commercial bank or traditional bank sits uncomfortably both in the narrow bank model, and in a universal bank scheme. Drawing on Tobin's proposals, a kind of tripartite banking structure can be envisaged, possibly within the same financial group, where the narrow bank could coexist with a commercial bank, appropriately redefined, and an investment bank. Though allowing this tripartite system is not the best solution, it may be what is political acceptable. The difficulty is finding a way to gradually move away from a financial system in which too big to fail results in government action to bailout any large financial institution.

The commercial bank would be engaged in a relatively wide range of activities, mostly short-term, but longer-term assets might include variable rate bonds and mortgages. It would be prevented, in principle, from investing in equities or taking stakes in nonfinancial companies. Derivative products would be used for bona fide hedging transactions only (Tobin 1987, pp. 174–175; Wilmoth 2002). It could not invest in complex structured products. This commercial bank would be subject to strict regulations on capital adequacy, would be deposit insured within certain limits, and would have access to the discount window.

Beyond it, the third leg of the banking structure would be the investment bank that, for the reasons mentioned above, could not be unregulated, and would be subject to a layer of supervision that would cover not only transparency and conduct of business, but also stability issues. These issues would have to be faced also in reference to the insurance component of the group.

Any discussion about the appropriate architecture of regulation goes well beyond the scope of this policy brief, but it can be said that we would have three concentric circles of regulation and supervision: regulation would be tight, but also relatively simple, in the inner circle; more prudentially articulated in the medium circle of the commercial bank; while the regulation of the outer circle—the securities and insurance business—would have an ample focus on conduct-of-business but should not escape the prudential side. The lender of last resort would be, in principle, not necessary in the inner circle; would be a basic feature of the medium circle; and probably would be unavoidable in the outer circle. For a recent discussion on a comparative basis of the current regulatory architecture in nine advanced countries, see Gola and Roselli, 2009, section 2 of chapter 8.

Conclusion

Reform of the financial system is once again on the agenda for Congress and the President. Bankers are rightly concerned that a return to New Deal-style regulation, while solving some immediate problems, may adversely affect banking operations in the long run. At the same time, the public is concerned about the safety and security of their money and their savings. Since the 1930s, the nation has relied on FDIC-insured banks to provide a safe and convenient payments system, while also channeling funds from savers to borrowers. The Fed has sought to maintain a monetary policy consistent with price stability and economic growth. As we have recently witnessed, our financial system has provided an unstable and risky banking structure which is supported through an extensive federal safety net. The recent taxpayer bailouts of the financial system indicate some of the weaknesses in this safety net. Would the separation of the deposit and credit functions provide a better financial system?

First, the Federal Reserve Board would be better able to control the basic money supply, currency, and demand deposits under a narrow banking system. The question remains whether such control would be economically relevant in a world of financial innovation and instantaneous transfer of financial wealth. Whether a monetary growth rule or policy discretion is adopted would still have to be decided by the Board and agreed to by Congress. Though the narrow banking system would obviously allow for some financing of government deficit spending by money creation, there would be greater transparency.

While regulation of narrow banks could be reduced, it would not mean the end of all financial system regulation, because regulation of lending or transaction-oriented institutions should continue. However, if the only insured deposits are in narrow banks, then the potential costs to the DIF would be greatly reduced. Though deposit insurance is redundant for narrow banks, it could be maintained with reduced premiums.

Under a narrow banking system, credit would be supplied by finance houses, separate lending institutions that could be mutual funds, finance companies, even separate windows of the bank—as suggested by Seidman—or, if desired, government owned corporations. An example of the latter is the Reconstruction Finance Corporation of the 1930s, which both took ownership stakes in private companies and provided direct loans to the private sector. A particular problem may be the availability of funds for small business loans and consumer loans. Alex Pollock of American Enterprise Institute has proposed that the Home Loan Banking Act be revived to create community-oriented lending institutions. These organizations would be established as mutuals, with members as shareholders and therefore owners of the institution, and would be oriented toward community needs.

Should government policy attempt to maintain the current role of banks in offering deposit and lending functions with federal deposit insurance or begin the evolution toward a financial system that separates the respective banking functions? A narrow banking system would not only protect depositors and forestall future bailouts but also create a way for bankers to compete in other areas without being hindered by too intrusive regulatory burdens.

References

Bossone B (2001) Should banks be narrowed? IMF Working Paper 01/159. http://www.imf.org/external/pubs/ft/wp/2001/wp01159.pdf

Bryan L (1991) Core banking. McKinsey Q 1:61–74

Buiter W (2007) Would narrow banking prevent another Northern Rock? FT.com 22 Sept

Burnham JB (1991) Deposit insurance: the case for the narrow bank, in regulation. Cato Rev Bus Gov 14(2):Spring

Cao J, Illing G (April 2009) Endogenous systemic liquidity risk. CESifo Working Paper Series No. 2627. http://ssrn.com/abstract=1393186

Economist Staff (2008) Confessions of a risk manager. The Economist, 7 Aug

Ely B (1991) The narrow bank: a flawed response to the failings of the federal deposit insurance, regulation. Cato Rev Bus Gov 14(2):Spring

Fisher I (1935) 100% money. Adelphi Company, New York, NY

Friedland J (1994) The law and structure of the international financial system: regulation in the United States, EEC, and Japan. Quorum Books, Westport, CT

Friedman M (1965) A program for monetary stability. In: Kendall LT, Ketchum MD (eds) Readings in financial institutions. Houghton Mifflin, Boston, MA, pp 189–209

Gola C, Roselli A (2009) The UK banking system and its regulatory and supervisory framework. Palgrave Macmillan, Houndsmill, UK

Harrod RF (1969) Money. Macmillan, London

Herring RJ, Litan RE (1995) Financial regulation in the global economy. The Brookings Institution, Washington, DC

Hetzel RL (1985) The rules versus discretion debate over monetary policy in the 1920s. Federal Reserve Bank of Richmond. Econ Rev 71(Nov/Dec):5–9

House of Commons Treasury Committee (2008) The run on the rock. Fifth Report of Session 2007–2008. I(Jan):13–14

James KR (2007) The case for narrow banking. Central Bank of Brazil, 2nd Annual Seminar on Banking, Financial Stability and Risk, Sao Paulo, 7 May. http://www.bcb.gov.br/Pec/seminarios/SemMetInf2007/Port/KevinJames.pdf

Jessup P, Bochnak M (1992) A case for a U.S. postal savings system. Challenge 25(Nov/Dec): 5–60

Kobayakawa S, Nakamura H (2000) A theoretical analysis of narrow banking proposals. Monet Econ Stud 18(1):May. http://www.imes.boj.or.jp/english/publication/mes/fmes00.html

Lawson N (2009) Capitalism needs a revived Glass-Steagall. Financial Times, March 16

Litan RE (1987) What should banks do? The Brookings Institution, Washington, DC

Miles W (2001) Can narrow banking provide a substitute for depository intermediaries? Federal Reserve Bank of St Louis, First Annual Missouri Economics Conference, 4–5 May. http://research.stlouisfed.org/conferences/moconf/papers/miles.pdf

Mishkin F (1999) Financial consolidation: dangers and opportunities. J Bank Finance 23(2–4): 675–691, Feb

Padoa-Schioppa T (2004) Regulating finance: balancing freedom and risk. Oxford University Press, Oxford, UK

Phillips RJ (1995a) The Chicago plan & new deal banking reform. M.E. Sharpe, Armonk, NY

Phillips RJ (1995b) Narrow banking reconsidered: the functional approach to financial reform. Levy Institute Public Policy Brief, no. 18/1995. http://www.levy.org/pubs/ppb17.pdf

Pierce JL, Leone RC (1993) The future of banking. Yale University Press, New Haven, CT

Pollock AJ (1992) Collateralized money: an idea whose time has come again. Challenge 35(Sept/Oct):62–64

Shy O, Stenbacka RA (June 2000) Bundling argument for narrow banking. http://ozshy.50webs.com/narrow26.pdf

Simons HC (1948) Economic policy for a free society. University of Chicago Press, Chicago, IL

Spong K (1996) Narrow banks: an alternative approach to banking reform. In: Papadimtriou DB (ed) Stability in the financial system. St. Martin's Press, New York, NY, pp 360–384

Tobin J (1987) The case for preserving regulatory distinctions. In: Restructuring the financial system: a symposium sponsored by the federal reserve bank of Kansas City, 20–22 August:167–183. https://www.kansascityfed.org/publicat/sympos/1987/S87TOBIN.PDF

Wallace N (1996) Narrow banking meets the diamond-Dybvig model. Federal Reserve Bank Minneapolis Q Rev (Winter) 20(1):3–13. http://www.minneapolisfed.org/research/QR/QR2011.pdf

Wilmoth AE (2002) Restructuring the American safety net after Gram-Leach-Bliley. In: Gup BE (ed) The future of banking. Quorum Books, Westport, CT, pp 101–130

Chapter 11
Regulation of Bank Management Compensation

David VanHoose

Introduction

The structure of management compensation influences agency problems involving both equity holders and debt holders. On the one hand, shareholders desire for managers to engage in actions that benefit the shareholders, which gives shareholders an incentive to tie managerial compensation to shareholder returns. On the other hand, tying management compensation to shareholder returns provides a potential mechanism for shareholders to shift risk to holders of the firm's debts. As documented by Demirgüç-Kunt et al. (2008), banking firms in most nations receive government-sponsored deposit insurance. Thus, among the potential debt holders on the receiving end of risk-shifting incentives potentially created by compensation arrangements aligning interests of bank managers with those of shareholders are the taxpayers who ultimately guarantee these deposit insurance systems.

Several actual and proposed regulations of bankers' pay have emerged in the aftermath of the recent panic and bailouts. Table 11.1 summarizes actual and proposed rules governing pay at U.S. banks. These include establishment of explicit pay ceilings for some institutions receiving "exceptional assistance" from the U.S. government, publication and distribution of new supervisory guidelines for bank compensation policies, incorporation of reviews of pay programs into supervisory examinations, and circulation of a proposal by the Federal Deposit Insurance Corporation (FDIC) to condition deposit insurance premiums on management compensation packages (see Adler (2010a, b)). As discussed by Hill (2009), similar regulations and proposals have been advanced in other countries.

Some observers—for example, Macey and O'Hara (2003)—suggest that there is a strong justification for explicit involvement of policymakers in the establishment of rules governing internal management of banks. Others, such as Grant and Grant (2008), view the establishment of curbs on executive compensation to be in the

D. VanHoose (✉)
Baylor University, One Bear Place #98003, Waco, TX 76798, USA
e-mail: david_vanhoose@baylor.edu

This chapter also appeared as Networks Financial Institute *Policy Brief* 2010-PB-06.

J.A. Tatom (ed.), *Financial Market Regulation*, DOI 10.1007/978-1-4419-6637-7_11,

Table 11.1 Proposed and actual regulations of bank management compensation

Law/rule/proposal	Form of regulation
Economic stabilization act of 2008	• Sets a strict $500,000 pay cap at institutions receiving "exceptional assistance" • Establishes a discretionary $500,000 pay cap at institutions receiving assistance under "generally available capital access programs"
American recovery and reinvestment act of 2009	• Limits bonus payments to no more than one-third of total compensation • Creates the office of Special Master of Compensation—or "Pay Czar"—to oversee employee-specific compensation decisions at 7 large institutions receiving "exceptional assistance" and to establish pay guidelines for institutions receiving assistance under "generally available capital access programs"
Federal reserve "Guidance on sound incentive compensation policies" (October 22, 2009)	• Requires reviews of incentive-compensation programs to evaluate risk-taking incentives • Subjects 28 specific large banks to detailed reviews of systems for incentive compensation, risk management, and corporate governance • Adds reviews of incentive-compensation programs of all banks to regular examinations and incorporates results into supervisory ratings
Dodd-Frank wall street reform and consumer protection act (2010)	• Directs the Federal Reserve to establish formal regulatory standards for pay practices • Rules must specify compensation practices that contribute to unsafe and unsound banking
Federal deposit insurance corporation 12 CFR Part 327: "Incorporating employee compensation criteria into the risk assessment system"	• Proposed adjustment of the FDIC's risk-rating system to "adequately compensate" the Deposit Insurance Fund for "the risks presented by certain compensation programs" • Proposal to set insurance premiums to provide incentives to adopt compensation programs that "align employees' interests with those of. . .other stakeholders, including the FDIC" and "reward employees for focusing on risk management"

Sources: Hill (2009), Mason (2009), FDIC (2010)

interests of shareholders as well as taxpayers. Others, such as Mason (2009), contend that efforts to regulate bank management compensation are at best misguided and at worst counterproductive.

This chapter provides an assessment of empirical and theoretical evaluations of the relationship between the structure of bank management compensation and bank risks and of possible effects of regulations. The following section surveys the current body of evidence regarding the relationship between the structure of bank management compensation and bank risks. The next section reviews theoretical rationales for regulation of bank management compensation. This is followed by an evaluation of the prospects for such regulatory policies to accomplish their intended objectives, both in light of available evidence and given the prevailing state of economic theory. The chapter concludes with a summary of the main conclusions.

Evidence on the Relationship Between Bank Management Compensation and Performance

Before considering theoretical rationales for regulating bankers' pay, it is useful to review evidence in the academic literature. What does this literature suggest about the relationship between the structure of bank management compensation and bank performance?

Table 11.2 lists a number of key academic studies published during the past two decades, discusses the data upon which empirical analyses have based, and provides, and summarizes notable findings. Among these are performance based on stock returns and operating profits (Barro-Barro 1990) and gains from actions such as mergers and acquisitions, with executives at larger banks receiving greater remuneration (Anderson et al. 2004); bank size (Barro-Barro 1990; Bliss-Rosen 2001); other manager characteristics, such as age and experience (Webb 2008); and features of corporate governance, with a lower degree of director independence being associated with higher management pay (Sierra et al. 2006; Cooper 2009).

The studies indicate that the sensitivity of compensation to performance in the banking industry has tended to lag behind the pay-for-performance sensitivity observed in other industries (Becher et al. 2005; Crawford et al. 1995 ; John-Qian 2003). Various factors have influenced the degree of sensitivity of bank manager compensation to observed performance. Several studies find evidence that the pay-performance sensitivity increased during periods of banking deregulation and widespread merger activity (Houston-James 1995). To some extent, the resulting increase in average bank size with the advent of interstate banking contributed to the higher pay-performance sensitivity (Chen et al. 2006; Hubbard-Palia 1995). Nevertheless, a broadening in the range of business lines also clearly played a role in leading to management compensation becoming more sensitive to performance (Harjoto-Mullineaux 2003).

Research clearly indicates that the primary means through which bank managers' pay became more sensitive to the performances of their institutions was via the use of equity-based incentives such as stock options. Some work indicates that pay-performance sensitivities generated by use of equity-based mechanisms tend to be higher for banks with lower ratios of debt to equity and in the presence of more intensive monitoring by debt holders and regulators (John et al. 2010; John-Qian 2003). The ultimate pay-for-performance actions—dismissals of management—occur for reasons that are not too surprising, including poor performance and increased indebtedness (Čihák et al. 2009) and weak performances in deregulated and hence more competitive markets (Hubbard-Palia 1995).

Table 11.2 A summary of key academic studies of the structure of bank management compensation and bank performance

Study	Data	Key findings
Anderson-Becher-Campbell (2004)	Sample of CEO compensation levels at U.S. banks with billions of dollars of assets that were involved in 97 mergers during the 1990s	There was a positive relationship between changes in CEO compensation and expected merger gains and actual changes in operating profits
Barro-Barro (1990)	Panel data for CEO compensation at 83 large U.S. banks during the 1982–1987 interval	The value of the elasticity of compensation with respect to assets was about one-third for new CEOs; changes in compensation reflected performance as measured by stock and accounting returns
Becher-Campbell-Frye (2005)	Sample of 700 U.S. banks and more than 13,000 nonbank firms during the 1992–1999 period	Directors of U.S. banking firms received less equity-based compensation than directors of other firms, but a consequence of banking deregulation was increased use of equity-based compensation with weak evidence of no increase in risk
Bliss-Rosen (2001)	Sample of 32 U.S. bank holding companies that were among the 30 largest in asset size in at least 1 year and existed for at least 5 years within the 1986–1995 sample period	Mergers had a positive effect on compensation mainly via an impact of bank size on compensation; CEOs with more stock-based compensation were less likely to enter into a merger
Bolton-Mehran-Shapiro (2010)	CEO deferred pay, pensions, and wealth at 27 U.S. financial institutions since 2007	Firms with larger shares of CEO deferred compensation experience lower credit default swap spreads, possibly indicating market perceptions of lower risk

Table 11.2 (continued)

Study	Data	Key findings
Chen-Steiner-Whyte (2006)	CEO compensation and other data for 68 U.S. banks and 70 CEOs during the 1992–2000 interval	There was greater use of stock option-based compensation for bank CEOs following deregulation; various measures of risk suggested that the result was increased management risk taking
Chen-Steiner-Whyte (1998)	Rolling samples of about 300 depository institutions per year between 1988 and 1993	There was a negative relationship between the extent of managerial ownership and risk in depository institution returns, particularly for savings institutions
Čihák-Maechler-Schaeck-Stolz (2009)	Banking executive (CEO, CFO, COO) turnovers at U.S. banks over the 1990–2007 period	Senior management dismissals were more likely to occur at banks experiencing greater risk, high losses, lower dividends, greater charter value, and higher levels of subordinated debt, with only limited evidence that forced turnovers resulted in better performance
Cooper (2009)	Data on the composition of boards of directors at 293 U.S. banks in 2006	An increased presence of management insiders on bank boards of directors boosted both director and executive compensation; directors were awarded for high ratings from regulators
Crawford-Ezzell-Miles (1995)	Data on compensation of 239 CEOs at 124 U.S. banks over the 1976–1988 period	Greater pay-performance sensitivity existed in the 1982–1988 subsample than in the pre-deregulation 1976–1981 subsample, particularly at low-capitalized banks
Gropp-Köhler (2010)	Data from 2007 and 2008 for 1,142 banks with more than $1 billion in assets located in 25 OECD countries	Shareholder-controlled banks took on more risk and obtained more government assistance than manager-controlled banks

Table 11.2 (continued)

Study	Data	Key findings
Hagendorff-Vallascas (2010)	Data on relationships between CEO wealth and pay-performance sensitivities inferred from 1,462 bank merger deals between 1993 and 2008	Limited evidence that greater pay-performance sensitivity reduces risk-taking mergers and evidence that CEOs at larger banks engage in riskier mergers
Harjoto-Mullineaux (2003)	CEO compensation at 84 U.S. bank holding companies between 1992 and 2000	There was an increased link between growth options and CEO compensation in the 1990s; greater pay-performance sensitivities at bank holding companies involved in securities underwriting; reduced pay-performance sensitivities as variability of returns increases
Houston-James (1995)	Data on CEO compensation for 134 of the largest U.S. commercial banks between 1980 and 1990	There was a strong positive relationship between equity-based incentives and bank charter value; there was no evidence that CEO compensation policies promoted excessive risk taking during the interval studied
Hubbard-Palia (1995)	CEO compensation at 147 U.S. banks during the 1980–1989 interval	Stronger pay-performance sensitivities were higher in interstate banking markets; CEO turnover increased substantially after deregulation
John-Mehran-Qian (2010)	Data on CEO compensation at 143 U.S. bank holding companies and 997 manufacturing firms during the 1993–2007 period	Consistent with the idea that pay-performance sensitivities respond to risk-shifting incentives, these sensitivities were declining in the bank's leverage ratio and increasing in the intensity of outside monitoring by holders of subordinated debts and regulators
John-Qian (2003)	CEO compensation at 120 U.S. banks between 1992 and 2000	Bank pay-performance sensitivity decreased with higher leverage ratios and greater bank size; bank pay-performance sensitivity was lower than at manufacturing firms
Laeven-Levine (2009)	Data on ownership structures of up to 279 large banks across 48 nations as of the end of 2001	Greater cash-flow rights by larger equity owners are associated with increased bank risk; an increased share of equity rights also is associated risk rising in response to tougher regulation and more access to deposit insurance

Table 11.2 (continued)

Study	Data	Key findings
Minnick-Unal-Yang (2009)	Compensation to CEOs involved in 178 acquisitions by 65 U.S. bank holding companies between 1991 and 2005	CEOs with compensation exhibiting greater pay-performance sensitivity were less likely to engage in value-reducing mergers
Palia-Porter (2004)	1991 CEO compensation data for 102 U.S. bank holding companies	Increases in the salary and bonus components of bank management and compensation packages were associated with lower risk
Saunders-Strock-Travlos (1990)	Data on the composition of shareholders at 38 U.S. bank holding companies between 1978 and 1985	Predominantly stockholder-controlled banks exhibited greater risk-taking behavior than predominantly managerially-controlled banks as a consequence of deregulation
Sierra-Talmor-Wallace (2006)	Compensation data for CEOs of 76 U.S. bank holding companies during the 1992–1997 period	Greater independence of a bank's board of directors from management was associated with stronger performance, lower levels of executive pay, and smaller rates of growth of executive pay
Webb (2008)	Compensation paid to top executives at 107 U.S. banks during the 1992–2004 interval	Pay-performance sensitivity was weakly affected by regulatory monitoring but varies inversely with the age of bank CEOs
Westman (2010)	A sample of 995 bank-year observations from 548 banks in 37 European nations	The extent of bank risk taking increases with a greater degree of interaction between concentration of bank equity ownership and greater availability of particularly generous deposit insurance programs
Williams-Michael-Rao (2008)	Data on stock option compensation paid to CEOs involved in 131 U.S. bank mergers between 1993 and 2002	The use of stock options within bank CEO compensation packages was associated with a higher post-merger level of equity risk

From a regulatory standpoint, a fundamental issue is the relationship between bank management compensation and risk. Some studies find no evidence that greater pay-performance sensitivities are associated with increased risk taking (Becher et al. 2005; Houston-James 1995). One study suggests that increasing the share of management compensation derived from salary and bonuses contributes to reduced bank risk (Palia-Porter 2004). Other research concludes that linking bank executives' pay to equities' values makes it more likely that they will take adverse actions such as potentially value-reducing mergers (Williams-Michael-Rao 2008) or generally engage in greater risk taking (Chen et al. 2006). Others reach contrary conclusions on whether greater pay-performance sensitivity increases the risk of value-reducing mergers (Bliss-Rosen 2001; Minnick et al. 2009, and Hagendorff-Vallascas 2010). In addition, there is a finding of a negative relationship between greater pay-performance sensitivity and variability of returns (Harjoto-Mullineaux 2003). There is also evidence that risk-taking behavior depends on the degree of management control generally exercised by equity holders (Saunders et al. 1990; Gropp-Köhler 2010) and by a few large equity holders (Laeven-Levine 2009; Westman 2010) and on whether management compensation is deferred (Bolton et al. 2010).

On net, the empirical literature indicates an increased dependence of bank management compensation on equity returns since the movement toward banking deregulation began in the 1980s. The literature yields more mixed conclusions, however, about whether this shift contributed to greater bank management risk-taking behavior. The academic literature's net conclusion is that the relationship between the structure of bank executive pay packages and management risk taking ultimately hinges on various other factors that differ across countries and that likely differ across individual institutions within any given nation (see Craig (2004) for a similar judgment).

Bank Management Compensation, Risk, and Regulation: Theory

There have been a limited number of theoretical analyses of the relationship among bank management compensation, risk, and a possible role for regulation. As discussed by Kay and Van Putten (2007), during the 1990s and early 2000s, companies made greater use of options in management compensation packages, and some of the studies listed in Table 11.2 document the utilization of options in bank manager contracts. Does incorporating options payments into compensation arrangements tend to make managers more or less averse to risk? The work of Ross (2004), which focuses on the general question of how payment of options to agents affects their risk aversion, suggests that the answer to this question is theoretically ambiguous. Ross finds that an options-based compensation package aimed at inducing an agent to operate along the risk-averse portion of the agent's preference function will, other things being equal, tend to achieve this aim. The difficulty is that other things are not equal, both because of slippage in the linkage from compensation to preferences and because of wealth effects caused by the ways in which compensation can enlarge or contract the magnitude of a marginal gamble on risk. Consequently, Ross concludes that the risk effects of options-based compensation packages cannot readily be determined from a purely theoretical perspective.

To examine the nature of the tension between the interests of holders of equity and debts in a more narrow setting relating to the structure of bank management compensation, Schreiber (1997) considers a framework in which equity holders and managers each hold call options on portions of the distribution of the value of a bank's risky assets net of the value of its liabilities over states of the world in which their net value is positive. A deposit insurer writes a call option on the portion corresponding to states in which the net value of assets in relation to liabilities is negative.

Schreiber studies settings in which the bank insurer is or is not aware of the bank's risk level when setting the bank's deposit insurance premium. In addition, a bank manager's salary is either predetermined or supplemented by a bonus conditioned on the bank's assets. When the deposit insurer knows the bank's risk level in advance of determining the deposit insurance premium, the setting of an actuarially fair premium that results means that the gross amount of funds available to be split between owners and the manager (whether or not a bonus is included) will be fixed and unrelated to risk. Owners will tend to prefer greater risk that pushes up the value of equity in good states of the world while transferring a large portion of risk to the deposit insurer in bad states, while the manager will prefer less risk. When the deposit insurer is unaware of the bank's overall risk prior to determining the insurance premium, however, the level of the premium will not be at the actuarially fair value, so the total pool of funds that will be available for splitting between owners and the manager will vary with risk.

Schreiber conducts simulations indicating, under this form of informational asymmetry, that a manager receiving a fixed salary prefers more risk in order to generate a higher salary up to a certain point, beyond which greater risk is less preferred by the manager. When the manager receives a bonus in this asymmetric-information situation, however, the manager's attitude toward risk matches the attitude of owners, resulting in a preference for more risk on the part of the manager.

In Schreiber's analysis, deposit insurance premiums are contingent on a bank's risk level but are not directly linked to the structure of the bank's management compensation package. The theoretical analysis provided by John et al. (2000) suggests a motivation for a deposit insurer and regulator to explicitly tie deposit insurance premiums to the bank's management compensation structure. John et al. consider a setting in which a bank with fixed equity (E) initially issues a fixed amount of deposits (D). Prior to allocating these funds to its asset portfolio, the bank pays a deposit rate premium π to a government agency that seeks to raise sufficient funds, on average, to protect the bank's depositors against realized outcomes in which the bank cannot honor payment guarantees to depositors. In advance of the bank's asset allocation choice, all banks contracts are written and priced in the market, so the deposit rate and the price of the bank's equity are determined.

To contemplate the bank's asset decision within the John et al. framework, let's consider a diagrammatic representation of their analysis. In Fig. 11.1, the bank can choose between either a risky asset that yields either a high (H) value or a low (L) value, or a "safe" asset that offers zero risk but yields a return with nonnegative net present value between H and L. There is a fixed probability of obtaining the high return H on the risky asset, with one less this probability being the probability of realizing the lower return L, and this probability is uniformly distributed between 0 and 1. The bank can also allocate its assets to combinations of the safe and risky assets, resulting in a continuum of feasible investment policies for the bank along the interval between 0 and 1 along the horizontal axes in the figure. Panel (a), which is drawn under the assumption that the certain return on the safe asset is less than the average return on the risky asset, depicts ranges of resulting expected values of the bank's end-of-period cash flows associated with alternative investment policies. Investment policy 1 corresponds to holding all safe assets, which yields the

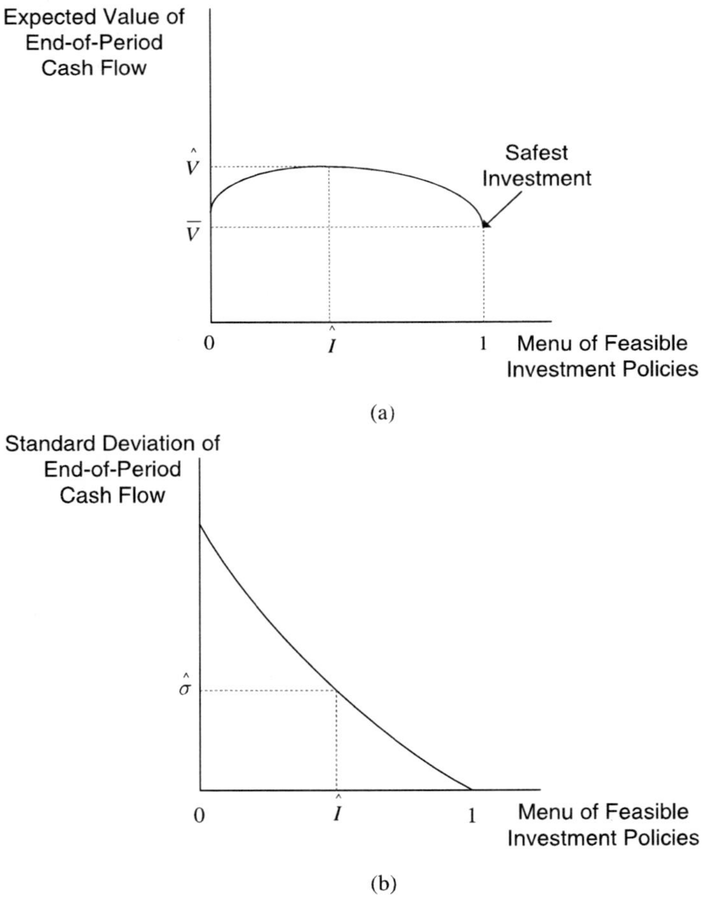

Fig. 11.1 Maximized expected value and standard deviation of a bank's cash

certain terminal cash flow $\overline{V}$, while investment policy 0 is associated with holding all risky assets.

Panel (b) of Fig. 11.1 depicts the standard deviations corresponding to the alternative investment policies, with bank investment policy 1 yielding a standard deviation of terminal cash flows equal to zero and investment policy 0 yielding the highest standard deviation among feasible investment policies.

John et al. assume that the bank's objective is to maximize the expected value of its end-of-period cash flows. In panel (a) of Fig. 11.1, the mix of safe and risky assets associated with attaining this objective is denoted as investment policy $\hat{I}$. Given the assumption that a uniform distribution governs the return on the risky investment, this optimal investment policy corresponds to the probability associated with receiving the high return on the risky asset. The investment policy $\hat{I}$ yields the highest feasible expected terminal cash flow $\hat{V}$ given the bank's asset mix. In panel (b), the resulting standard deviation of the bank's end-of-period cash flow is denoted $\hat{\sigma}$.

John et al. also assume that at the end of the period, the bank must make a promised fixed payment F to its depositors—presumably equal to D plus interest payments at the market rate of interest—and that the value of F exceeds the value of L. This means that if the bank holds a sufficiently large mix of its asset portfolio as risky assets, there is the potential for the expected value of its end-of-period cash flow to be less than what the bank owes depositors. Thus, the bank potentially can fail. To protect against this possibility, the deposit insurer would have to set the deposit insurance premium at an actuarially fair value, $\hat{\pi}$, that would cover expected losses to the bank given the investment policy $\hat{I}$.

John et al. consider a situation in which the bank possesses inside information about the probability governing the return on the risky asset. To simplify, they assume that the bank's managers can select this probability—that is, select a particular risky asset possessing this probability—contingent on other information available to them. To contemplate the complications this possibility raises, suppose that Fig. 11.1 applies to a setting in which the bank possesses no inside information, so that the probability governing the returns on the risky assets is known to everyone. Consequently, the investment policy $\hat{I}$ displayed in Fig. 11.1 and the resulting expected value of and standard deviation of the terminal cash flows given by $\hat{V}$ and $\hat{\sigma}$ can be viewed as benchmarks for evaluating the implications of possession of inside information by the bank.

Figure 11.2 explains the implications of inside information and evaluates the implications of bank capital regulation and fair-value deposit insurance pricing in John et al.'s model. The bank's managers select an investment policy in light of the known payment obligation to depositors. This investment policy is given by $I(F)$ in Fig. 11.2. Because $I(F) < \hat{I}$, the bank's managers select riskier assets—that is, assets with a lower probability of yielding the high return H and hence a higher probability of yielding the low return L. The bank's managers do so because this choice yields a higher expected residual payoff—over and above the amount F owed to depositors out of the bank's overall expected end-of-period cash flow—to holders of the bank's equity.

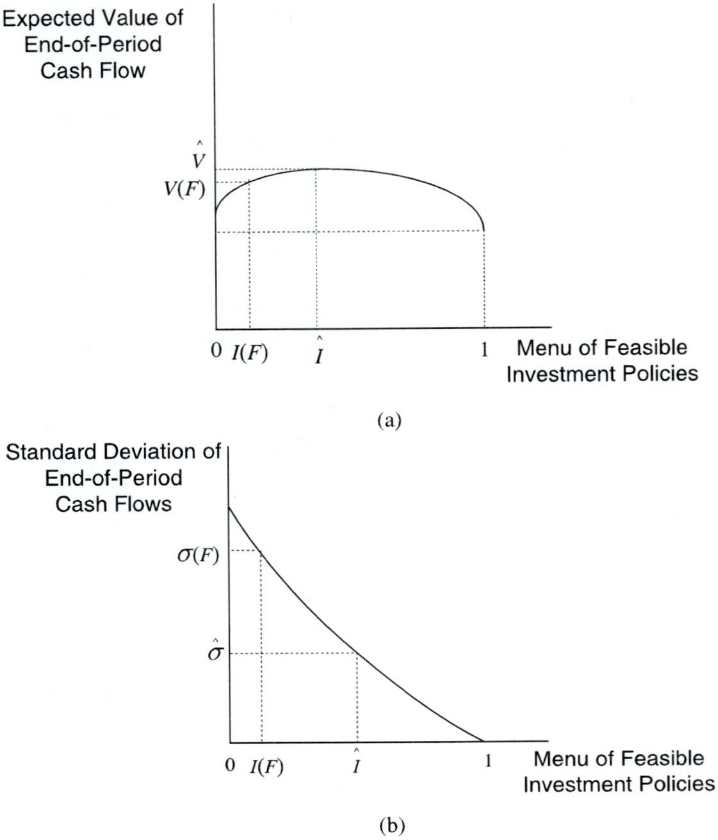

Fig. 11.2 Bank risk shifting with inside information and a fixed payment owed to depositors

The expected end-of-period cash flow when the bank's managers have inside information is $V(F)$, which as shown in panel (a) of Fig. 11.2 is less than $\hat{V}$, and standard deviation of the bank's end-of-period cash flow is $\sigma(F)$, which as shown in panel (b) is smaller than $\hat{\sigma}$. Thus, the simultaneous presence of deposit insurance and inside information on the part of the bank's managers induces the managers to opt for a riskier asset mix in pursuit of higher potential returns for shareholders facing the outside debt to depositors F. Deposit insurance, therefore, creates a moral hazard problem—an incentive for the bank's managers possessing inside information about the distribution of asset risks to choose a riskier portfolio and to shift the higher risks to the deposit insurer.

John et al. point out that one way to try to partially offset this risk-shifting incentive of deposit insurance is to engage in capital regulation. In their model, with the overall size of the bank's liabilities fixed at $D + E$, ex ante, this can be done by requiring a higher value of E, thereby reducing D and hence the contracted value of F. The effect of an exogenous reduction in F, they demonstrate, would be to raise the value of $I(F)$ in Fig. 11.2, thereby boosting the expected value of the bank's terminal cash flow closer to $\hat{V}$ and reducing the standard deviation nearer to $\hat{\sigma}$.

With such a capital requirement in force, John et al. demonstrate, an actuarially fair deposit insurance premium covering the expected deposit insurance payout, given the riskier investment policy$I(F)$ can be calculated. Nevertheless, the premium rate is calculated *given* this risk-shifting investment policy—and hence is a function of F, or $\pi(F)$. The setting of this actuarially fair premium does nothing, therefore, to offset the moral hazard problem of deposit insurance, so it will still be the case that $V(F) < \hat{V}$ and that $\sigma(F) > \hat{\sigma}$. Bank equity owners will still prefer the risk-shifting investment policy $I(F)$ that yields these outcomes, and as long as the bank managers' incentives are aligned with those of the equity owners, the managers will deliver this policy.

To induce bank managers to opt for the investment policy $\hat{I}$ —that is, to induce bank managers to select the same asset allocation they would make if they did not possess inside information—John et al. propose relating the deposit insurance premium charged to the bank to the structure of compensation paid to its managers. They consider management compensation structure depicted in Fig. 11.3. Up to the point at which the bank's end-of-period cash flow is less than the fixed payment F due depositors, the bank's managers receive a fixed salary, S. As remuneration for generating a cash flow sufficiently high to cover F, the managers can earn a bonus as high as the value B. If the terminal cash flow exceeds the sum of the salary and the bonus, $S + B$, then the managers receive a fraction e of the resulting addition to stockholders' equity.

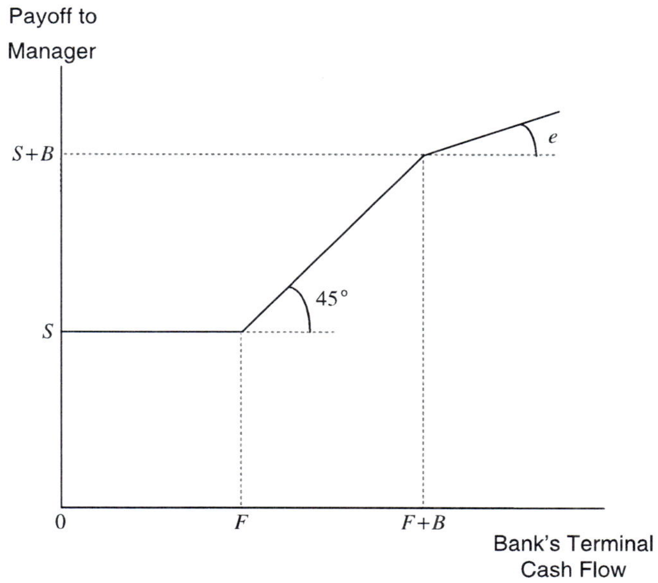

Fig. 11.3 Proposed structure of bank management compensation

Under John et al.'s proposed deposit insurance policy, the premium rate selected by the deposit insurer is set with an aim to inducing the bank's equity owners to select a combination of contract terms involving S, B, and e consistent with management replication of the investment policy $\hat{I}$. In the context of their specific framework, John et al. calculate that a bank management compensation structure consistent with this outcome satisfies the condition $\hat{B} = \frac{\hat{e}}{(1-\hat{e})}(F - L)$. This condition implies that larger shares of additional returns to equity holders generated by terminal cash values over and above the fixed payment to depositors and fixed manager bonus should accompany a value of a higher manager bonus. Suppose that the condition above is satisfied and then the bonus is decreased to a value, $\hat{B}'$, while $\hat{e}$ is held unchanged. Then the bonus is "too low," which gives the manager an incentive to opt for a riskier investment policy; reducing $\hat{e}$ to a smaller value thereby will realign the manager toward a less risky investment policy that is more likely to ensure a terminal cash flow sufficient to cover both the depositor payment and the smaller bonus.

A diagrammatic depiction of the condition $\hat{B} = \frac{\hat{e}}{(1-\hat{e})}(F - L)$ for generating management replication of the investment policy $\hat{I}$ is displayed in Fig. 11.4. The figure also depicts a specific point along this locus of $\hat{B}$-$\hat{e}$ combinations in which $\hat{e}$ is set equal to ½, so that equity owners grant managers a 50 percent share of their gross equity return. This compensation arrangement aligns the managers' incentives closely with their own preferences. In this case, $\frac{\hat{e}}{(1-\hat{e})} = 1$, so the condition requires that the bonus be set at the value $\hat{B} = F - L$. Thus, if the bank's assets yield the low return L, the bank's managers have an incentive to generate a sufficient terminal cash flow to pay off depositors and cover their own bonus payment before generating additional returns for equity holders.

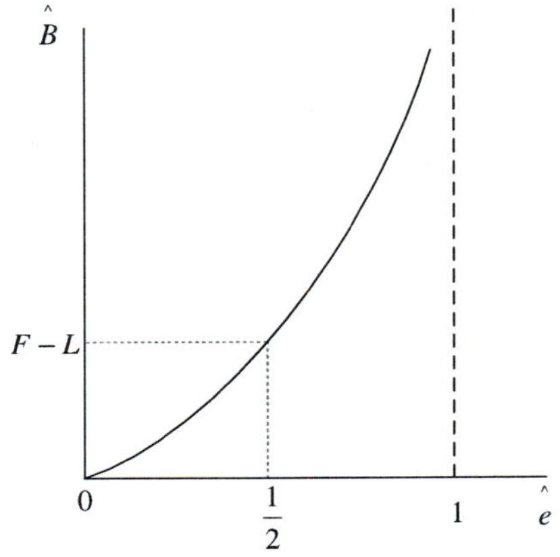

Fig. 11.4 Management compensation terms to eliminate bank risk shifting

Interestingly, John et al.'s compensation arrangement is comparable to one proposed by Raviv and Landskroner (2009), which analogously includes a fixed payment to be paid to bank managers for maintaining solvency supplemented by an options-based form of compensation. Raviv and Landskroner add to these components of their proposed compensation package a third, fixed component that would be payable if the value of the bank's assets at maturity remains between two upper thresholds. Raviv and Landskroner add this additional component to encourage an "interior level of volatility" between the extremes associated with "a long 'cash or nothing' call option... that pays a fixed amount of money at maturity if the value of assets is above some upper threshold and a short position in a similar option with a higher strike price" (Raviv and Landskroner, p. 6). Raviv and Landskroner do not discuss their proposal in the context of the structure of deposit insurance premiums, but their suggested policy is cited within the FDIC's (2010) recent proposal.

Regulation of Bank Management Compensation: An Evaluation

Does the academic literature in economics and finance support actual and proposed regulation of the structure of bank management compensation? From an empirical standpoint, the answer is ambiguous. There is some evidence that making bank executives' pay more closely attuned to shareholder interests may contribute to greater risk taking as well as increased risk shifting onto bondholders and taxpayers. There is also some evidence against this conclusion, however. Consequently, the available empirical evidence fails to provide strong support for government management-compensation regulation aimed at limiting bank risk-taking behavior.

What guidance does theory offer? At the most basic level, economic theory identifies three potential pitfalls of regulations aimed specifically at restraining bank management compensation. One pitfall is that explicit ceilings that constrain executive pay below market clearing levels—which already show signs of adjusting to altered perceptions of risk (see, for instance, Davis (2010))—are likely to prove to be counterproductive in relation to the overriding objective of producing a safe and sound banking industry. As any first-year economics student learns, establishing a ceiling wage rate beneath the equilibrium level paid to suppliers of labor of a particular skill causes employers to desire to obtain more units of labor at the ceiling wage. Such a policy simultaneously induces a reduction in the quantity of labor supplied at the lower wage rate. The consequence is a shortage in the market for labor possessing the particular skill utilized by the industry in question. In the case of the banking industry, there would be a shortage of labor possessing talents in managing risks.

The second pitfall is the danger of assuming that the effects of bank pay regulation can be evaluated without reference to the rest of the economy. A shortage of executive talent would not result because a number of people possessing risk management skills would not usefully employ them. Instead, a number of these people would opt to provide those skills to other industries, including firms in other financial industries as well as companies in nonfinancial industries seeking financial officers that would be able to offer higher, unregulated wages. Of course, these nonbanking industries would be willing to hire only skilled individuals offering levels of productivity per unit of labor commensurate with the higher rates of compensation they would pay. Thus, a predictable effect of restraining executive compensation in the banking industry to a "below market" level would be the departure of the most productive managers to other industries. Among these executives would be people with the best skills in managing risks. The loss of this talent pool would hardly promote improved risk management capabilities within the banking industry.

The third pitfall is a failure to account for feedback effects of wage regulations. The potential for a labor shortage within the management ranks and the impending loss of some of the most talented managers to other industries would give banking firms a strong incentive to engage in regulatory avoidance behaviors. Undoubtedly, some institutions likely would respond to regulations on explicit executive compensation by developing implicit forms of compensation—improved benefit packages and miscellaneous forms of executive "perks"—not covered by laws or regulatory rules. Other banks might respond by leaving the "banking" business and reconstituting themselves as an alternative form of uninsured financial institution not subject to compensation restrictions.

Of course, economic staffs of bank supervisory agencies are well aware of these basic economic pitfalls associated with pay restrictions that might effectively impose ceilings on managers' wages. This recognition is surely the reason that bank regulators are always careful to state that, aside from the statutory restrictions imposed on a few bailout recipients by the Economic Stabilization Act of 2008 (see Table 11.1), there is no intent to place arbitrary "caps" on bankers' pay. Nevertheless, even rules intended to subtly redistribute the forms of compensation received by bank executives ultimately could under some circumstances have the unintended effect of pushing allowed rates of pay beneath levels consistent with market wage rates for skilled financial managers.

For the sake of argument, however, suppose that regulations of bankers' pay could indeed be constructed in some way that ensures that on average there would only be a *redistribution* of the aggregate rate of managerial compensation without restraining the *overall* compensation rate below the equilibrium level. Such a policy outcome probably is the implicit intent of recent guidelines issued by the Federal Reserve and the FDIC's current proposal to condition a bank's deposit insurance premium rate on the bank's managerial compensation structure. Could the FDIC counter moral-hazard-based risk shifting by charging lower premiums to banks adopting bonus-shares arrangements—potentially consistent with a general rule combining bonuses and shares of returns as in Johns et al.-type rule or with a specific multipart compensation package such as the one proposed by Raviv and Landskroner? It is not apparent that the answer to this question is yes. One difficulty is that the Johns et al. deposit-rate-setting rule is derived under several constraining assumptions:

(a) *The payment owed to insured depositors (F) is fixed.* Flannery (1982) and others have provided evidence that retail deposits are quasi-fixed factors of production, suggesting that expenses associated with these deposits are indeed fixed. Nevertheless, recent expansions in deposit insurance coverage have encompassed many negotiable deposit instruments with variable payments determined on a continuous basis in the money markets. In these deposit markets, one key determinant of these variable payments is the demand for deposits by banks, implying that such payments in fact vary endogenously alongside bank decision making. It is unclear how incorporating endogeneity of payments to depositors would affect a Johns et al.-style compensation-structure-based rule for setting deposit insurance premiums.

(b) *The bank optimizes only on the asset side of the balance sheet.* Since early in the literature on bank behavior dating back to Klein's (1971) analysis (see VanHoose (2010, Chapter 3) for a recent review), it has been understood that the assumption that there is no interdependence of asset and liability decisions—commonly called the assumption of portfolio separation—can generate artificially narrow conclusions about the bank decision-making process. Sealey (1985) showed that three conditions must be met for portfolio separation to hold: (a) shareholder unanimity regarding portfolio decisions, (b) separability of the bank's resource cost function, and (c) access by the bank to a market for funds with equal ex post borrowing and lending rates. Many applications of financial theory to the banking firm—including the analysis of John et al.—rely explicitly or implicitly on the assumption of portfolio separation. Nevertheless, at best the empirical evidence regarding its real-world applicability is mixed; see, for instance, Elyasiani et al. (1995). Relaxing the assumption of portfolio separation undoubtedly would greatly alter the specific conclusions obtained by John et al. and certainly would considerably complicate the structure of the optimal compensation arrangement forthcoming from their analysis.

(c) *Bank equity is fixed.* There are two potential problems associated with John et al.'s assumption that equity is exogenous. The first possible difficulty relates to their analysis of the interplay between capital regulation and the setting of deposit insurance premiums. They envision capital regulation as requiring the assumed exogenous level of deposits to be lower relative to equity, which then generates lower asset risk in their model. This interpretation of capital regulation, however, is inconsistent with forms of capital regulation utilized under Basel I and II, in which capital requirements relate the required equity capital to loans and other risk-based assets. Their analysis of joint determination of capital regulation and deposit insurance premiums would be considerably altered if a more realistic capital-regulation setting were contemplated. The second possible problem amounts to a reformulated perspective on point b above. In the event of interdependence between the asset and liability side of the bank's balance sheet—and Basel-style capital regulation forces such interdependence even if the conditions identified by Sealey hold true—then endogeneity involving loans and bank capital would yield a wider set of margins along which a bank must optimize. Whether the analysis of John et al. would generalize to an environment with interdependence between bank loans and equity also is unclear.

(d) *Equity Holders Care Only about the Expected Value of Cash Flows.* The John et al. analysis presumes unanimity of equity holders in seeking to maximize the expected value of cash flows. A majority concern among shareholders about the standard deviation of their share of cash flows in John et al.'s framework undoubtedly would result in outcomes more attuned to the interests of risk-averse regulators, even in the presence of deposit insurance, and hence reduced effects of implicit regulation of management pay structure via settings of deposit insurance. Indeed, it is conceivable that extending John et al.'s model to include risk aversion on the part of a sufficient fraction of shareholders could yield diminishing benefits to such regulation as the degree of risk aversion rises.

Thus, potential social benefits of regulations on bank management compensation are likely to be ambiguous even for a subtly crafted effort to alter the distributional structure of pay packages. Even if regulations might succeed in avoiding damaging resource allocation effects while redistributing sources of compensation in ways aimed at preventing undesired risk shifting owing to the moral hazard owing to deposit insurance, the ultimate impacts of such rules remain uncertain. Within sufficiently constrained theoretical frameworks, such regulations potentially could alter risk-shifting incentives in ways that would enhance bank safety and soundness. If real-world elements from which previous academic analyses have abstracted were taken into account, however, it is not apparent that proposed restrictions on bank pay practices would necessarily accomplish this objective.

Conclusion

Deposit insurance structured without appropriate consideration of risks magnifies shareholders' incentives to shift risks onto debt holders. In theory, tying management compensation to equity returns could increase the extent to which banks shift risks to bond holders and depositors—and consequently to deposit insurers. These considerations provide motivation for recent actual and proposed government restrictions on bank management compensation.

Nevertheless, the case for regulating bankers' pay is not very strong. Empirical findings to date provide mixed conclusions regarding the relationship between the structure of bank management compensation and risk-taking behavior. Although there has been an increase in the sensitivity of bank managers' pay to performance in recent years, there is very mixed evidence regarding the effect of this development on banks' risk-taking behavior. Furthermore, research suggests that effects of the relative shares of shareholders, debt holders, and managers in bank risk-taking decisions depend considerably on factors such as the magnitude of the moral hazard problem created by deposit insurance and the governance structure in place at banks. These results suggest that a variety of factors that heretofore have not been studied carefully likely influence how greater sensitivity of managers' pay to performance affects bank risk-taking behavior.

Despite the uncertain evidence regarding the relationship between bank management compensation and risk, the U.S. government has subjected the pay of executives at a few banks accepting the most substantial government bailouts to explicit caps. In addition, the government has issued guidelines for management compensation at all other banks accepting assistance. Furthermore, the Federal Reserve has incorporated analysis of management compensation programs into its supervisory examination process (see, for instance, Hopkins 2010) and under pending legislation could be required to establish explicit standards for evaluating such programs. In response, some banks have shifted toward greater emphasis on salary over bonuses in management-compensation package—even though some of the theoretical contributions reviewed above that support the idea of factoring bankers' pay into regulations suggest that certain types of bonus packages can contribute to lower risk. Finally, the Federal Deposit Insurance Corporation has proposed conditioning deposit insurance premiums on the structure of bank management compensation, both to take into account the risk implications of alternative pay plans and to try to influence the pay structures that banks select so as reduce risks.

Even from a purely theoretical standpoint, however, the risk implications of regulatory and supervisory involvement in bank management compensation are debatable. Theoretical research suggests that the effects of performance-based pay on risk depend on a number of factors, such as the relationship between managers' preferences regarding compensation and risk, the strength of wealth effects, and the nature of informational asymmetries faced by shareholders, debt holders, and regulators. Conditioning deposit insurance premiums on a bank's pay structure might alter risk-shifting incentives created by moral hazard arising from deposit insurance. Nevertheless, to date theoretical predictions about the effects of this policy proposal potentially hinge on a number of simplifying assumptions of questionable validity.

Perhaps the most important difficulty, however, is that any restriction likely would push overall compensation levels for bank executives below market levels. Effective ceilings on bankers' pay would push the quantity of executive talent demanded by banks above the quantity supplied, resulting in a shortage of qualified managers. The reduction in the pool of available executive talent if this eventuality were to arise likely would contribute to higher rather than lower risks in the banking industry.

References

Adler J (2010a) FDIC board split on exec pay plan. American Banker, 13 Jan

Adler J (2010b) FDIC plan to link premiums to compensation already under fire. American Banker, 8 Jan

Anderson C, Becher D, Campbell T II (2004) Bank mergers, the market for bank CEOs, and managerial incentives. J Financ Intermediation 13:6–27

Ang J, Lauterbach B, Schreiber B (2001) Internal monitoring, regulation, and compensation of top executives in banks. Int Rev Econ Finance 10:325–335

Barro J, Barro R (1990) Pay, performance, and turnover of bank CEOs. J Labor Econ 8:448–481

Becher D, Campbell T II, Frye M (2005) Incentive compensation for bank directors: the impact of deregulation. J Bus 78:1753–1777
Bliss R, Rosen R (2001) CEO compensation and bank mergers. J Financ Econ 61:107–138
Bolton P, Mehran H, Shapiro J (2010) Executive compensation and risk taking, Columbia University, Federal Reserve Bank of New York, and University of Oxford, 27 May
Chen C, Steiner T, Whyte AM (2006) Does stock option-based executive compensation induce risk-taking? An analysis of the banking industry. J Bank Finance 30:915–945
Chen C, Steiner T, Whyte AM (1998) Risk-taking behavior and management ownership in depository institutions. J Financ Res 21:1–16
Čihák M, Maichler A, Schaeck K, Stolz S (2009) Who disciplines bank managers? IMF Working Paper WP/09/272, Dec
Cooper EW (2009) Monitoring and governance of private banks. Q Rev Econ Finance 49:253–264
Craig V (2004) The changing corporate governance environment: implications for the banking industry. FDIC Bank Rev 16:121–135
Crawford A, Ezzell J, Miles J (1995) Bank CEO pay-performance relations and the effects of deregulation. J Bus 68:231–256
Crittenden M (2010) FDIC moves to tie fees to bank pay. Wall St J 13 Jan
Davis P (2010) Seeking new balance on pay policies. American Banker, 5 Apr
Demirgüç-Kunt A, Kane E, Laeven L (2008) Deposit insurance design and implementation: Policy lessons from research and practice. In: Demirgüç-Kunt A, Kane E, Laeven L (eds) Deposit insurance around the world. MIT Press, Cambridge, pp 3–26
Elyasiani E, Kopecky K, VanHoose D (1995) Costs of adjustment, portfolio separation, and the dynamic behavior of bank loans and deposits. J Money Credit Bank 27:955–974
Federal Deposit Insurance Corporation (2010) Incorporating employee compensation criteria into the risk assessment system. Advance Notice of Proposed Rulemaking, 12 CFR Part 327, 12 Jan
Flannery M (1982) Retail bank deposits as quasi-fixed factors of production. Am Econ Rev 72:527–526
Grant CT, Grant G (2008) Can regulations curb excessive executive pay? Strateg Finance (September):31–39
Grocer S (2010) Banks set for record pay, Wall St J 16 Jan
Gropp R, Köhler M (2010) Bank owners or bank managers: who is keen on risk? Evidence from the financial crisis, Center for European Economic Research Discussion Paper No. 10-013, Feb
Hagendorff J, Vallascas F (2010) CEO pay incentives and risk-taking: evidence from bank acquisitions, 31 Mar. Available at SSRN: http://ssrn.com/abstract=1625689
Harjoto M, Mullineaux D (2003) CEO compensation and the transformation of banking. J Financ Res 26:341–354
Hill J (2009) New trends in the regulation of executive remuneration. Working Paper, Vanderbilt Law School
Hopkins C (2010) Fed finds flaws in big banks' pay packages. American Banker 22 June
Houston J, James C (1995) CEO compensation and bank risk: is compensation in banking structured to promote risk taking? J Monet Econ 36:405–431
Hubbard RG, Palia D (1995) Executive pay and performance: Evidence from the U.S. banking industry. J Financ Econ 39:105–130
John K, Mehran H, Qian Y (2010) Outside monitoring and CEO compensation in the banking industry. J Corp Finance 16:383–399
John K, Qian Y (2003) Incentive features in CEO compensation in the banking industry, Federal Reserve Bank of New York Economic. Policy Rev (April) 9:109–121
John K, Saunders A, Senbet L (2000) A theory of bank regulation and management compensation. Rev Financ Stud 13:95–125
John K, Saunders A, Senbet L (1995) Perspectives on bank capital regulation and managerial compensation. J Bank Finance 19:735–737
Kay I, Van Putten S (2007) Myths and realities of executive pay. Cambridge University Press, Cambridge, MA

Klein M (1971) A theory of the banking firm. J Money Credit Bank 3:205–218
Laeven L, Levine R (2009) Bank governance, regulation, and risk taking. J Financ Econ 93: 259–275
Macey J, O'Hara M (2003) The corporate governance of banks, Federal Reserve Bank of New York. Econ Policy Rev 16:91–107
Mason D (2009) Why government control of bank salaries will hurt, not help, the economy. Backgrounder, Heritage Foundation, No. 2336, 4 Nov
Minnick K, Unal H, Yang L (2009) Pay for performance? CEO compensation and acquirer returns in BHCs, FDIC Center for Financial Research Working Paper No. 2009-03, Dec
Palia D, Porter R (2004) The impact of capital requirements and managerial compensation on bank charter value. Rev Quant Finance Account 23:191–206
Raviv A, Landskroner Y (2009) The 2007–2009 financial crisis and executive compensation: analysis and a proposal for a novel structure. Working Paper, New York University, 15 June
Ross S (2004) Compensation, incentives, and the duality of risk aversion and riskiness. J Finance 59:207–225
Saunders A, Strock E, Travlos NG (1990) Ownership structure, deregulation, and bank risk taking. J Finance 45(2):643–654
Schreiber B (1997) The owner-manager conflict in insured banks: Predetermined salary versus bonus payments. J Financ Serv Res 12:303–326
Sealey CW Jr (1985) Portfolio separation for stockholder-owned depository financial intermediaries. J Bank Finance 9:477–490
Sierra G, Talmor E, Wallace J (2006) An examination of multiple governance forces within bank holding companies. J Financ Serv Res 29:105–123
VanHoose D (2010) The industrial organization of banking: bank behavior, market structure, and regulation. Springer, Heidelberg
Webb E (2008) Regulator scrutiny and bank CEO incentives. J Financ Serv Res 33:5–20
Westman H (2010) The role of ownership structure and regulatory environment in bank corporate governance. Working Paper, Hanken School of Economics
Williams M, Michael T, Rao R (2008) Bank mergers, equity risk incentives, and CEO stock options. Managerial Finance 34:316–327

Part IV
Legislation and Implications: The View from the Top

Chapter 12
The Lure of Leveraging: Wall Street, Congress, and the Invisible Government

James A. Leach

It is my intent to review the legislative framework of financial regulation, assess public and private sector accountability for the economic trauma loosed in 2008, and appraise the legislative aftermath.[1] My thesis is that the economy and the financial security of the country were unnecessarily jeopardized by the unchecked greed of a few; that, at critical moments, politics and ideology dominated regulatory decision making; that the regulators, the invisible government, allowed excess leveraging out of excess confidence in risk-based mathematical modeling; that a conflicted Congress emboldened risk taking at Fannie Mae and Freddie Mac; and that problems in commercial bank regulation related less to what Congress did than what it didn't do. As both a participant and observer in the legislative process, I have designed this review in part as a chronicle of Congressional interactions between the parties and with the Executive branch, and in part as a take on regulation itself. Accordingly, I apologize for presumptuous overuse of the "I" word and the presentation of an unavoidable personal perspective.

The Pre-2010 Framework of Financial Regulation

Let me begin with a counterintuitive observation. The institutional framework of our financial regulatory system—the mix of federal and state regulatory bodies—has

J.A. Leach (✉)
National Endowment for the Humanities, Washington, DC, USA
e-mail: jleach@neh.gov

This chapter also appeared as Networks Financial Institute *Policy Brief* 2010-PB-04.

[1] A former 15-term Congressman, Leach chaired the Banking and Financial Services Committee from 1995 to 2000. Currently he is chairman of the National Endowment for the Humanities. The views expressed are of the author and are not to be construed as an official reflection of the views of the National Endowment for the Humanities or the United States Government. The perspective taken is based in part on two addresses the author delivered, one to a conference on "Regional and National Financial Crises: Roots, Results and Responses," held at the Policy Research Institute at the Woodrow Wilson School at Princeton University on November 7, 2008, and one prepared for the "Symposium on Shaping Global Financial Reform," sponsored by the Bretton Woods Committee and the Boston University School of Law, held in Washington, DC, on April 22, 2009.

J.A. Tatom (ed.), *Financial Market Regulation*, DOI 10.1007/978-1-4419-6637-7_12,

changed little in the past half century. Markets have changed dramatically but the regulatory governance structure has not. The Gramm-Leach-Bliley Act of 1999 (GLBA), for instance, changed part of the competitive but little of the regulatory framework of the Glass Steagall Act, which dates to the early years of the Great Depression. Indeed, it added to, rather than subtracted from, federal oversight authority over fast-changing markets.

By background, Glass Steagall and the Bank Holding Company Act had defined three cocoons of financial activity—commercial banking, investment banking, and insurance. While investment banks were allowed under these two acts to combine and compete against insurance companies, commercial banks were not allowed to engage in investment banking or insurance underwriting. What GLBA authorized was increased competition within the financial community with the maintenance of historically tested functional regulation. Banking activities in newly authorized multipurpose financial companies would be regulated by state and federal banking authorities, securities functions by state and federal securities commissions, and insurance by state insurance departments.

The GLBA restructured the competitive framework to recognize technological changes in the economy and reflect market place changes that had taken place, including changes in state law and federal rule making.

During the twentieth century, the most profound competitive changes in the banking arena related to the manner Americans chose to save and invest. At the beginning of the century, three fourths of American savings were managed by commercial banks. By the century's end, only one quarter of the saved dollar entered the banking system, jeopardizing in many parts of the country its capacity to tap community savings to reinvest in the community itself.

Driving consensus in the 1990 s on the need for a statutory review of competitive legal constraints in the financial industry was a graduated series of preemptive determinations of the Treasury Department's Office of the Comptroller of the Currency (OCC) allowing national banks to engage in aspects of investment banking. In a cumulative manner, these OCC determinations coupled with Federal Reserve regulatory approvals of various activities often described in the legal rubric "incidental to banking" had significantly begun to breach Glass Steagall's competitive walls. These unilateral authorities and the manner in which they were structured were seen as inducements to conflicts of interest within banks, particularly national banks. They were also competitively disadvantageous to other parts of the financial industry: securities and insurance firms and community banks. Hence, Congress chose to adopt a new approach designed to advance competitive equality for each part of the financial industry and provide an umbrella of equalitarian regulation.

Contrary to popular assumption, Glass Steagall was modified rather than repealed. Much remained intact. Restrictions, for instance, on investment banks accepting deposits and commercial banks investing in commercial activities were maintained. And what was then considered a loophole in law, a provision that allowed commercial firms to own unitary thrifts, was closed with passage of GLBA.

The most controversial provision under consideration during the GLBA debate was whether banks or bank holding companies could merge with commercial companies—i.e., whether a Citicorp could merge with a Wal-Mart or Microsoft or

Enron. If this feature of federal law had been removed, enormous new incentives would have been given to the biggest American banks, or the industrial firms that would inevitably come to control them, to leverage depositor dollars to buy corporate assets rather than lend to American families and job-making entrepreneurs. The mission of banking would have been transformed from stimulating innovation and entrepreneurship to precipitating asset conglomeration, and the American ideal would have shifted from spreading opportunity to concentrating wealth in fewer hands.

In the end, as chairman of the House Banking Committee, I was barely able to keep this radical breach of the wall between banking and commerce from occurring. But it was a close call. Congressional leadership of both parties in both bodies largely supported this change, as did the other two chairmen of the relevant committees of jurisdiction and several of the most powerful bank lobbying groups. At one point, the Treasury was in full and the Federal Reserve (Fed) in partial agreement, proposing what it described as a step-by-step "basket" approach, but fortunately each, with the passage of time, reconsidered, in part perhaps because I had indicated that I would do my utmost to pull the plug on any bill that contained such a provision.[2]

If the prohibition on the repeal of mixing commerce and banking—the heart of Glass Steagall and the Bank Holding Company Act—had been repealed, the recent financial contagion could have tripwired even more adversely from Wall Street to the industrial heartland. What did not happen in Glass Steagall reform was more important than what did.

Like cicadas, insider advocates of merging commerce and banking resurface periodically in Washington. The public has never paid much attention to the issue and its consequences, but in a political system where money power games are not unknown, it is the kind of mischievous initiative that can suddenly take legislative hold outside the public spotlight.

The regulatory edifice established by GLBA was intended to bring greater order to the financial market place where (1) despite a prohibition in banking law against a bank buying an insurance company, the Clinton Administration had allowed a large insurance company, Travelers, to do the reverse in a merger in which it became the technical purchaser of our largest commercial bank, Citicorp; and (2) the OCC had through aggressive rule making began in the 1990 s to erode barriers between

[2]In an effort to reduce the intensity of banking industry lobbying for this change in the late 1990s, I sent letters to the CEOs and general counsels of the largest banks with an analysis of the relative value of commercial firms to banks on public exchanges. Only one bank (Citicorp) at the time was in the top 20 (it was 20th) in market value of companies on the New York Stock Exchange. At the risk of presumption, I suggested that it was naïve for bankers to assume that a law suddenly allowing the merging of commerce and banking would put bankers in the mergers and acquisitions driver's seat. Wouldn't, I asked, companies like Amoco, Microsoft, Wal-Mart, and G.E. not quickly move to control major financial institutions? Months later, at a luncheon in which I addressed a Federal Reserve advisory committee composed of major bank CEOs, a banker wryly noted that my letter had been widely discussed. The consensus, he noted, was that while he and his colleagues disagreed with my position, they understood this might be an inopportune time to proceed with so profound a breach of Glass Steagall. Nevertheless, the lobbying on Capitol Hill never abated.

bank and nonbank financial activities under a regulator-empowering Supreme Court ruling, the Chevron decision, which, in effect, held that the courts should give deference to federal regulators as long as their judgments were not capriciously derived. The OCC also allowed newly authorized insurance and securities activities to be conducted within the bank itself, i.e., without the necessity for a bank to establish separately capitalized and regulated subsidiaries.

To reduce internal banking conflicts of interest, GLBA demarcated activities traditionally subject to deposit insurance from activities of a different nature and required nontraditional banking activities to be separately funded and regulated. The reform intent of GLBA was to require banks to have adequate capital, transparently reviewable in separable categories to match whatever new risks developed with new activities.

In addition, GLBA established the most extensive privacy regulation in the history of Congress and required that every financial enterprise have a primary regulator to insure, among other things, that no product slipped through a regulatory crack, a provision that had become compelling because an increasing number of hybrid products had come to market that were part insurance, part banking, and part securities in nature.

In this context, GLBA called for the Federal Reserve to be the umbrella regulator of financial holding companies. As a consolidated supervisor, the Fed was given responsibility for imposing holding company capital requirements and insuring that all aspects of any multi-purpose financial holding company were subject to appropriate regulatory oversight. Analogously, the GLBA authorized the U.S. Securities and Exchange Commission (SEC) to be the consolidated regulator of investment bank holding companies.

To reduce industry capacity to seek the least level of regulation by arbitraging regulatory agencies, the act called for greater regulatory cooperation and commonality of approaches. Of particular importance, it mandated in key areas joint Federal Reserve and Treasury Department decision making. Government-to-industry regulatory order was not only expected to be maintained, but enhanced and streamlined.

One of the most important things that the legislation did in relation to the financial meltdown of the past few years is help to insulate smaller banks from the liquidity traumas that inevitably follow erosions in public confidence. By allowing smaller, but not larger, institutions to tap Federal Home Loan Banks for liquidity through the option of selling or collateralizing agricultural and small business loans, an extra liquidity backstop was given community banks.

In sum, financial markets changed dramatically in the post World War II era but except for the addition of more coherence under GLBA, the superstructure of regulation changed little.

The Invisible Government

There are many ways to organize regulation. The current regulatory regime can and should be improved and I will touch later on various approaches, most of which were pressed to little avail during my career in Congress. Nonetheless, if one assumes that the framework of regulation defined by GLBA is rooted in history and steeped in precedent, why have we just witnessed the greatest regulatory failure in the history of the planet?

In banking regulation, the one judgment that cannot be ducked over the last decade might be described as the nurture versus nature question. Is it the organization of decision making that failed or is it the invisible government—the panoply of federal regulatory bodies—that erred in reducing reliance on capital ratios for supervision of large financial institutions and giving deference instead to risk-based, mathematical modeling that accommodated ever riskier off-balance sheet and derivatives investment strategies?

Assessment of whether regulatory failure is principally judgmental or organizational matters, for it has everything to do with applying lessons to failed circumstances. Are the lessons to be learned first and foremost about arrangement of regulatory boxes or about imprudent regulatory judgment in the public sector and improvident risk taking in the private?

For those who hold that modification of Glass Steagall is part of the problem at hand, several points deserve review. The year before Glass Steagall was modified in 1999, Travelers had used a legal loophole to merge with Citicorp, and 2 years before the current financial collapse, the holding company, Citigroup, had divested itself of Travelers. There is no evidence: (a) that the securities industry got into trouble doing too much commercial banking, or marketing and underwriting of insurance; (b) that the insurance industry erred by doing too much investment or commercial banking; or (c) that commercial banks and insurance companies got into fundamental difficulty engaging in activities they couldn't have engaged in before Glass Steagall was modified. Commercial banks and insurance companies, after all, have always been able to deal in mortgage products and, since their invention, in mortgage and other finance-related derivatives.

Likewise, GLBA did not change the types of financial products that could be sold to investors by government sponsored enterprises (GSEs) in housing or Wall Street securities firms which were able under Glass Steagall to invest in and trade the kinds of assets that wreaked such recent financial havoc. As for individual entities from Fannie Mae and Freddie Mac to American International Group (AIG) to Lehman Brothers and Bear Stearns, all could have made the same problematic investment decisions under the pre-GLBA structure. None were subject to commercial bank regulation.

As for commercial banks doing investment banking, the most talked about legislative issue in the 1990 s was whether it was appropriate to allow them to compete with securities firms in merger and acquisition activities. Such activities—the golden egg of investment banking—have not caused commercial bank solvency problems. They proved to be profitable, increased competitive choices for American industry, and allowed consumers more decentralized financial options.

Not only is evidence lacking that changes in Glass Steagall precipitated this crisis, it is because of Glass Steagall reform that a far greater cratering of investment banking did not occur. For instance, J.P. Morgan Chase was able to assume Bear

Stearns and Bank of America was able to take over Merrill Lynch. And, after others assumed most of the loss-embedded investments of Lehman Brothers, Barclays embraced its structural and operating assets. The elimination of these investment banks, which would have been quite conceivable if Glass Steagall had not been reformed, could have caused a far greater confidence crisis than otherwise proved to be the case. Now each is subject to bank holding company capital requirements, activity restrictions, and general oversight, as are Goldman Sachs and Morgan Stanley.

What Then Happened?

What is impressive as post-mortem reviews take place is not what is newly figured out, but how many of the problems that precipitated the current financial crisis were known in advance. With few exceptions, it was widely understood in financial circles that:

(a) ethical lapses can quickly erode public confidence in finance more than in any field of commerce because finance depends so completely on trust;
(b) at a macro level, for a number of years we Americans have been spending approximately 5% more than the country produces, mortgaging our future with twin fiscal and trade deficits;
(c) at a micro level, housing prices over much of the country increased faster than household income or inflation, spurred by a monetary policy designed to keep interest rates low, a sudden adoption by an historically conservative mortgage industry of lax lending standards, and a spike in fraud among mortgage brokers;
(d) at a political level, an American administration had lost worldwide confidence related to a war financed with tax cuts against a country that did not attack us;
(e) Congress had adopted an egregiously inadequate regulatory framework for the two housing-related GSEs, Fannie Mae and Freddie Mac.
(f) the ability of Wall Street firms to market mortgage portfolios rated by agencies with inherent conflicts got ahead of their willingness to do disciplined due-diligence reviews of products sold, with gross inattention to the quality of appraisals and income verification of borrowers;
(g) like any manufactured item produced without adequate quality controls, mortgage portfolios could plummet in resale value if defective standards existed;
(h) trade in sliced and diced mortgage portfolios and an assortment of derivatives products grew at a rate that was inherently destabilizing, given the lack of widespread product standardization and absence of generalized clearing capacities;
(i) U.S. money center banks were allowed to adopt leverage ratios far higher than community banks and use, sometimes imprudently, nontransparent off-balance sheet accounting techniques;
(j) at the turn of the new millennium, international financial regulators in Basel, with the approval of the U.S. Federal Reserve, authorized unprecedented

leveraging for multinational banks, allowing them to move away from reliance on traditional capital ratios to untested risk-based modeling approaches developed at individual institution discretion;

(k) in the middle of the 2004 presidential campaign, the SEC, citing Basel standards, gave a green light for the largest securities firms to increase their leverage and then failed to provide adequate oversight of their investment and accounting practices;

(l) a division of the Treasury Department, the Office of Thrift Supervision (OTS), was given responsibility to share with the New York Insurance Department oversight responsibility for the London branch of AIG and neither regulatory body understood the nature of the risk implicit in credit default swaps;

(m) in a little noted regulatory initiative in another election year (2000), the Treasury Department's OCC bypassed traditional administrative procedures and without public or Congressional input gave national banks the power to skirt law and invest in equity securities as part of their derivative strategies,[3] thus providing an unlegislated green light to national banks to do proprietary trading—i.e., speculating—implicitly with insured deposits; and

(n) despite legislative authorization for the creation and oversight of swaps clearing facilities in the Commodity Futures Modernization Act (CFMA) of 2000, regulators did not begin to press the establishment of such clearing facilities until the last months of the Bush administration when it was too late to stem the financial meltdown.

In sum, from a regulatory perspective, the debasement of bank standards abroad sanctioned in the Basel process was matched by standards reduction at home. Leveraging excesses were exacerbated by the irresponsible marketing and insuring of faulty mortgage portfolios and the failure to recognize the macroeconomic liabilities associated with a mushrooming derivatives market that had no universal clearing mechanisms.

There was also a largely unnoted failure of law enforcement. In the wake of 9/11, much public attention was properly given to problems of coordination between the federal agencies responsible for reviewing international threats (principally the Central Intelligence Agency) and the federal agencies responsible for domestic threats (principally the Federal Bureau of Investigation) and local law enforcement. An analogous problem arose in finance. The parts of the national government most responsible for threats to the financial system (principally the Treasury Department and the Federal Reserve) appeared not to give priority attention and/or lacked the capacity to press coordination with the Justice Department and local law enforcement on the implications of unprecedented fraud, particularly but not exclusively in inner cities, that had developed in the mortgage brokering industry.

---

[3] In my last year as the term-limited chairman of the House Banking Committee, I objected strenuously both to the judgment and rule-making process that regulators followed and to no avail provided Treasury's Inspector General with a detailed complaint.

The mortgage development process had for generations been assumed to be principally one where a prospective home owner would approach a commercial bank or savings and loan (S&L) and in a careful, often cumbersome, process be required to document income, with the financial institution doing an independent appraisal of the property. But as a consequence of the development of computer modeling and swift capacities to sell mortgages up the financial chain to secondary and tertiary markets, a mortgage brokering industry that skipped federally insured intermediaries expanded significantly. Instead of working almost exclusively with comprehensively regulated institutions that had a vested interest in mortgage quality due in no small part to the extensive maintenance of mortgages in internal portfolios, Wall Street and the housing GSEs found themselves increasingly dealing with lightly regulated brokers who lacked skin in the game as they quickly sold their mortgage contracts into a secondary market.

When brokers developed the immediate capacity to unload upstream their mortgage contracts, they effectively transferred contract liabilities to others. The same situation applied at the secondary level for products bundled and resold to tertiary markets. If these products were subsequently found to be overvalued either because of wrenches in the economy or because of fraudulent origination numbers, the losses were assumed to be transferred to secondary or tertiary holders of mortgage portfolios.

The principal long-term damage to Wall Street is the deterioration in the reputation of individual firms, with those who maintained large mortgage portfolios also suffering substantial financial losses. Some were such good salesmen that they fooled themselves. The losses to Fannie Mae and Freddie Mac were substantially larger than any Wall Street institution because they were bigger market players, because they maintained a greater percentage of the mortgages they bought, and because they often guaranteed payment streams on mortgage portfolios they sold.

The same inadequacy of coordination between regulators and law enforcement agencies applied to identity theft and Internet gambling offenses. The lack of coordination in these areas where laws were also routinely breached was at most a tangential aspect of the financial trauma of 2008. But both of these unlawful elements of finance, especially Internet gambling, could grow in significance for many American families and the economy itself in coming years.

Congressional Accountability

Aside from the macro issues of war and the deficits, it is laws at the intersection of finance and housing where Congressional accountability for the financial meltdown is most stark. While financial institutions such as Fannie Mae, Freddie Mac, and AIG initially recorded sizable profits in purchasing, marketing, and insuring packages of housing products, their losses came in the end to be so large that taxpayers have been forced to pick up hundreds of billions of dollars in liabilities.

If one were to define the current economic trauma as a single industry debacle, it is a close call whether to describe it as principally a result of excesses in the housing or financial industry. At the heart of Congressional responsibility is the captive regulator model established by statute in 1994 for Fannie Mae and Freddie Mac. The legislation that set up the regulatory scheme for these housing GSEs was an egregious example of Congressional capitulation to interest group pressure. More constraints were put on the regulator than the regulated.

But the marketing of sliced and diced mortgage portfolios was complicated by the growth in markets of new kinds of derivative products. Concerned for the stability of these markets, I issued in 1993 as the ranking member of the then-named Committee on Banking, Finance, and Urban Affairs a 902-page report on regulating derivatives.[4]

What came to be called the Leach Report, I later learned, was widely read by regulators in the principal financial capitals around the world because government agencies everywhere were apprehensive of putting out comprehensive approaches that might offend affected parties. Based on interviews and written exchanges with academia, industry, and the regulatory community, the 30 recommendations for derivatives regulation which it contained represented at the time the most wide-ranging series of recommendations any governmental body had publicly set forth on the subject.

Relevant today in the recommendations made 17 years ago were calls for strong capital standards for financial institutions regardless of the development of other risk-based approaches, the application of capital requirements for off-balance sheet instruments, the establishment of comparable standards and market rules for nonbanks as well as banks, the international harmonization of standards, the standardization of documentation, and the development of protections against systemic risk.

Following up on the report that winter, I introduced a bill to establish a Derivatives Commission to enhance the federal framework for regulation of derivative activities. In introducing the bill on the House floor, I noted in my opening statement that:

> [M]y operating assumption is that derivatives are the new wild card in international finance. There is an American adage: "I wouldn't do that for all the money in the world." Interestingly, the multitrillion dollar derivatives activities of the ten largest American commercial banks alone amount to double the annual [gross national product] of the United States which, in turn, is more money than all the money in the world. If this doesn't define a pyramidal house of cards—particularly in the event of a market shock sparked abroad by warmongers or at home by private sector speculators or public pandering protectionists—what does?
>
> Everett Dirksen once commented that a billion here and there pretty soon added up to real money. With regard to derivatives, it would appear that a trillion here and there may add up to a real problem.

---

[4]The report was printed as an appendix to a hearing before the Committee on Banking, Finance, and Urban Affairs. See *Safety and Soundness Issues Related to Bank Derivative Activities: Hearing Before the Committee on Banking, Finance, and Urban Affairs*, House of Representatives, One Hundred Third Congress, first session. Washington, U.S. G.P.O., 1994.

> As the federal deficit bears proof, Congress has yet to understand how to manage figures followed by [nine] digits. With derivatives it is asked to understand quantumly larger figures—numbers followed by [twelve] digits.
>
> Derivatives pose a conundrum in that the problems they present may be too sophisticated for a Congress of generalists to deal with in any detail. However, this does not mean that legislators do not have the responsibility to set forth a general framework of concerns with the understanding that the executive branch and Federal Reserve must be held accountable for responsible oversight of the financial markets."[5]

Half a decade after these observations, Brooksley Born, a relatively new head of the U.S. Commodities Future Trading Commission (CFTC), broke with her administration and her predecessors at the CFTC to indicate in a highly publicized "concept" release that her agency was contemplating taking the lead in regulating swaps based contracts with an implicit unilateral assertion of jurisdiction over these markets by her agency. The Federal Reserve, Treasury and U.S. Securities and Exchange Commission (SEC) bitterly objected on legal and competence grounds.

In a contentious 1998 hearing, they pointed out that if the CFTC attempted to take such a step without statutory change, the legal certainty of trillions of dollars of existent swaps contracts could be challenged, potentially causing an international financial tremor, with the trading of swaps likely to move quickly to lightly regulated foreign jurisdictions. Privately, they added that they considered the CFTC, with its slim bench of professional talent, cozy relationship with Chicago traders, and lack of perceived heft in the banking system, to be the least suitable Federal agency to oversee swaps trading, particularly among commercial and investment banks.

Amidst as great angst between governmental witnesses as I ever witnessed, the most sober observation was that of Chairman Greenspan. "I have no doubt derivatives losses will mushroom at the next significant downturn as will losses on holding of other risk assets, both on and off exchanges," he observed. But in an understated assessment, he further noted that swaps contracts involved a "wholly different type of market process" than trading in commodities, the pointed implication being that, in the Federal Reserve's judgment, the capacity of the agriculture-oriented CFTC to oversee financial markets was a stretch.[6]

Confronted with unprecedented public splintering of financial policy views within the Executive branch, I tried to broker a consensus memorandum of understanding that each could approve. Initially suggesting a "standstill" approach close to that of the Federal Reserve and Treasury and later embracing several perspectives of the CFTC, I developed a series of draft approaches to resolve differences in an effort to avoid legislative intervention. I have never known a committee of Congress

[5] For statement and bill, see the *Congressional Record* 140.2 (January 26, 1994), statement 29.Available at http://www.gpo.gov/fdsys/pkg/CREC-1994-01-26/html/CREC-1994-01-26-pt1-PgH54.htm.

[6] See Testimony by Alan Greenspan, Chairman, Board of Governors of the Federal Reserve System, before the Committee on Banking and Financial Services, U.S. House of Representatives, July 24, 1998. http://financialservices.house.gov/banking/72498fed.shtml.

to ever undertake the refereeing of Executive branch differences in this manner, but I felt it important that the government speak with one voice when the prospect of riling markets and moving a multitrillion dollar market abroad was at issue.

Amongst the regulators, it was three to one, with Treasury, the Federal Reserve and SEC accepting some of the concerns of the CFTC that I had pressed into a final (fourth) draft approach. I thought we were close to agreement but the three exceptionally frustrated banking and securities regulators balked at the "standstill" constraints Chairman Born ironically insisted be placed on their regulatory discretion as a condition of her backing off the processes the CFTC had set in place.

Since issuing the 1993 study on derivatives and introducing my first bills on the subject in 1994 and 1995, I had been concerned with the challenges of derivatives clearing, but was reluctant to insist prematurely on utilization of clearinghouses until the legal risks that the Federal Reserve and Treasury enumerated could be legislatively resolved.

As the decade ended, the Agriculture Committees of the Senate and House, which have jurisdiction over the CFTC, generated a bill that came to be known as the Commodity Futures Modernization Act (CFMA) of 2000. The bill resolved the legal certainty issue that applied to existent swaps contracts and authorized the establishment of clearing facilities to be regulated exclusively by the CFTC. Based on Congressional precedent and overlapping jurisdictions, the bill was sequentially referred to the Senate Banking Committee and the House Committee on Banking and Financial Services.

On the Senate side, Chairman Phil Gramm demanded that certain products bought and sold by large institutions be exempted from case-by-case oversight but acquiesced to SEC chairman Arthur Levitt's insistence that his agency be provided compensating powers. For the first time, the SEC was thus provided anti-fraud and anti-manipulation authority over all derivatives contracts and given insider trading enforcement powers over all securities-based swaps agreements.

On the House side, I concluded that the CFMA, while a flawed bill, could, if properly amended, provide a framework to establish clearing facilities overseen by competent federal regulators. The Banking and Financial Services Committee would not concur, I indicated, with House consideration of the bill unless the Federal Reserve and Treasury in addition to the CFTC were properly empowered to authorize and oversee swaps clearing facilities.

Opposition quickly developed within and outside the Congress to the clearing option I pressed. Various Wall Street lobbying coalitions, principally the Ad Hoc Coalition of Commercial and Investment Banks, worked with members of the Agriculture Committee to object to the prospect of what they feared would be comprehensive Federal Reserve or Treasury supervision of clearinghouses. But I held firm and this provision with balancing empowerment given later in the legislative process to the SEC was placed in the CFMA of 2000.

The importance of swaps clearing cannot be underestimated. The greatest challenge in derivatives markets is to get a handle on individually tailored products sold in multicountry, multiparty markets. The creation of clearing facilities allows for the prospect that swaps, including credit default instruments, can be pressed into a regulated environment where various standards can be insisted upon as a condition of institutional participation. The value of derivatives transactions in notional terms is more than the combined gross domestic product (GDP) of all countries of the world. But when netted out, that is, cross discounted with counter parties, multi-trillion dollar figures can in some cases be discounted by factors of 100 or more, depending on the contract design and individual party relationships.

Clearing facilities not only serve as a grease to make the engine of finance work more fluidly, they also provide incentives for market standardization and a hook to bring governmental oversight to market participants, including nonbanks and foreign firms.

The concern for derivatives clearing in troubled times also led me to introduce over a series of Congresses a bill to allow a timely netting of derivatives contracts in the event a firm enters bankruptcy. Without a special exemption under our bankruptcy laws for orderly netting of derivatives contracts, these contracts could be caught up in months, perhaps years, of bankruptcy turmoil, potentially spurring a bankruptcy contagion. Legislative language I had crafted on this point was originally accepted on the House side as part of the CFMA of 2000 but subsequently stripped at the insistence of the Senate Judiciary Committee. I finally got the language passed half a decade later as a provision in an otherwise controversial bankruptcy reform act.

Whether it was wise to let Lehman Brothers go under—and many on Wall Street and a number of economists now believe the government erred in not intervening or working more assiduously to incentivize a merger partner—and whether the methodologies undertaken to shed certain investment assets of Lehman Brothers resulted in fair asset distribution, the exemption just referenced freeing derivatives contracts from becoming tied up in lengthy bankruptcy proceedings coupled with the flexibility provided by the clearing capacities authorized in the above mentioned amendments to the CFMA take pressure off the government to prop up financial firms facing insolvency challenges.

The Responsibility of Regulators

What I am suggesting that again may be counterintuitive to many is that while clearing facilities were not administratively in place, the statutory framework nevertheless existed during the recent financial meltdown for mutualization of derivatives counterparty risk, supervision of derivatives clearing, and for resolution and clearing of derivatives contracts involving insolvent entities.

The CFMA is a law that critics have properly focused on as a problematic statute. But the most problematic aspect of the law relates to its implementation—the failure of the SEC to implement the anti-fraud, anti-manipulation, and insider trading authority that it was accorded and, most importantly, the failure of relevant federal regulators to press on a timely basis the creation of clearing facilities for swaps.

These failures do not mean that the Senate Banking Committee was correct to insist in negotiations on the CFMA that discrete derivative products developed and traded exclusively between large, federally regulated banking and securities firms should be exempted from direct oversight. Nevertheless, it was the failure to implement provisions authorized by statute that proved to be more systemically consequential than the constraints the law placed on regulatory capacity to review individual credit default arrangements.

A fair question is why, until the crisis, was there so much reluctance of the four regulatory bodies—the Federal Reserve, the Treasury, the SEC and the CFTC—to implement fully authorized capacities.

The CFMA removed the cloud of legal uncertainty that would otherwise have hindered utilization of swaps clearinghouses and allowed any resulting clearing to be regulated federally. Yet, for most of the first decade of the twenty-first century, a period in which derivatives markets swelled to glittering heights, industry intransigence coupled with regulatory turf concerns impeded the development of swaps clearing facilities. Powerful financial institutions preferred to market individually tailored product approaches where margins could be expected to be high rather than standardized, more easily clearable products.

It wasn't until the spring of 2009, based on concerns expressed by the New York Federal Reserve the summer before, that multiparty derivatives clearing institutions finally began to get off the ground with the chartering of a special purpose Federal Reserve supervised clearing bank designed to serve large financial institutions, and CFTC-supervised facilities to serve nonbank traders and smaller financial entities.

The refusal of the Executive branch in the last months of the Clinton Administration and early Bush years to advance mechanisms to mutualize credit risk with standardized products and establish clearing facilities for derivatives contracts is one of the greatest judgmental failures in the history of regulation.

Derivatives aside, what is principally but by no means exclusively at issue on the regulatory front today are two failures and the manner each informs the question of whether and how to reorganize regulation of finance. The first failure was inadequate regulation of housing finance, particularly Fannie Mae and Freddie Mac, and inadequate oversight of the worldwide marketing and insuring of mortgage portfolios that presumably were designed to reduce cost to home buyers and risk to financial institutions. The second was the green light given large financial institutions to radically increase their leveraging ratios. The first mistake precipitated the financial crisis; the second deepened and lengthened it.

For over a decade, the Federal Reserve warned Congress to no avail of problems inherent in Fannie Mae and Freddie Mac regulation and market dominance. But just as Congress and to a partial degree the Treasury ignored the Federal Reserve's judgment on housing GSEs—perhaps influenced by the favors and campaign contributions Fannie Mae and Freddie Mac showered on the Hill—regulators failed to comprehend the macroeconomic as well as criminal implications of the reports of mortgage fraud filtering in from around the country. Many members of Congress heard anecdotally about fraud in the mortgage brokering industry in their districts and brought their concerns to the attention of regulators in hearings and meetings, especially during the late 1990s.

Warnings about the existence and implications of mortgage fraud and the need for viable swaps clearing facilities were largely ignored. The pervasive attitude seemed to be that since so many bright people were involved in money center finance and since finance was one of the few areas of commerce that America was competing well in around the world, traditional concern for prudential capital standards and more contemporary concern for derivatives processing could be dropped in favor of benign corporatist neglect.

Just as the Treasury and Federal Reserve were disinclined to object to the thin layers of capital which had seemed to be successfully managed by money center banks, so the SEC, despite the green light it gave to greater investment bank leveraging, was disinclined or lacked sufficient financially trained professionals to implement the anti-fraud, anti-manipulation, and insider trading enforcement powers over securities-based swap agreements provided it under the CFMA.

While the CFMA exempted credit default swaps from being considered securities under federal securities laws, it neither exempted principal market participants nor all aspects of the derivatives market from regulation. And it never exempted the banking regulators, SEC, or state insurance departments from responsibility for institution viability, which necessitates a company-wide assessment of all the risks undertaken by a financial firm under a regulator's purview.

Regulator accountability is particularly vexing in the context of swaps because definitional boxes are not neat. The jurisdictional concerns of those accountable for overseeing insurance, banking, commodities, and securities activities overlap.

For instance, in the case of AIG's London office where so few lost so much, its insurance regulator (the New York Insurance Department) should have understood that just as a casualty insurance company must keep deep reserves and/or have comprehensive reinsurance to protect against hurricane claims, AIG should have had deeper reserves to protect against man-made financial disasters. Likewise, Treasury's OTS, which oversaw AIG's London operations due to a British law requiring a national regulator to assert responsibility for foreign financial firms in British jurisdiction, should have understood that the company was massively over-leveraged relative to the risk it was assuming.

AIG had a lucrative business as long as there were no adverse economic occurrences. But adverse things do happen, and while both the state insurance regulator and the Treasury Department might have been handicapped in not being able to review the micro dimension of a particularly incendiary financial product, they should have had the macro judgment to recognize the nature of the business and the systemic risk it posed.

There is an old saw to the effect that success has a thousand chest thumpers while failure has no one raising a hand. With regard to the collapse of AIG, it is the New York Insurance Department and the Treasury Department (OTS) that held the door open while a small group of AIG traders in London cracked the public safe and Congress blinked as the getaway car sped past. In the aftermath, it was the decision of the Treasury Department to increase substantially taxpayer liabilities to protect fully AIG counterparties (investment and commercial banks, foreign and domestic) and provide surprising shelter for AIG shareholders.

Collective responsibility exists for the current crisis but the collectivity of it all should not limit individual institution accountability. Regulators simply cannot shirk responsibility for institutions failing under their jurisdiction.

Regarding Congressional accountability, it is instructive to review the House debate that occurred in 1993 and 1994 on the bill creating the regulatory apparatus to oversee Fannie Mae and Freddie Mac. As the only member of the Banking Committee to vote against the bill in committee, I led a quixotic debate on the House floor against the measure. A review of that debate as well as of the comprehensive approach I proposed in a following Congress to restrain the multibillion dollar perquisites provided annually to these two GSEs might be helpful in revealing the array of egregious advantages Congress handed no other corporations of any kind in American society.[7]

To date, the major systemic issues that will cost taxpayers significantly will come outside of the traditional bank regulatory system. Commercial banks, particularly money center institutions, have suffered significantly and several large and a number of smaller banks and S&Ls have failed in this crisis. But if the economy continues to recover, it looks as if virtually all public funds, including Troubled Assets Relief Program (TARP) resources, infused in commercial banking will be returned with interest. The Federal Deposit Insurance Corporation (FDIC) has lost enormous resources in dealing with a number of failed banks but these funds were derived from assessments over the years on banks rather than taxpayers.

It is in three institutions—Fannie Mae, Freddie Mac, and AIG—where public funds are least likely to be recovered. Losses embedded in these institutions underscore the housing and mortgage product dimension of the financial implosion. If Congress's industry-pandering approach to regulation of Fannie Mae and Freddie Mac had been structured more prudently; if banks, securities and insurance companies had come under more restrictive leveraging guidelines, particularly in the trading of derivatives products; if swaps clearing facilities had been created and vigilantly regulated; and if mortgage fraud had been more diligently pursued and

---

[7]There are many examples of the extraordinary reach of Fannie Mae and Freddie Mac on Capitol Hill. Three personal anecdotes are illustrative: Late 1 week, I circulated a battery of amendments to Fannie Mae and Freddie Mac legislation that would have radically reformed their manner of operating. The next Monday I received phone calls from three of my party's leaders in the House with the same message: the approach, even if it got out of committee, would not be scheduled for consideration in the House. The same day an ex-Member called to underscore how much he shared the views of House leadership, but after going down his talking points, he burst out laughing to tell me how fortuitous it was for him that I had proposed the reform initiative. Upon learning of its existence, Fannie Mae management, which had extensive ties to Democrats on the Hill, decided they needed more Republican assistance and offered my ex-colleague what he described as a much appreciated retainer to join their stable of lobbyists. Several weeks later I received a letter from the mayor of Washington, DC objecting to my approach, even though one of its provisions would have removed the unprecedented exemption the two housing GSEs have to paying state and district income taxes, a change in law that would have provided multimillion dollar benefits to the budget of the District of Columbia as well as every state in the country.

mortgage portfolios properly valued, the depth and consequences of the current financial crisis could have been substantially mitigated.

Foreigners often wonder why the United States does not go to a single regulatory model. But total simplicity isn't always a panacea. As events have shown, the British experiment with a single regulator has produced results more disastrous than ours. Indeed, the most decentralized part of our regulatory system—state regulation—has in this crisis held up better than national regulatory bodies. Unlike Europe, we are a geographically robust society with a federal political structure and tradition. Just as in our federal political system, there are regulatory counterparts at the state level.

The vastly more prudential approach taken by state regulators of community banks over the last decade informs review of the recent crisis because of the contrast it provides with the regulation applied to our largest national banks and with the errors state authorities were accountable for during the (S&L) crisis a generation ago.

The S&L crisis was initially triggered by an inflation-driven increase in the cost of funds for institutions that borrowed short and lent long. It was then compounded by capricious regulation and law making in a small number of states like California, Texas, Louisiana, and Arkansas, where instead of insisting on recapitalization, state authorities allowed institutions to attempt to work their way out of insolvency by providing an unprecedented right to use federally insured deposits to make direct investments. These investments generally proved misguided, thus deepening losses that had to be picked up by an inadequately capitalized federal fund that had to be bolstered with taxpayer resources. Relatively small institutions caused surprisingly large public losses.

By contrast, the current financial trauma has been alleviated rather than accentuated by interest rate changes and disproportionately involves one group—nationally regulated institutions characterized by bigness. The level of imprudence in the regulation that precipitated the worldwide financial crisis was in direct proportion to size of institutions regulated.

It is conjectural whether any financial institutions should be considered "too big to fail" and an open question whether some are "too big to manage." But what is clear in the last decade was that mega-banks were "too big for Washington to understand."

Community banks, on the other hand, are in a relatively stronger position today for a number of reasons, one being a singular reliance of state regulators on prudential capital standards.

For years I used to be labeled a "capital hawk" because I argued that large banks should be subject to the same capital standards as community institutions. To apply looser standards to the big not only increased systemic risk, it incentivized the movement of capital from more prudentially capitalized institutions to banks with comparatively smaller capital cushions. But for decades there had been an assumption in Washington, magnified during the Bush years, that because money center banks had ready access to capital markets and were run by people of enormous talent able to limit industrial risk with diverse lending portfolios and operating options, they ought to be allowed to leverage to a far greater extent than community banks.

Today, if one were sitting on the moon and observing the multitrillion dollar contraction in world economic activity precipitated in no small measure by the biggest American financial institutions, it would appear self evident that institutions that are so large as to be able to systemically jeopardize the economy should be required to maintain capital standards not only equal to but stronger than nonsystemically challenging ones. When the public welfare has been so extraordinarily damaged by the lure of leveraging, new rules need to be written. The game should not be replayed the same way.

Industry participants are prone to contend that, in an emergency, liquidity in a financial institution matters more than capital. There is certain logic to this proposition in that banks have an everyday challenge to manage liquidity demands. But if a bank has solid capital, it generally has ready access to liquidity through inter-bank borrowing, or the pledging of assets to the Federal Reserve or a Federal Home Loan Bank, or through public or private equity offerings. On the other hand, if it is perceived to lack sufficient capital to cover losses, a run of substantial magnitude can occur on an institution in a blink of an eye. There is no substitute for the strength that tangible equity capital provides.

The public interest must be the preeminent regulatory concern, but it is a myth that all public policy concerns are necessarily at odds with shareholder interests. While greater institutional leveraging in stable times can spur per share bank stock returns, the reverse can be the case in volatile circumstances. When financial traumas occur, the economy can contract and the shareholder and, more importantly, the public can be on the line for losses of a vastly larger magnitude. This is why the use of mathematical models to help assess risk has to be considered exceptionally useful but only with the understanding that the lesson of this past crisis is that care must continually be taken to insure that such modeling augments rather than replaces reliance on traditional capital standards.

The big picture is that intense competition is underway for leadership of international banking. In order to reestablish worldwide financial preeminence, protect the taxpayer, and reclaim investor confidence, the principal responsibility of regulators must be to constrain the lure of leveraging. The case for deferring to a management that may prefer to operate with minimum levels of capital is frail to nonexistent.

The tarnishing of the reputation and leadership of the United States that has had such extraordinary repercussions in all fields of commerce and geopolitics must be repaired.

Congressional Initiatives

Whatever regulatory scheme is in place at any point in time, the challenge for the Executive and Congress should always be to avoid populist irrationality and, at the same time, steer clear of interest group captivity.

There are a number of approaches that can be taken to organizing financial regulation, including various ways to consolidate commercial bank supervision. Clearly the Washington alphabet soup institutions—the Fed, SEC, CFTC, OTS, OCC, and FDIC—that evolved over many decades present a confusing picture. The existence of too many regulators can cause a lack of accountability and at the same time increase the capacity of private sector parties to game the system through regulatory arbitrage—the movement or implicit threat of movement of a financial institution to the least intrusive regulator.

The central reform initiatives that demanded the greatest attention of Washington policy makers in 2010 were the need to press forward with prudential oversight, including strong capital standards, of systemically significant financial enterprises, nonbank as well as bank; to utilize more extensively clearing facilities for derivative contracts; and to develop further emergency approaches to resolving problems of failing financial institutions of all kinds, preferably without infusions of taxpayer resources.

Congress's approach in 2010, the Dodd-Frank bill, gives systemic risk authority to a committee chaired by the Treasury. The determination to establish a committee to oversee systemic risk mirrors to a large extent a framework bill I introduced in the mid 1990s. H.R. 20, the Risk Management Improvement and Derivatives Oversight Act of 1995, would have created an interagency Federal Derivatives Commission to be chaired by the chairman of the Federal Reserve, consisting of the federal banking agencies plus the SEC and CFTC. The proposed Commission was empowered to establish strong capital standards and limits on leverage and to advance common rules related to accounting, disclosure, sales practices, including appropriateness, and such other regulatory actions the Commission deemed relevant to the supervision of financial firms engaged in derivatives activities. The dual goal was to establish cross-industrial commonality of standards and collective Executive branch accountability for these standards.

H.R. 20 also provided relevant regulators the legal authority to net out or otherwise deal with clearing contracts of failed financial institutions. The bill required the Derivatives Commission to provide risk management and derivatives activities training for regulators and called on the Federal Reserve to lead in international negotiations aimed at seeking commonality of standards worldwide. The bill included a host of other provisions, including an amendment to the Federal Deposit Insurance Act stipulating that engaging in derivatives activities with inadequate technical expertise could be deemed to constitute "an unsafe or unsound" banking practice.

As the newly designated chairman of the Banking and Financial Services Committee, I had hoped that H.R. 20 would be the principal agenda item for the committee in the 104th Congress. But because the bill fetched vibrant industry and conservative opposition and could not garner support from either the Clinton administration or liberals on the committee, it could not muster sufficient momentum for Congressional movement at the time.

The Dodd-Frank approach calling for the Treasury to head a comparably empowered committee is a thoroughly constructive initiative although the Federal Reserve would have been a more suitable, less political choice to chair regulatory coordination. No matter how able a particular Secretary of the Treasury may be at any moment in time, the Treasury by its nature is at the epicenter of politics. The Federal Reserve, on the other hand, is an institution ensconced in the art of economics. Politics is circular; repetition is the norm. Economics is linear; experience can more readily add to judgment.

These distinctions are relevant for if the regulatory policies of the prior two presidencies are a guide, it would appear that the Treasury under both political parties has an institutional predilection to shower discreet, outside the public glare favors on Wall Street during presidential election years. The Federal Reserve has likewise at times been overly deferential to Wall Street concerns, particularly relating to leveraging, but because mistaken judgments have generally been more ideological than political, lessons are more easily grasped and changes in approach more readily implemented.

Chairman Bernanke manages the most impressive assembly of economic talent in the world and has ready access to the expertise of America's relevant academic and financial institutions. Most importantly, the Federal Reserve's quasi-independent status positions it to be more above politics than any other governmental body. This circumstance alone is worth its weight, figuratively and nonmetaphorically, in gold.

As this financial trauma has shown, the Federal Reserve has the greatest financial discretion to act in an emergency of any governmental body. It has multitrillion dollar pockets and the legal discretion to move with alacrity. By contrast, Treasury's very name can be a misnomer. It has more regulatory than financial discretion. It has no money unless Congress first acts.

While the Dodd-Frank bill provides certain new powers to the SEC and CFTC, greater consideration could have been given the prospect that these two regulatory cousins be part of a three-way merger, with the third party being an infusion of a substantial number of new professionals with backgrounds in math, economics, and accounting. The CFTC has impressive leadership at the top and extraordinary jurisdiction but a staff that has historically been responsible for nonfinancial markets. Size- and personnel-wise it may not be large and experienced enough to manage the responsibilities it has been given. The SEC is also well led today and has an estimable history, much bigger staff, and an impressive record of shareholder protection, but it has an analogous problem of the CFTC—the existence of surprisingly few professionals devoted to oversight of the securities industry, let alone all the other areas of finance that have grown so substantially in recent years.

The Byzantine Congressional hurdle that blocked a consolidation approach in 2010 relates to reluctance of powerful Capitol Hill figures to cede jurisdictional authority of committees upon which they sit. The exchanges in Chicago, for instance, are active political contributors and want to maintain their cozy relationship with the CFTC and their close ties to the agricultural committees of Congress. The political key is to provide a way for the various committees of Congress to keep in place jurisdiction over the activities they have today while at the same time providing greater depth and enhanced independence to consolidated administrative units within the Executive.

Appropriately, under Dodd-Frank, the Treasury's OTS has been merged into its OCC. Wisely, mortgage lenders are required to keep a 5% stake in loans they sell into secondary markets. And, controversially, banks are allowed to invest 3% of their capital in private equity and hedge fund activities.

This investment provision is tangentially reminiscent of the commerce and banking "basket" breach that the Federal Reserve advocated in the mid 1990s but is substantially more constrained. Investments are limited to 3% of fund value as well as 3% of capital. In theory, this provision touches on the concerns that former Federal Reserve Chairman Paul Volcker has articulated about banks doing proprietary trading and potentially entering speculative markets. While the double 3% limits are designed to keep equity investing as a *de minimis* part of banking, the larger theoretical issues will come more to the fore if and when these percentage constraints are allowed to increase. This "nose in the tent" prospect is likely to garner extensive attention in the years ahead with proponents arguing that proprietary trading wasn't a major factor in the housing related losses where the taxpayer faces the biggest liabilities today. Nevertheless, at increasing issue is the question of whether banking should exclusively be structured as a financial services industry or an enterprise that also is allowed to compete, even become conflicted with its customers.

The functional fate of the $6.5 trillion behemoths, Fannie Mae and Freddie Mac, where the Congressional Budget Office predicts that taxpayer are set to lose $380 billion, perhaps more, remains unresolved. And the corporate future of AIG is still unclear.

One of the reasons that concern is so great over the government's responsibility in the failure to prudently regulate Fannie Mae, Freddie Mac, and AIG is that the subsequent decision to fully back the liabilities of these three institutions tripwired counterparty bailouts not only of Wall Street firms but foreign banks. The perspective that is hardly noted abroad because of the anger that has developed against American financial leadership is that as a consequence of the manner the Treasury Department chose to assist domestic counterparties, the bailouts of Fannie Mae, Freddie Mac, and AIG produced the largest foreign assistance program since the Marshall Plan.

The principal difference between President Truman's approach in 1948 and Secretary Paulson's 60 years later is that the Marshall Plan was in reaction to the need to build up European economies in the wake of Nazi aggression and the imminent threat of Soviet imperialism. The Paulson Treasury decision also had significant international implications, but it was not triggered by adversaries. Rather, a breach in the economic order was precipitated by aggressive American private sector financial strategies unchecked by prudential regulatory judgment. Perhaps cognizant of its own regulatory accountability as well as concern for an international financial contagion, the U.S. Treasury responded to the growing financial fire by calling on the taxpayers to hold as harmless as possible those affected by these strategies, at home and abroad, as well as those accountable for them.

Historical perspective is difficult to apply to recent events, but it is hard to visualize any other country in the world bailing out American banks investing in faulty foreign financial instruments. Under agreement, every government is responsible for its domestic bank traumas. Before this crisis, no one ever suggested that another country should be responsible for the difficulties of banks outside its sovereign jurisdiction or common market framework.

It is understandable that Wall Street salesmanship of improperly valued mortgage portfolios should outrage foreign institutions. But at a minimum, one would think the U.S. taxpayer would get a little credit abroad for unwittingly bailing out foreign banks, and that Wall Street should realize that, in exchange for the massive public assistance it received, the taxpayer has compelling reason to unequivocally demand that systemically consequential institutions operate in the future with more prudence, fewer conflicts, and less leverage. A requirement that mega financial entities maintain strong capital cushions is a small price to pay for those institutions that cost so many American jobs, so much taxpayer money, and so much loss of national reputation.

With regard to Fannie Mae and Freddie Mac, Congress decades ago had legislatively provided a backstop not given any other publicly traded companies—a right to draw down $2.5 billion from Treasury in an emergency. It was this right plus a host of other advantages given these GSEs that allowed them to borrow from the public for so many years at close to Treasury rates. But, prior to this crisis there were no grounds to believe that these two entities could tap into the Treasury nearly a hundred times more than these legislated commitments. Every sophisticated bank in the world knew our law and its precise limits.

This circumstance doesn't mean that the Treasury was wrong in its determination to move quickly to stabilize the financial system after it compelled the demise of Lehman Brothers. But fairness judgments must also come into play. Should shareholders of failed institutions enjoy taxpayer protections? Should financial discounts have been more actively pursued with the counterparties of AIG, Fannie Mae, and Freddie Mac to protect the taxpayer? Should contingency plans and procedures of various kinds have been set in place, especially those authorized by statute, prior to rather than after financial problems erupted?

The questions that surround both the causes of the financial system's unraveling and the methodologies of dealing with individual institution failures underscore why it is so troubling that big institutions were allowed to leverage so excessively in the Bush years and so cavalierly given aggressive investment rights during the Clinton administration, including the discretion to invest in the stock market as part of derivatives hedging strategies, as if the failure a few years earlier of long-term capital management and earlier yet of S&L investment excesses were not alarming precedents. It is why there is such concern that large financial institutions not be given legislated powers that misalign their business interests with those of their customers and that of the public.

Over the last several decades, for instance, the committees of jurisdiction in the financial overhaul debate were lobbied not to reform an obscure charter for industrial loan companies (ILCs). Authorized to be issued in only a half dozen states, ILC charters allow parties to escape Federal Reserve rule making and/or Treasury supervision. They provide a back door avenue both to merging commerce and banking and to exercising banking powers without the oversight that goes with traditional banking. Companies that hold ILC charters should be placed under the Bank Holding Company Act. Such an approach would force the divestiture of firms that breach commerce and banking and place any financial firms holding the charter under the jurisdiction of the Federal Reserve.

Having attempted on numerous occasions to advance such an approach, I know how influential a few interest groups and a few legislators can be on the other side of the issue. So, if Congress considers this approach too politically uncomfortable but finds it compelling to advance a compromise that goes beyond the 3-year moratorium on new ILC charters that the Dodd-Frank approach establishes, it could permanently preclude the issuance of further charters, place limits on the size of existing ILCs, restrict charter transferability, and insist on backup Federal Reserve regulation for all.

Internet Gambling

Oddly, the most challenging issue in finance today, where capricious public policy could most jeopardize the viability of financial institutions, their customers, and the public at large, was outside the jurisdiction of the recent financial overhaul bill. The subject is Internet gambling. It behooves the public and the financial community to think through whether it is wise to uphold or eviscerate the last statute I passed as a Member of Congress, the Unlawful Internet Gambling Enforcement Act (UIGEA) of 2006. Gambling interests have weighed in on committees of jurisdiction in Congress in a considered effort to overturn or, at a minimum, delay the implementation of its prohibition on credit card companies, banks, and other financial intermediaries from processing or facilitating payments to Internet casinos.

The prospect of Internet gambling suddenly mushrooming in America hinges on a public decision that relates directly to what kind of society we want to have. Einstein is said to have observed that the only real miracle is compound interest. Failure to save, on the other hand, can have compound social implications. Internet gambling is an analogue to predatory lending. It is a predatory savings practice with "deposits" going to off-shore gambling institutions operating in violation of a host of state and federal laws rather than into an individual retirement account (IRA) or federally insured savings account.

If legalized, Internet gambling could grow rapaciously and rob far more Americans of the capacity to buy and maintain a family home than all the predatory lenders combined. What everyone has missed in the debate over UIGEA is that there is a quantum distinction between bricks and mortar casinos and Internet gambling. Internet gambling brings the casino to the college dorm, the work station, the kitchen, and bedroom of the American home. It has the potential to become the most omnipresent and invasive financial industry in the world, competing for the disposable dollar with the corner shoe store and community bank as well as Wall Street. Yet Internet gambling does not involve the making, distributing or facilitating of any meaningful services or products.

Advocates of legalizing Internet gambling have come to Congress and suggested that it could provide a new federal revenue source. This is true if one assumes that a massive expansion of Internet gambling will have no effect on other governmental revenue. But such reasoning is nonsensical. As Internet gambling revenues go up, tax receipts from service industries tied to finance, manufacturing, and retail marketing go down, while the need for expanded social services caused by business and family bankruptcies escalate.

Yet because UIGEA puts a modest enforcement obligation on banks, the American Bankers Association (ABA) so chafes at the prospect of an exaggerated new regulatory burden that it is willing to play Russian roulette with the American economy and the role of banks in it. The prospect that immature regulatory carping could lead to an unnecessary crippling of our economy and social fabric is real.

Lobbying

There is an assumption everyone understands that lobbying organizations are designed to represent the parochial rather than the national interest. But in my years in Congress I found that now and again lobbyists could be as confused about their own vested interests as legislators can be about the national interest.

Gambling interests, for interest, have huge behind the scenes influence in American politics. Could it be that when bank lobbyists and Internet casino lobbyists come down on the same side in trying to block anti-Internet gambling legislation and the rules to enforce it, that one or the other is being duped?

This confusion also seemed to be the case with regard to the ABA's objection to placing one of the banking industry's most sophisticated competitors—Industrial Loan Companies—under the Bank Holding Company Act.

Could it be that one reason Merrill Lynch got in such difficulty is that its multibillion dollar ILC operated without Federal Reserve oversight and without comparable rules applying to comparable financial activities of traditional banks?

Could it be that allowing certain foreign institutions—commercial as well as banking—to gain entry into American finance with advantaged ILC charter rules jeopardizes other parts of American banking and commerce as well as basic systemic stability?

But the real trauma of lobbying is less the problem of bewildering misdirection and more the consequences that unfold when industry concerns are pitted by design against the public interest. Here it is a myth to assume in finance that one party is more aligned with the public interest on Capitol Hill than another. Interest groups shower attention on both sides of the aisle on committees of jurisdiction, generally with more favors thrust on members of whichever party is momentarily in the majority. Over my time in Congress—18 years in the minority and 12 in the majority—the more liberal party had the close attention of GSEs, S&Ls, and investment banks. The more conservative party was more attuned to commercial banking. Sometimes competitive advocacy would spring up with rivalries generally advanced at the top where, largely unnoted by the public, senior members of committees are asked to raise substantial funds to assist party campaign treasuries[8] in so-called "leadership" political action committees (PACs) which they control. Unless one doesn't believe in human nature, a citizen might surmise that gifting to member-controlled PACs might precipitate quid pro quos of an even greater magnitude than direct campaign contributions.

Keynes vs. Friedman

In the wake of what some will suggest is a legislative over-reaction in 2010 to the financial meltdown and what others will consider the taking of inadequate fiscal and regulatory steps, the question remains whether a roller coaster double or even triple or quadruple dip recession is ahead, and whether the banking system is stabilized enough to weather the challenges and be in a position to put bounce back into the economy.

American economic viability is based on a competitive financial system which in turn is dependent on how judgments are reconciled between the two principal economic paradigms of the twentieth century—that set forth by John Maynard Keynes and that suggested by Milton Friedman.

Philosophically, Keynes was never as liberal as his adherents often assume. He believed in fiscal intervention to spur productive potential in an economic downturn or national emergency. At the same time, he argued that debt should be paid back after an economy stabilizes. Friedman, for his part, also believed in economic stimulus in faltering times, but he would rely more on interest rate cuts than spending increases and he maintained an abiding conviction that even more important than a budget in balance was that government not grow too large relative to the size of the economy.

What is new in the current Keynesian/Friedmanesque debate is the manner in which the Federal Reserve has led not only with traditional monetary policy tools but with innovative techniques to infuse more money into the economy than Congress's fiscal approaches provided. What is also new is that most of the Federal Reserve's stimulus and some of Congress's so-called TARP funds will be paid back, with interest. As, or more precisely, if the economy recovers, an unprecedented amount of "borrowed" resources could be returned on rather short notice to the government.

The contrast of Keynes vs. Friedman on economic matters mirrors the contrast of liberals vs. conservatives in politics. Fiscal and monetary policy can move in tandem to spur or constrain an economy. Likewise, the two can move in contrast. Today, both approaches are designed to stimulate. Big deficits at the state as well as national level are coupled with low interest rates. Whatever judgmental tacks are

[8]On issues like abortion rights and the Iraq War, I was philosophically out of step with my party but my position as chairman of the Banking Committee was more jeopardized by refusal to play the political action committee funding game than any stance on any issue.

considered in the future will be made in a setting in which options for policymakers become narrower because demographically the population is aging; because the modest recovery underway may be insufficient to significantly bring the unemployment rate down; because debt-to-GDP has grown to troubling levels; because for the first time problems in governance at state levels could exacerbate problems at the national level and vice versa; and because, for whatever reasons, political winds shift.

At some point, sparked rationally or perhaps irrationally, triggered by a small local or big international event, confidence can stutter and the recession just ended could reignite.

Hence, a crucial challenge is the maintenance of social cohesion. Now is not a time to polarize. We can vigorously disagree as a people on what the most appropriate governmental action should be and perhaps credibly shift policy gears, but we should never abandon the pursuit of common ground. Little could jeopardize the economy more than a governance breakdown.

The "Who" and "What" of Regulation

As important as the locus of regulation is, it is vastly more consequential to concentrate on the question of the independence and judgmental capacities of those regulating than the design of the institutional boxes where authority is placed. The "who" and "what" matter more than the "where."

Here I want to postulate a premise that goes against the dominant genetic bias of Washington. Experience tells us that there is a difference between linguistic and numerical capacities, and scientists inform us that discrete activities are concentrated in various parts of the brain—creative instincts in the right lobe; numerical competency in the left. Accordingly, in reference to neuron activity rather than partisanship, it may be that the failure of regulation in the last decade relates in part to the disproportionate dominance of right-brainers in positions of financial oversight. Financial regulation, after all, is more about understanding numbers and their implications than words and their meaning.

In this regard, there is a difference in education and training of individuals with varying interests and aptitudes. From a nurture perspective, the most appropriate regulatory background for nature's linguistically oriented is law school. Regulatory bodies need quality attorneys trained in process considerations to insist on compliance with law. But the regulatory tragedy of the decade is not only the lack of regulatory personnel but the lack of balance in the background of regulators. A paucity of attention had been given to complementing the legal expertise of many regulators with left-brain talent—certified public accountants (CPAs), economists, and mathematicians.

It is hard, for instance, to imagine how a quality CPA could have walked into Bernie Madoff's office and not demanded to follow the money, to know where assets were and how they could be verified. It is hard to visualize a sophisticated economist would not have recognized that AIG did not have sufficient reserves to guarantee either the magnitude or the integrity of the credit default insurance it was selling. And it is hard to see how an experienced mathematician could have reviewed many of the mortgage portfolios Wall Street firms hawked and concurred with the triple-A ratings applied.

Uniquely, lawyers and CPAs represent professions that have precise obligations to the law which go beyond their obligations to employers and clients. A lawyer is ethically bound by his or her profession to represent a client to the fullest extent but remains an officer of the court and is ethically bound not to lie or commit a felony to protect a client. A CPA's obligations go even further. While a lawyer may, and in some cases must, be silent about a client's circumstance, CPA attestations imply that obligations to reflect a truthful picture to the public trump concerns for the interests of employers or clients.

Risk factors are inherent in financial numbers, but to avoid garbage-in, garbage-out modeling, the quality of loans and their relationship to macroeconomic vulnerabilities must be prudently assessed. Mathematicians must work with economists using numbers scrubbed by CPAs to create financial products that lawyers can attest to, and regulators can conclude don't increase institution or systemic risk.

A Final Perspective

The Dodd-Frank legislation that passed in 2010 maintains the framework of Glass Steagall as modified by Gramm-Leach-Bliley. Several changes in the alphabet soup of regulatory bodies occurred. The most irresponsible Treasury regulator—the OTS—was eliminated and two new authorities were created. A consumer protection bureau was thrust on a reluctant Federal Reserve and a committee of regulators was empowered to oversee systemic risk. The oversight jurisdiction of both the newly authorized consumer bureau and the systemic risk committee will cover nonbanks as well as banks. The creation of a consumer protection bureau is welcomed or hated, depending on one's philosophy, but it is the expanded rule making jurisdiction over nonbanks and the added resolution capacity provided the government if financial institutions fail that is the most profound augmentation of federal authority in the Dodd-Frank legislation.

Regulatory changes, assuming they occur, will principally be of a judgmental rather than organizational nature. Rule making instead of definitive law will define the breadth and scope of what could become a more comprehensive regulatory regime.

The assumption is that stronger capital adequacy will be required in large financial institutions and that swaps clearing capacities will be strengthened. But banks, while encouraged, are not mandated to clear all transactions through exchanges or clearinghouses. And, ironically, insiders and their interest group allies were able in an inexplicable power play to remove, with one "grandfathered" exception, the most progressive provision in the CFMA of 2000, the authority of banking regulators to charter and oversee clearing facilities. If the single, fledgling Federal

Reserve supervised special purpose clearing bank "grandfathered" under this Dodd-Frank provision chooses to change charters or is bought out by a CFTC supervised entity, the Federal Reserve will lose its direct capacity to oversee a key part of the derivatives market.

A citizen might ask what difference a regulator makes. In the case of derivatives clearing, it is profound. Integral to the development of rules for the financial industry is the knowledge a regulatory body must have of individual financial institutions and their potential counterparties. Key as well is an understanding of the incentives and disincentives that may exist for parties to use clearing facilities, and the authority or influence a regulator may have to advance policy in the public interest. A decade ago when markets seemed tamable, mega financial institutions fought coming under Federal Reserve jurisdiction of all kinds, especially derivatives clearing. Today in the wake of the financial disaster of the new century, they recognize their dependence on the Federal Reserve and Treasury

In this context, the case for the Federal Reserve to oversee derivatives clearing facilities for large banks is compelling. Only the Treasury is a credible alternative. How realistically can a nonbank regulatory body understand the standards individual banks should be required to meet and maintain to clear within a bank-centric clearinghouse? And as prescient as a nonbank regulator might be at a point in time, how could such a regulator have near the influence over banks that a bank regulator maintains because of the host of rules and regulations it must on a daily basis enforce?

As consequentially, what other governmental entity has the authority of either the Federal Reserve or the Treasury in international negotiations related to the development and maintenance of comparable standards for clearinghouses abroad so that financial institutions will not be incentivized to gravitate to clearing bodies outside the United States if they have less intrusive rules?

In the development of finance related statutes, I understood as a legislator that wordsmithing nuances could affect not only the national interest but various private sector competitive relationships, which is one of the reasons lobbyists galvanize like locusts on Capitol Hill. Competitive differences could at times be galling, but a company's or industry's concern for the bottom line was rationally explicable. By contrast, what frequently amazed me was the seemingly irrational intensity of competitive power considerations that would surface within the government. In turf battles for authority and hence jobs, rival regulators often had differences, sometimes vibrant hostility toward each other. Like the profit motive that governs private sector concerns, power considerations, sometimes microinstitutional, sometimes macropolitical, appeared too often to dominate regulatory judgments.

In the case of oversight of derivatives clearing, the revoking of critical authority from the two principal banking regulators represents a bureaucratic win for the CFTC and an interest group victory for the trading groups it oversees. But, despite a backup role potentially reserved for the Federal Reserve, this approach is at odds with the general direction of the Dodd-Frank bill which, above anything else, is intended to be an effort to strengthen the spine and broaden the jurisdiction of financial regulators.

While approaches to reform differed between the political parties in 2010, the one consensus goal of legislators was to avoid the prospect of further AIG-like bailouts. The common hope was that regulators would be in a position to rely on normal bankruptcy processes or the resources that banks provide the FDIC for resolution of failing institutions. The problem is that the FDIC fund that had been built up over decades has largely been exhausted. Accordingly, the Dodd-Frank bill confers on the FDIC authority to borrow from the Treasury up to an amount equal to the assets of any firm being liquidated.

Critics of the Dodd-Frank approach hold that governmental intervention provides less incentive for natural bankruptcy proceedings to unfold and thus increases the possibility that, in the name of stability, new burdens could be placed on taxpayers. Supporters, on the other hand, point out that this borrowing right is designed to give regulators discretion to develop techniques to help stabilize the impact a failing institution might have on the economy without imposing sudden new liabilities on the financial industry.

If the economy resumes solid growth, there is a credible prospect that over time the private sector can refurbish relevant insurance funds and that the risk of tapping the public can be reduced. But if new economic traumas are imminent, the prudential case for greater governmental discretion would appear compelling. It is to address the risk of future challenges as well as new dimensions to old problems that Dodd-Frank is in no small measure targeted.

What is clear today in finance is that regulators must use sophisticated techniques to understand modern markets and at the same time apply old-fashioned regulatory discipline to oversee a technologically changing financial system. In the last decade, however, the assumption was that modern financial engineering had so outstripped public sector ability to understand markets that regulators had no choice except to defer to private sector judgments. This meant deferring to the notion that risk-based financial modeling could be so prescient that the dangers of leveraging could be mastered. This in turn meant that management of financial institutions could increase per share earnings based on asset growth that lacked attendant capital cushions.

In addition to a more sophisticated understanding of modern markets, regulators and the institutions they oversee must have a more realistic understanding of the ramifications for finance of changes in geopolitics. For decades, concerns for such concepts as interest rate risk, credit risk, and country risk have dominated risk management committees within government and financial institutions. Now we are in a world where terrorism has for the first time been globalized, where experience is showing that protective steps can be taken but perfect insulation is impossible. Given the proliferation of weapons of mass destruction at one extreme and the potential damage that an angry few can inflict from any corner of the world with TNT and chemical compounds at the other, the premium risk factor that all in finance have to be concerned with for the foreseeable future is political risk of a very different dimension than was applied in a pre-9/11 framework.

There are few places in America where the consequences of 9/11 were discussed more than in the board rooms of financial institutions and their regulators. But, ironically, of the many aspects of the terrorist attack on New York and Washington, D.C., the one systemic response to protecting the financial system that was either not considered, or not insisted upon, may have been the most important: the necessity of developing greater capital cushions in the banking system.

It might be unfair to suggest that a governmentally sanctioned lowering of the guard occurred. Terrorism, after all, did not precipitate the financial crisis of 2008. But 6 years earlier, 19 terrorists struck at the heart of our financial and political capitals. It is historically premature to assess whether our interventionist response to those who transformed commercial planes into suicide bombs has made us politically secure. But the decision to defer the multitrillion dollar costs of two wars to subsequent generations and to compound these obligations with wartime tax cuts has clearly left us more vulnerable to a financial trauma. The surprise of 2008 was not that another blow was struck against the American way of life, but that it was self-inflicted. We were not prepared.

Regulators have often been considered financial police. Today the more appropriate analogy, at least for our largest banks, is to an international highway patrol. Driving in a fast lane can jeopardize the national defense. We cannot afford to have anything except strong banks. They are critical to economic security and job creation. Accordingly, when financial risk tests are considered, there is little alternative except to begin with concern for the implications of a multiplicity of easily imaginable, terrorist generated events as well as inflation/deflation challenges and the interconnectivity of international markets. In this setting, fragile capital cushions are inadequate security.

National security aside, two profound problems have unfolded with deferential regulation of the financial industry, one increasingly apparent, and the other less so. The increasingly apparent one is that when the invisible government accommodates highly leveraged approaches aimed at achieving greater per share near-term earnings for a few, the risks of higher social losses at a later point for the public increase, especially when systemic problems surface. The less recognized one is that finance has capricious as well as rationally foreseeable dimensions.

Even in systemically stable times, some seemingly well-run institutions are likely to falter when similar institutions may be quite profitable. The dichotomies of success or lack thereof are vastly complicated by the circumstance that banking institutions compete increasingly against a variety of nonbank financial firms, a number of which may be quicker witted with faster capacities to move capital than traditional banks.

While risk-reducing instruments have been developed to protect individual market participants, the sum total of their usage can at times increase systemic risk and, at all times, be misunderstood or misused by some financial parties. Hence, another irony of finance is that those who develop and market risk-reducing tools are unlikely to be able to protect themselves fully from all significant risks. The failure prospect of high end financial institutions may thus be greater than in years past.

Analogously, in an economy hallmarked by change and its acceleration, banks, particularly community institutions, are having difficulty finding enterprises to extend loans that are good credit risks. The Austrian economist Joseph Schumpeter's notion of creative destruction in capitalism may be jobs-neutral or better, but the faster the destruction rate, the greater the liabilities for financial intermediaries. Losses associated with unrecoverable loans to failing companies can quickly exceed profits based on loan spreads to companies that succeed. Traditional banking as well as other sectors of modern finance has thus become an increasingly risk-intensive enterprise.

There is always a tendency for reform legislation that passes Congress in the wake of a crisis to overreach. Critics believe that, like Sarbanes-Oxley, this may be the case with Dodd-Frank which, given the extent of public anger, awkwardly clips bank pricing discretion, perhaps moving banking closer toward a public utility model of regulation. Nevertheless, supporters convincingly point out that the bill adds important safeguards to the financial system. Support is provided for greater oversight of systemically consequential nonbanks; greater resource options are given regulators to deal with failing institutions; advocacy is stated for higher capital standards; and, if regulatory cooperation can be obtained, increased use of clearing facilities is incentivized.

While the legislation is characterized by stated intent rather than legislative mandate, this intent is important. But it is not new. The discretion of bank regulators to insist on honest numbers and prudential leverage ratios has been fully authorized for more than half a century and methodologies for regulating derivatives have been available to the Executive branch and comprehensively advanced without consensus on Capitol Hill since the mid 1990s. Now under Dodd-Frank, prudential approaches will again be pointed to, but at a time governmental resources are dangerously stretched and economic stability sorely threatened.

Over the last two administrations, the size of derivatives markets mushroomed and the degree of recklessness in developing and marketing mortgage portfolios grew. Washington responded with a deregulatory bent. Regulatory bodies chose to accede to the leveraging instincts of large financial institutions in deference, if not awe, of Wall Street. In part, the loosening of regulatory standards was a reflection of an insider political/money game; in part, it related to an ideological reluctance to constrain markets; and in part, it was an offshoot of a manpower circumstance where markets and those participating in them increased in size and sophistication while Washington couldn't keep up.

While the economy and the financial security of the country were unnecessarily jeopardized by the unchecked greed of a few, statutorily directed deregulation did not occur. Regulation is fundamentally about the right and power of government to oversee markets. This right and power never diminished. Multipurpose institutions were authorized in 1999 but few came into being and the parts of each that did were subject to functional regulation that had been in place for half a century. Standards reduction was invisibly authorized.

Where Congressional accountability stands out is in the establishment of a problem-inducing GSE regulatory framework, in the exemption of credit default swaps from individual contract review, and in unsustained oversight of derivatives markets. The principal mistake of Capitol Hill was not what it did. It was what it failed on a timely basis also to do.

To a different degree, the same "not do/did do" perspective could be applied to the Dodd-Frank law. What it did not do was deal with housing finance where the woefully inadequate regulatory framework for GSEs helped precipitate the 2008 trauma. What the overhaul act did do was adopt the general framework of approaches to derivatives oversight that was laid out in comprehensive proposals and bills introduced in the 1990s on the House side of Capitol Hill but opposed by the two prior administrations and the majority of relevant committee members on both sides of the aisle in prior Congresses.

To recapitulate, the Dodd-Frank approach helps propel derivatives trading onto exchanges and into clearinghouses; gives regulators greater capacities to oversee mega nonbanks; provides greater discretion in dismantling failing firms; and empowers a council of regulators to coordinate governmental policies. These approaches were all legislatively pressed a decade or more ago and in some aspects, such as clearinghouses, had been fully authorized by the end of the Clinton administration. As for dismantlement provisions, the key exemption of derivatives products from bankruptcy turmoil was legislatively authorized 3 years before the financial debacle occurred. And, while never precisely legislated, a council of regulators was utilized on an informal discretionary basis during several administrations, but it had never been as fully empowered as legislation of the 1990s envisioned and Dodd-Frank provides.

What this perspective suggests is that Congress was a day late in reaching consensus on aspects of regulation but the Executive branch and Federal Reserve were more than a dollar short in failing to exercise prudential authorities that they had accumulated over the last half century. Dodd-Frank fills in certain regulatory gaps and could help deter financial contagion in the future. But it is a mistake to assume that regulators and law enforcement did not have the legislated power before the financial calamity to enforce rules that would have substantially reduced the magnitude of the crisis that precipitated new legislation.

This perspective is crucial for the legion of new rule writers within the invisible government to think through. It implies that if calamity could have been significantly limited by applying more prudential judgment under the prior regulatory regime, the principal need today is less for social engineering than for the application of renewed attention to the regulatory basics. The emphasis should be on derivatives clearing, counterparty and terrorist risk, due diligence in marketing asset portfolios, and most importantly, on strong capital.

Financial industry stability is part and parcel of overall systemic stability. The public interest can be expected to be at variance with industry perspectives, but it is not identical with punitive rule making that could shutter the extension of credit. The meaning and affects of the Dodd-Frank legislation will not be known until the required 243 rule makings and 67 studies are completed. Too little balance in rule making or too much uncertainty in process could prove counterproductive for the economy. In particular, care must be taken to insure that so many studies and so much rule writing not cause the eye of regulators to be taken off the fundamental issue, capital adequacy. Invested capital and retained earnings remain the principal buffer between institutional misjudgment, systemic wrenches, and the public treasury.

The capital problem is highlighted if sophisticated derivatives strategies are used to leverage rather than protect capital. The temptation of the weak is to bet the house, knowing the speculator wins with a lucky hand but the taxpayer loses if there is an unfortunate turn of events. Without adequate skin in the game, derivatives market players could become like owners of weakly capitalized S&Ls a generation ago who speculated with taxpayer insured funds. There are times in history that capital is king. In the wake of war and a stuttering economy, this is such a time in finance.

In the months since the financial trauma was sparked in 2008, regulators have understandably given attention in the United States and abroad to stress testing banks for similar events. While events of this nature can be simulated, their depth and consequences are difficult to predict with confidence. Predictions are unreliable because confidence factors are difficult to measure and the prospect of follow-on traumas difficult to gauge. Just as with nature where hundred year floods now seem to occur every decade, and where hurricanes seem to have higher force levels and frequency, manmade financial ruptures may be abbreviated from a once in a generation circumstance that used to confront Wall Street to more rapid fire challenges.

For more than half a century, regulators have had full authority to set prudential capital standards. From the perspective of community banks, our largest financial institutions have been granted unpardonable forbearance. In addition to off-balance sheet accounting gimmickry, they have been allowed to count long-term debt as part of Tier 1 capital. This definitional approach defies Webster's. Instead of debt being considered a liability and expense for a bank, it is arbitrarily designated a leverage-able asset, making mockery of reported leverage ratios. A step forward would be to insist that bank borrowings be convertible to stock at bank or regulator discretion. Still, unless and until conversion, the question remains whether prudence should allow debt to be considered capital, at least for Tier 1 purposes.

In the final measure, regulation as well as public confidence is based on the integrity of numbers and the manner capital is deployed. The financial crisis that America sprung on the world was in no small measure about too little capital in one place and too much in another. Too little capital with too much leverage was infused in large financial institutions. At the same time, too much capital with even greater leverage was employed in the American political system. The dual imbalance jeopardized the national interest. Hence, the cases for stronger capital standards in finance and progressive reform in campaign spending are entwined and compelling.

The principal oversight that now matters is of the public over its government.

References

Greenspan A (1998) Testimony by Alan Greenspan, Chairman, Board of Governors of the Federal Reserve System, before the Committee on Banking and Financial Services, U.S. House of Representatives, 24 Jul. http://financialservices.house.gov/banking/72498fed.shtml

Hale T (ed) (2008) Regional and national financial crises: roots, results and responses. Policy Research Institute, The Woodrow Wilson School at Princeton University, 7 Nov

Leach JA (1994) Derivative regulations. Congressional Record Online (26 Jan) 140(2), House, Page H. http://www.gpo.gov/fdsys/pkg/CREC-1994-01-26/html/CREC-1994-01-26-pt1-PgH54.htm

Leach JA (1995) H.R. 20 risk management improvement and derivatives oversight act. U.S. House of Representatives. http://frwebgate.access.gpo.gov/cgi-bin/getdoc.cgi?dbname=104_cong_bills&docid=f:h20ih.txt.pdf

Leach JA (2009) Address at the symposium on shaping global financial reform. Sponsored by the Bretton Woods Committee and the Boston University School of Law, Washington, DC, 22 Apr. http://www.brettonwoods.org/events/index.php/54/Shaping_Global_Financial_Reform

Paulson HM Jr, Steel RK, Nason DG (2008) Blueprint for a modernized financial regulatory structure. The Department of the Treasury, Mar. http://www.ustreas.gov/press/releases/reports/Blueprint.pdf

United States. Congress. House. Committee on Banking, Finance, and Urban Affairs (1994) Safety and soundness issues related to bank derivatives activities: hearing before the Committee on Banking, Finance, and Urban Affairs, House of Representatives, One Hundred Third Congress, first session. U.S. G.P.O, Washington, DC

About the Editor

John A. Tatom is the director of research at Networks Financial Institute in the Scott College of Business at Indiana State University and associate professor of Finance at Indiana State University. He has held both positions since June 2005. Previously, he was an adjunct professor in the Economics Department at DePaul University in Chicago from 2000 until 2005. In 2003–2004, he was also a senior fellow at the Tax Foundation in Washington, D.C.

Dr. Tatom served from 1995 to 2000 in various capacities for UBS in Zurich, including chief U.S. economist in the asset allocation and currency group at UBS Asset Management in Chicago, executive director and head of country research and limit control in Zurich, and chief economist for emerging market and developing countries in Zurich. From 1976 to 1995, he served as assistant vice president and policy adviser in the research department of the Federal Reserve Bank of St. Louis. He has taught at several other colleges and universities. He holds a Ph.D. from Texas A&M University.

He has published over 100 articles on international and domestic monetary and fiscal policy issues, inflation, capital formation, productivity and growth, energy price shocks, and other macroeconomic and international topics. His focus at Networks Financial Institute is on financial sector performance and regulatory reform, the link between the financial sector and economic growth, and financial literacy. He has edited (with James Barth and Glenn Yago), *China's Emerging Financial Markets: Challenges and Opportunities*, Springer Publishing (September 2009), *In Search of Effective Corporate Governance*, (November 2007), *The Health Care Financing Bomb: Where's the Money (or the Solution)?* (August 2006), *Assessing Adult Financial Literacy* (March 2006), *Is Your Bubble About to Burst?* (October 2005), *The Social Security Dilemma* (September 2005) for Networks Financial Institute and (with Costa Vayenas and Heinrich Siegmann) *The UBS Guide to the Emerging Markets*, Bloomsbury (1997).

J.A. Tatom (ed.), *Financial Market Regulation*, DOI 10.1007/978-1-4419-6637-7,

About Networks Financial Institute

Networks Financial Institute at Indiana State University (NFI) exists to facilitate broad, collaborative thinking, dialogue, and progress in the evolving financial services marketplace through three targeted initiatives:

1. Develop future financial services industry leaders
2. Improve financial literacy of current and future consumers
3. Improve financial services industry decision-making innovation and progress.

With innovative programs and services, NFI provides an unprecedented link among educators, students, professionals, policymakers, and citizens. Launched in 2003 as an outreach of the Scott College of Business at Indiana State University, NFI is made possible through a grant from Lilly Endowment Inc., an Indianapolis-based, private philanthropic foundation.

NFI has three principal programs: the thought leadership program, the Networks Scholars program, and an outreach program to promote financial literacy.

The thought leadership program focuses on financial research and conducts public programs in Indiana, around the region, and in Washington D.C., addressing critical public policy issues affecting the financial industry, and about financial literacy. Research is conducted by distinguished experts drawn from around the nation who serve as Fellows of the Institute, and by other experts who join us for public policy events or other research projects. The Institute has extensive *Policy Brief* and Working Paper series; it also publishes other research reports and books on financial issues.

NFI provides 4-year scholarships for qualified students accepted to Indiana State University, who choose to pursue a career in the financial services industry. Networks scholars participate in an innovative 4-year experiential learning program that focuses on team leadership development and career development. The financial literacy outreach program offers accessible financial literacy educational programming for children, college students, and young adults. NFI's Kids Count® Program is a comprehensive and integrated curriculum complete with hands-on and web-based games, a family component, and a mobile classroom.

Networks Financial Institute® is a not-for-profit organization. It is headquartered in the Donald. W. Scott College of Business on the campus of Indiana State University in Terre Haute with offices in Indianapolis and Washington, D.C.

More information can be found on the web site: www.isunetworks.org.

About the Contributors

Kabir Hassan is Professor of Finance at the University of New Orleans and also holds a visiting research professorship at Drexel University, Philadelphia. He is a financial economist with consulting, research, and teaching experiences in development finance, money and capital markets, corporate finance, investments, monetary economics, macroeconomics, and international trade and finance. He has published five books, over 70 articles in refereed academic journals and has presented over 100 research papers at professional conferences globally.

Ihsan Isik is Professor of Finance in the Rohrer College of Business at Rowan University. He received his B.S. in Management from Middle East Technical University, his M.S. in Finance from Texas Tech University, his M.A. in Economics, and his Ph.D. in Financial Economics from University of New Orleans (December 2000). Dr. Isik was an assistant professor of finance and accounting at New Jersey Institute of Technology for 2 years before joining Rowan University. His research and teaching interest is in the field of Financial Markets and Institutions. Dr. Isik is a research fellow of the Economic Research Forum.

Edward J. Kane, Ph.D. is Professor of Finance at Boston College. He received his Ph.D. from Massachusetts Institute of Technology. Previously, Kane occupied the Everett D. Reese Chair of Banking and Monetary Economics at Ohio State University and also taught at Princeton University and Iowa State University. Kane has held several visiting professorships and is a past president and fellow of the American Finance Association and a former Guggenheim fellow. He serves on the editorial boards of several journals and is a founding member of the Shadow Financial Regulatory Committee. Currently, he consults for the World Bank and is a Senior Fellow in the FDIC's Center for Financial Research.

George G. Kaufman is the John F. Smith Professor of Finance and Economics and Director of the Center for Financial and Policy Studies in the School of Business Administration, Loyola University, Chicago. Before teaching at Loyola, he was a research fellow, economist, and research officer at the Federal Reserve Bank of Chicago and has been a consultant to the Bank since 1981. Kaufman received his B.A. from Oberlin College, M.A. from the University of Michigan, and Ph.D. in economics from the University of Iowa. Professor Kaufman's teaching and research interests are in financial economics, institutions, markets and regulation, and in the Federal Reserve and monetary policy. He has lectured widely in the United States and abroad and published extensively in professional journals, as well as having been an editor or a member of the editorial board of several major journals. He is also the author or editor of numerous books. In May 2003, the *Economist* identified Kaufman as one of "America's leading financial economists." Professor Kaufman has served as a consultant to numerous government agencies and private firms. He has frequently testified before Congress and other legislative and policy groups.

James A. Leach is Chairman of the National Endowment for the Humanities. Prior to being nominated by President Obama for the post, Leach was a Professor at the Woodrow Wilson School at Princeton University and Interim Director of the Institute of Politics and Lecturer at the Harvard Kennedy School. Leach's brief stint in academia was preceded by 30 years of service as a representative in Congress where he chaired the Banking and Financial Services Committee, the Subcommittee on Asian and Pacific Affairs, and the Congressional-Executive Commission on China. Leach attended Princeton, the School of Advanced International Studies of Johns Hopkins, and the London School of Economics. He holds 10 honorary degrees, has received decorations from two foreign governments, and is the recipient of the Wayne Morse Integrity in Politics Award, the Adlai Stevenson Award from the United Nations Association, the Edger Wayburn Award from the Sierra Club, the Norman Borlaug Public Service Award, and a Woodrow Wilson Award from both Princeton and Johns Hopkins. Leach served on the board of several public companies and a series of non-profit organizations, including the Century Foundation, the Carnegie Endowment for International Peace, the Social Sciences Research Council, Pro Publica and Common Cause, which he chaired. He is a member of the Council on Foreign Relations and formerly served as a trustee of Princeton University.

Abdullah Mamun is an Associate Professor of Finance at the University of Saskatchewan in Canada. He also taught at Massey University in New Zealand. He earned his Ph.D. in financial economics from the University of New Orleans in 2003. His primary areas of research interests are in financial markets and institutions and investments. He has a good number of publications to his record.

Martin Mayer, Brookings Institution Guest Scholar since 1993, is the author of 35 books. His first financial books date back to the 1950s. While for several years he worked mostly in the field of education, he returned to financial markets in 1975 with *The Bankers*. His book *The Builders* led to his service as a commissioner on Ronald Reagan's National Commission on Housing. *The Fate of the Dollar*, published in 1979, detailed the decline of the currency in the 1960s and '70s, and *The Money Bazaars* in 1983 predicted the dominance of the capital markets over the credit markets. *Markets: Who Plays, Who Risks, Who Gains, Who Loses* told the story of the 1987 crash and the rise of Chicago and Tokyo, while *The Greatest Ever Bank Robbery* in 1990 told the savings and loan story. *Stealing the Market* (1991) worried about front-running, and *Nightmare on Wall Street* dealt with the Salomon Brothers' attempt to corner the market in an auction of 2-year Treasuries. In 1997,

The Bankers: The Next Generation centered on the oncoming derivatives disaster and was followed by *The Fed*, published in 2002. Through most of those years he was also a professional music and opera critic and historian.

Ronnie J. Phillips is a Senior Fellow at Networks Financial Institute. He is a Professor of Economics at Colorado State University. Most recently he was a Visiting Research Fellow at the American Institute for Economic Research in Great Barrington, Massachusetts. Previously, he has been Scholar in Residence at the Ewing Marion Kauffman Foundation in Kansas City, Missouri and a Visiting Scholar at the FDIC, the Comptroller of the Currency, and at the Jerome Levy Economics Institute of Bard College. He is a past president of the Association for Evolutionary Economics (AFEE). His publications on financial system issues have appeared in books, academic journals, newspapers, magazines, and public policy briefs. Phillips holds a B.A. from the University of Oklahoma and a Ph.D. from The University of Texas at Austin.

Alessandro Roselli is an Honorary Visiting Fellow, Faculty of Finance, Cass Business School, London, UK and has been a Visiting Fellow, Nuffield College, Oxford University. From 1972 to 2007, he worked for the Bank of Italy in various positions including UK Representative, Observer for the Republic of Ireland and Governor's Secretariat, Deputy Head of Department/European Central Bank. He is the co-author with C. Gola of *The UK Banking System and Its Regulatory and Supervisory Framework*, Palgrave Macmillan, 2009.

John A. Tatom is the Director of Research at Networks Financial Institute at Indiana State University and Associate Professor of Finance at Indiana State University. He has published widely on international and domestic monetary and fiscal policy issues, particularly inflation, capital formation, productivity and growth; the macroeconomics of supply, especially oil and energy price shocks; the relationship of exchange rate movements to international competitiveness, capital flows, trade, and international economic policy; and on financial innovations and their effects on monetary policy and the economy, among other areas.

David VanHoose is a Senior Fellow at Networks Financial Institute. VanHoose earned his Ph.D. at the University of North Carolina at Chapel Hill and is currently the Herman W. Lay Professor of Private Enterprise and Professor of Economics at the Hankamer School of Business at Baylor University. He has published articles in such professional journals as the *Quarterly Journal of Economics*, the *International Economic Review*, the *Southern Economic Journal*, the *Journal of Money, Credit, and Banking*, *Economic Inquiry*, and the *Scandinavian Journal of Economics*.

Peter J. Wallison, co-director of the American Enterprise Institute's program on financial policy studies, researches banking, insurance, and securities regulation. As general counsel of the U.S. Treasury Department, he had a significant role in the development of the Reagan administration's proposals for financial services industry deregulation. He served as White House counsel to President Ronald Reagan and is the author of *Ronald Reagan: The Power of Conviction and the Success* *of His Presidency* (Westview Press, 2002). His other books include *Competitive Equity: A Better Way to Organize Mutual Funds* (2007); *Privatizing Fannie Mae, Freddie Mac, and the Federal Home Loan Banks* (2004); *The GAAP Gap: Corporate Disclosure in the Internet Age* (2000); and *Optional Federal Chartering and Regulation of Insurance Companies* (2000). He also writes for AEI's *Financial Services Outlook* series.

Christopher Whalen is cofounder of Institutional Risk Analytics (IRA), the Los Angeles based provider of risk management tools and consulting services for auditors, regulators, and financial professionals. Whalen leads IRA's risk advisory practice and consults for global companies on a variety of financial and regulatory issues. He volunteers as a regional director of Professional Risk Managers International Association and is a board adviser to I-OnAsia, a global business security and risk consultancy based in Hong Kong. Whalen currently edits *The Institutional Risk Analyst*, a weekly news report and commentary on significant developments in and around the global financial markets. He has testified before Congress and the U.S. Securities and Exchange Commission on a variety of issues and contributes articles and commentaries to publications such as *The International Economy*, *American Banker*, and *The Big Picture*. His forthcoming book is titled *Inflated: How Money and Debt Built the American Dream* (John Wiley & Sons).

Index

G